Global Movement

Critical research and theorizing on the Anti- or Alter-Globalization Movement has exploded over the last two decades. This volume provides a platform for scholar-activists themselves to share insights from engaged research and to critically reflect on movement histories and internal dynamics. It also highlights ways in which activists are reaching beyond their geographical and issue boundaries to link with others in struggle, to construct a broader global movement of the left–and beyond. Case studies span the social movement spectrum from more traditional concerns with class, the primacy of the labor movement, economic redistribution and justice, through the so-called 'new' movements of identity and post-materialist issues of peace, the environment, gender, and indigenous struggles, to the newest currents in (post-)autonomy, (post-)anarchism, and de- or anti-coloniality.

Together these studies show that what began in Chiapas with the Zapatista cry of *basta ya!* as an 'anti-globalization' movement morphed for a time into 'alter-globalization' and 'global peace and justice', and may now be emerging as a counter-hegemonic project of and for global democratization.

This book was published as a special issue of *Globalizations*.

Ruth Reitan is Assistant Professor of International Studies at the University of Miami, USA. She is author of *Global Activism* (Routledge, 2007) and *The Rise and Decline of an Alliance: Cuba and African American Leaders in the 1960s* (Michigan State University, 1999) and conducts participatory research at World Social Forums and other international activist sites.

Rethinking Globalizations
Edited by Barry K. Gills, Newcastle University, UK

This series is designed to break new ground in the literature on globalization and its academic and popular understanding. Rather than perpetuating or simply reacting to the economic understanding of globalization, this series seeks to capture the term and broaden its meaning to encompass a wide range of issues and disciplines and convey a sense of alternative possibilities for the future.

1. Whither Globalization?
The vortex of knowledge and globalization
James H. Mittelman

2. Globalization and Global History
Edited by Barry K. Gills and William R. Thompson

3. Rethinking Civilization
Communication and terror in the global village
Majid Tehranian

4. Globalization and Contestation
The new great counter-movement
Ronaldo Munck

5. Global Activism
Ruth Reitan

6. Globalization, the City and Civil Society in Pacific Asia
Edited by Mike Douglass, K.C. Ho and Giok Ling Ooi

7. Challenging Euro-America's Politics of Identity
The return of the native
Jorge Luis Andrade Fernandes

8. The Global Politics of Globalization
"Empire" vs "Cosmopolis"
Edited by Barry K. Gills

9. The Globalization of Environmental Crisis
Edited by Jan Oosthoek and Barry K. Gills

10. Globalization as Evolutionary Process
Modeling global change
Edited by Geroge Modelski, Tessaleno Devezas and William R. Thompson

11. The Political Economy of Global Security
War, future crises and changes in global governance
Heikki Patomäki

12. Cultures of Globalization
Coherence, hybridity, contestation
Edited by Kevin Archer, M. Martin Bosman, M. Mark Amen and Ella Schmidt

13. Globalization and the Global Politics of Justice
Edited by Barry K. Gills

14. Global Economy Contested
Power and conflict across the international division of labor
Edited by Marcus Taylor

15. Rethinking Insecurity, War and Violence
Beyond savage globalization?
Edited by Damian Grenfell and Paul James

16. Recognition and Redistribution
Beyond international development
Edited by Heloise Weber and Mark T. Berger

17. The Social Economy
Working alternatives in a globalizing era
Edited by Hasmet M. Uluorta

18. The Global Governance of Food
Edited by Sara R. Curran, April Linton, Abigail Cooke and Andrew Schrank

19. Global Poverty, Ethics and Human Rights
The role of multilateral organisations
Desmond McNeill and Asunción Lera St. Clair

20. Globalization and Popular Sovereignty
Democracy's transnational dilemma
Adam Lupel

21. Limits to Globalization
North-South divergence
William R. Thompson and Rafael Reuveny

22. Globalisation, Knowledge and Labour
Education for solidarity within spaces of resistance
Edited by Mario Novelli and Anibel Ferus-Comelo

23. Dying Empire
U.S. imperialism and global resistance
Francis Shor

24. Alternative Globalizations
An integrative approach to studying dissident knowledge in the global justice movement
S. A. Hamed Hosseini

25. Global Restructuring, Labour and the Challenges for Transnational Solidarity
Edited by Andreas Bieler and Ingemar Lindberg

26. Global South to the Rescue
Emerging humanitarian superpowers and globalizing rescue industries
Edited by Paul Amar

27. Global Ideologies and Urban Landscapes
Edited by Manfred B. Steger and Anne McNevin

28. Power and Transnational Activism
Edited by Thomas Olesen

29. Globalization and Crisis
Edited by Barry K. Gills

30. Andre Gunder Frank and Global Development
Visions, remembrances and explorations
Edited by Patrick Manning and Barry K. Gills

31. Global Social Justice
Edited by Heather Widdows and Nicola J. Smith

32. Globalization, Labor Export and Resistance
A study of Filipino migrant domestic workers in global cities.
Ligaya Lindio-McGovern

33. Situating Global Resistance
Between Discipline and Dissent
Edited by Lara Montesinos Coleman and Karen Tucker

34. A History of World Order and Resistance
The Making and Unmaking of Global Subjects
André C. Drainville

35. Migration, Work and Citizenship in the New Global Order
Edited by Ronaldo Munck, Carl-Ulrik Schierup and Raúl Delgado Wise

36. Edges of Global Justice
The World Social Forum and Its 'Others'
Janet Conway

37. Land Grabbing and Global Governance
Edited by Matias E. Margulis, Nora McKeon and Saturnino Borras Jr.

38. Dialectics in World Politics
Edited by Shannon Brincat

39. Crisis, Movement, Management: Globalising Dynamics
Edited by James Goodman and Jonathan Paul Marshall

40. China's Development
Capitalism and Empire
Michel Aglietta and Guo Bai

41. Global Governance and NGO Participation
Charlotte Dany

42. Arab Revolutions and World Transformations
Edited by Anna M. Agathangelou and Nevzat Soguk

43. Global Movement
Edited by Ruth Reitan

44. Free Trade and the Transnational Labour Movement
Edited by Andreas Bieler, Bruno Ciccaglione, John Hilary and Ingemar Lindberg

Global Movement

Edited by
Ruth Reitan

LONDON AND NEW YORK

First published 2013
by Routledge
2 Park Square, Milton Park, Abingdon, Oxfordshire OX14 4RN
Simultaneously published in the USA and Canada
by Routledge
711 Third Avenue, New York, NY 10017

First issued in paperback 2014

Routledge is an imprint of the Taylor and Francis Group, an informa business

© 2013 Taylor & Francis

This book is a reproduction of *Globalizations*, vol. 9, issue 3. The Publisher requests to those authors who may be citing this book to state, also, the bibliographical details of the special issue on which the book was based.

All rights reserved. No part of this book may be reprinted or reproduced or utilised in any form or by any electronic, mechanical, or other means, now known or hereafter invented, including photocopying and recording, or in any information storage or retrieval system, without permission in writing from the publishers.

Trademark notice: Product or corporate names may be trademarks or registered trademarks, and are used only for identification and explanation without intent to infringe.

British Library Cataloguing in Publication Data
A catalogue record for this book is available from the British Library

ISBN 978-0-415-63773-2 (hbk)
ISBN 978-0-415-84026-2 (pbk)

Typeset in Times New Roman
by Taylor & Francis

Publisher's Note
The publisher would like to make readers aware that the chapters in this book may be referred to as articles as they are identical to the articles published in the special issue. The publisher accepts responsibility for any inconsistencies that may have arisen in the course of preparing this volume for print.

Contents

Citation Information ix

1. Introduction: Theorizing and Engaging the Global Movement: From Anti-Globalization to Global Democratization
   Ruth Reitan 1

2. Coalescence of the Global Peace and Justice Movements
   Ruth Reitan 15

3. The Global Social Forum Rhizome: A Theoretical Framework
   Peter Nikolaus Funke 29

4. 'Workers of the World, Unite'? Globalization and the Quest for Transnational Solidarity
   Andreas Bieler 43

5. Transnational Feminisms Building Anti-Globalization Solidarities
   Janet Conway 57

6. Climate Change or Social Change? Environmentalism, Leftist Praxis and Participatory Action Research
   Ruth Reitan & Shannon Gibson 73

7. An Indigenous Movement to Confront Climate Change
   Ben Powless 89

8. 'No One Is Illegal!' Resistance and the Politics of Discomfort
   Maurice Stierl 103

9. Balkanization of Politics, Politics of Balkanization
   Andrej Grubačić 117

10. The Living and Being of the Streets: Fanon and the Arab Uprisings
    Anna M. Agathangelou 129

Index 145

Citation Information

The chapters in this book were originally published in *Globalizations*, volume 9, issue 3 (June 2012). When citing this material, please use the original page numbering for each article, as follows:

Chapter 1
Introduction: Theorizing and Engaging the Global Movement: From Anti-Globalization to Global Democratization
Ruth Reitan
Globalizations, volume 9, issue 3 (June 2012) pp. 323-336

Chapter 2
Coalescence of the Global Peace and Justice Movements
Ruth Reitan
Globalizations, volume 9, issue 3 (June 2012) pp. 337-350

Chapter 3
The Global Social Forum Rhizome: A Theoretical Framework
Peter Nikolaus Funke
Globalizations, volume 9, issue 3 (June 2012) pp. 351-364

Chapter 4
'Workers of the World, Unite'? Globalisation and the Quest for Transnational Solidarity
Andreas Bieler
Globalizations, volume 9, issue 3 (June 2012) pp. 365-378

Chapter 5
Transnational Feminisms Building Anti-Globalization Solidarities
Janet Conway
Globalizations, volume 9, issue 3 (June 2012) pp. 379-394

Chapter 6
Climate Change or Social Change? Environmental and Leftist Praxis and Participatory Action Research
Ruth Reitan and Shannon Gibson
Globalizations, volume 9, issue 3 (June 2012) pp. 395-410

CITATION INFORMATION

Chapter 7
An Indigenous Movement to Confront Climate Change
Ben Powless
Globalizations, volume 9, issue 3 (June 2012) pp. 411-424

Chapter 8
'No One Is Illegal!' Resistance and the Politics of Discomfort
Maurice Stierl
Globalizations, volume 9, issue 3 (June 2012) pp. 425-438

Chapter 9
Balkanization of Politics, Politics of Balkanization
Andrej Grubačić
Globalizations, volume 9, issue 3 (June 2012) pp. 439-450

Chapter 10
The Living and Being of the Streets: Fanon and the Arab Uprisings
Anna M. Agathangelou
Globalizations, volume 9, issue 3 (June 2012) pp. 451-466

INTRODUCTION

Theorizing and Engaging the Global Movement: From Anti-Globalization to Global Democratization

RUTH REITAN
University of Miami, USA

Critical research and theorizing on facets of the Anti-/Alter-Globalization Movement (AGM) has proliferated over the last two decades. Fewer accounts, however, have been written by scholar-activists themselves engaged in and reflecting on the constituent movements they are helping to forge within this amorphous, global network of networks.[1] This volume provides a platform for doing so, and thus gives new empirical insights into the history and internal dynamics of the movements themselves along with the ways in which they are reaching beyond their geographical and issue boundaries to link with others in struggle, and thus constructing a broader global movement.

In this introduction, I will first survey the burgeoning literature on transnational activism and global civil society in order to situate, analyze, and theorize the AGM within the three historical traditions—and contentious relations—of the political left: namely liberal reformism, marxian revolution, and anarcho-autonomist radicalism. Doing so helps us to understand this diverse and dispersed mobilization cycle as growing out of, and still rooted in, the left and thus constitutive of it today. I argue that what is unique about this 'global left' is that it has not fractured into its historical three tendencies, but instead has woven itself into a metaphorical frayed braid, which is now entwining with transgressive and potentially transformative strands *beyond* the traditional left–right spectrum, those of indigenous and other anti- and de-colonial struggles.

The current cycles' weaving began in the mid-1990s, at the height of neoliberalism's material and ideational power. Thus it was characterized largely by resistance and indignation: the cry of *basta ya!* and the stance of 'anti-globalization'. But in the last decade, US–NATO imperial overstretch has combined with casino capitalism's catastrophic effects at last coming home to roost in the economic core. What is emerging is something that was always latent, as an aspiration, in the movement strands. But with time it has grown more pronounced, as the movements have moved from resisting to experimenting, from protesting to proposing and, in some places, imposing: coalescing into a demand and the practice of *democracy, now!* Thus, what began nearly two decades ago as *anti-globalization* morphed for a time into *alter-globalization* and *global peace and justice* or simply the *movement of movements*, and now seems to be congealing into a counter-hegemonic project of and for *global democratization*.[2]

This theoretical contextualization and survey of the diverse left—and 'beyond the left'—helps us better situate and appreciate this volume's empirical contributions, which span the social movement spectrum from what are considered more 'traditional' or older leftist struggles defined by class conflict, the primacy of the labor movement, and economic redistribution or justice, through the so-called 'new' movements of identity and post-materialist issues of peace, the environment, gender, and indigenous struggles, to the 'newest' currents in (post-)autonomy, (post-)anarchism, and de- and or anti-coloniality.

Arranging the volume in this way also demonstrates the oversimplification in this common rendering of social movement evolution from 'old' to 'newest'. Rather, we will see the considerable continuity among them, including a shared concern with and targeting of neoliberalism; engaging with multiple and overlapping issues rather than being single-issue movements; demands for and experiments with dispersing power into more democratic forms; and a desire for building *inter*-movement solidarity and broader alliances, while retaining *intra*-movement identity and autonomy. Finally, this work combines a critical globalization studies orientation and participatory research methodologies, which will be briefly overviewed at the end.

'The Frayed Braid': Three Strands of the Historic Left entwined in Today's Global Movement[3]

This most recent cycle of global contention in which the AGM is forging itself can be marked as beginning with the Zapatista uprising in Chiapas, Mexico, against the NAFTA on New Year's Day in 1994. It was nurtured within the World Social Forum (WSF) process beginning in 2001 and its ongoing regional and local manifestations since then, and has continued via mass mobilizations such as the 'Battle in Seattle' against the WTO in December 1999, the 15 February 2003 global day of action against the war in Iraq, the 2005 Gleneagles and 2007 Heiligendamm anti-G8 protests, and the 2009 UN climate summit mobilization in Copenhagen. The 2011 'Arab Spring' youth uprisings across the Middle East and North Africa (MENA) region and the Occupy Wall Street movement it helped inspire that autumn are better understood as a continuation and reinvigoration of this cycle, rather than the start of a new one.

The AGM is made up of myriad social movement organizations and networks that rebel, resist, petition, campaign, and create alternative practices that, although incredibly diverse, are quite clearly of the 'left': that is, against neoliberal globalization and state and corporate power and for greater equality, dignity, democracy, devolution of power, autonomy, peace, sustainable living, environmental protection, and social justice at the local, national, and transnational levels and across economic, political, social, cultural, and environmental spheres. Below I will historically situate, analyze, and theorize this amorphous movement (of movements) within the three broad traditions and fractious relations of the political left, namely liberalism, marxism, and anarcho-autonomism.

Theorizing to date has tended to privilege one of these traditions to the exclusion or marginalization of the others, for example in the social democratic reformism and liberal cosmopolitanism of Florini and Simmons (2000) and Albrow and Seckinelgin (2010), the neo-marxism of Hardt and Negri (2000, 2004) and Boswell and Chase-Dunn (2000), or the neo-anarchism of Graeber (2004) and Curran (2007). These valuable, though partial or partisan, works aside, scholars in the main have been hesitant to theorize the global left—autonomous from political parties or trade unions and beyond simply the 'transnational advocacy networks' led by professional non-governmental organizations (NGOs)—as a coherent formation.

This reticence is warranted for at least three reasons: the empirical challenge of sufficiently grasping the breadth and depth of a dispersed network of millions of actors in flux; the postmodern and postcolonial ethical aversion to grand narratives, which necessarily diminish the very diversity, egalitarianism, complexity, and contingency championed by alter-globalization activists; and the awareness of and sensitivity to activists' hesitancy in advancing an overall strategy or attempting to forge a united organization, which many deem not only impossible at the current juncture but also *impolitic*: that is, counter to the prevailing political ethos of the contemporary left which would only lead to the derision and failures of the past. Mindful of these caveats, I nevertheless offer a theorization here, drawn from engaging with and reflecting on the AGM for over a decade now.

Contemporary activism is as diverse, complex, and historically rooted as the global processes, actors, and power flows they contest. In this environment, activists have recognized the necessity for multiple and flexible approaches to resist, engage, and ultimately decapitate and replace the Janus-head of neoliberal globalization, connected to the much larger and longer-tailed monster of capitalism feeding off of other hierarchies of oppression. Yet what is remarkable about the most recent cycle of contention is the degree to which the global left has *not* fractured into its historical constituent parts of liberalism, marxism, and anarcho-autonomism. On the contrary, activists are reflecting on and debating together, hybridizing, experimenting with and challenging the limits of these traditions in unique ways. Groups and individuals inspired by each tendency hone their tactics, refine positions, and strengthen identities, while simultaneously seeking alliances, coordinating actions, and articulating nascent strategies with a wide range of others. Throughout this mobilization cycle they have sought to dialogue, build trust, craft consensus declarations, and act in coalitions when possible or in parallel affinity blocs when not.

While tensions are ever present, activists make ongoing efforts to mitigate, manage, bridge, or downplay them toward joint action—or at the very least to not work at cross-purposes. Thus, some focus on lobbying, advising, or challenging governance actors at all levels. Others experiment with alternative and autonomous modes of political, economic, and social relations. Their cumulative efforts amount to a multi-pronged strategy entailing dynamic, loose, and limited coordination across the spectrum from reform to radicalism. Their aim is to challenge and, for some, collectively wield power at the transnational level while drawing power *downwards* and pushing it *outwards* to local communities and daily struggles. This 'networked fragmentation', notes one scholar-activist, allows diverse groups to retain their 'oppositional autonomy within a network of oppositional unity' (Curran, 2007, p. 56).

The above trend can be visualized as a *frayed braid* woven from the three leftist strands, as their adherents dialogically define themselves and contentiously interact with others. Yet in observing and reflecting theoretically upon the interplay of liberal, post-marxist, anarchist, and autonomist traditions manifested in contemporary activist praxis, one also sees how they have entwined with potentially transformative strands *beyond* the traditional left–right spectrum, those of indigenous and other anti- and de-colonial struggles. Two recent 'twists' in this braid come, first, from deep ecology and autonomist leftist traditions articulating with indigenous activists—who themselves are in contentious relations with 'twenty-first century socialism' in places like Bolivia and Ecuador—and second, from the rapid diffusion of occupying public squares sparked by the Arab Spring youth uprisings and spreading through the *indignado* movement in Spain and Southern Europe and on to inspire the 'occupy' encampments in North America. These recent and dramatic turns have woven 'old', 'new', and 'newest' leftist social movement strands together with non-, anti-, and hybridized-Western resistance traditions, and, in South America, with new state-socialist experiments in a *diagonal* way.

Popular resistance to capitalism and demands for self-determination and democracy are by no means recent phenomena. Both can be traced back across centuries of contestation and proposition that Polanyi (2001 [1944]) called 'the double movement', Laclau and Mouffe (2001 [1987]) hailed as a counter-hegemonic movement of 'radical and plural democracy', and Boswell and Chase-Dunn (2000) termed the 'spiral of capitalism and socialism'. Social movement researchers have observed how each wave of progressive movements since the French and Russian revolutions has emerged out of preexisting groups, networks, identities, and solidarities (Bonnell, 1983; Gould, 1995; Heirich, 1968; Jasper, 1997; Levitsky, 2007; McAdam, 1982; Morris, 1984). Another line of scholarship shows that the left–right dichotomy, also emanating from the French revolution, has remained an enduring feature in public debate at the domestic and international levels and continues to shape both individual and collective orientations between progressives and conservatives (Noël and Thérien, 2008). Drawing these two strands together, I argue that each wave of movements has been shaped by—but also by its praxis, *shaped*—the left–right dichotomy inherited from the French liberal revolution, as well as the distinctions *within* the left itself following the communist revolution in Russia.

In today's AGM, the latter distinctions manifest in, first, the liberal, social democratic NGOs and the transnational advocacy networks they lead aimed at influencing national and intergovernmental policy, and second, the diminished Marxist-Leninist parties and trade unions and the various mobilization groups they organize. Both of these 'old left' or 'modernist' tendencies are concerned with rights, redistribution, and, at the margins, revolution. They thus view capturing, or at least influencing, the national state—and, more recently, inter-state bureaucracies—as a necessary step toward socializing the increasingly global means of production and democratizing the global polity. Both conceptualize power as hegemonic and hierarchical, yet ultimately consensual—once the liberals construct their perfect institutions or the marxists destroy capitalism. Both also view the state as either a prototype for, or as a necessary evil through which to pass to, a cosmopolitan world order characterized by equality, freedom, justice, democracy, and peace.

The two above modernist strands have largely set the parameters of theoretical debate and practice for twentieth century leftist struggles. A third strand, however, has again asserted itself in the most recent cycle of contention, characterized as late-, post- pre-, or anti-modern and anti- and de-colonial: it is comprised of autonomists, direct-actionists, post-anarchists, and post-marxists, as well as some indigenous, anarcha-feminist, and anti-colonial tendencies. This very broad strand views power as networked, biopolitical, prefigurative, and, in the current global order, parasitic—yet ideally horizontal. For them the state is one of many hierarchical and interlinked structures or relations of domination—along with capitalism, patriarchy, Western (neo)colonialism and racism, and the pro-growth and anti-environment development model—that must be abandoned, challenged, destroyed, or transformed if 'a world in which many worlds can fit', to quote Zapatista *subcomandante* Marcos, is to be realized.

These twirling three strands have been ubiquitous in leftist or progressive political praxis for well over a century, with enumerable examples of both *braiding* and *fraying*, of one strand thickening while another is thinning—and at times of one trying to strangle the other(s). Socialist folklore traces their genesis to the beginning of modern transnational activism, when Karl Marx himself, representing revolutionary communism, purged the anarchist group surrounding Mikhail Bakunin after the first Communist International for opposing Marx's call to participate in parliamentary elections with an eye toward seizing state power. Instead, the father of collectivist anarchism Bakunin (1996 [1873]) advocated direct action on the part of workers to abolish the state and capitalism simultaneously, and thus presciently rejected the intermediate stage of the 'dictatorship of the proletariat' on the grounds that it threatened to permanently enslave the very workers it purported to free. The second schism to emerge early on was between anti-capitalist revolution and social democratic reformism. It broke out in the wake of World War I and was exacerbated by the competing solidarities between national citizen and international proletarian. The terms of this polemical debate, leftist history tells us, were set by German Social Democratic Party members Eduard Bernstein (1993 [1889]) arguing for the reformist path to socialism as opposed to Rosa Luxemburg (1973 [1900]) advocating the workers' revolution.

The contemporary AGM is steeped in this legacy of debates and fractures among tendencies; thick constructivists and post-structuralists would go further in saying that the AGM *is* (constituted by) these three strands, and thus *embodies* the contemporary global left. It follows that, via their discursive actions, AGM activists have shaped and even transformed the left in unique ways.[4] As Curran (2007, p. 50) avers, the AGM 'draws from a variety of oppositional strands—old and new—and then reweaves them into a distinctive politics' in virtual spaces of the Internet and geographic convergence locales such as the WSF, both of which are based on horizontal, affinity, participatory, anarchistic, anti-capitalist, and radically democratic ethos which prize diversity (Ibid., pp. 50–3). Indeed, contentious dialogue among the three strands, rather than sectarianism or splittism, is evidenced in the ongoing 'space vs. movement' debate within the WSF (see Reitan, 2009; Smith et al., 2011; WSF, 2008), which to a certain extent mirrors that between the new and newest left vs. old left (Curran, 2007, p. 71).

Thus, this articulation among ideological tendencies is simultaneously a reweaving of the three generations of social movements on a dynamic and more egalitarian basis: the 'old left' of industrial trade unionism and communist political parties severely weakened by the collapse of state-socialism and the global spread of neoliberal capitalism is more open to seeking alliances with 'new left' identity-based movements such as feminists and ethnic minorities along with the 'post-materialist' concerns of peace and the environment, and both the 'old' and 'new' are infused with the vibrant networking processes and ethos of the 'newest left' (see Curran, 2007; Day, 2005) characterized by a resurgent anarchism and autonomy, along with militant indigenous and de-colonial activism.

In the context of contemporary leftist activism, these ideological and generational tendencies animate the global backlash against corporate and financial interests in their drive to construct a single integrated economy and international legal order via neoliberal globalization. And, as stated at the outset, as they mature and diversify, they have moved from resisting to proposing and doing, and from anti-globalization—the one 'no!' heard and amplified by the Zapatistas—to the many 'yeses' of alternative and democratic experiments that amount to an emergent, counter-hegemonic project of global democratization. Specifically, these strands manifest in the color-coded blocs and diverse tactics of black (anarchists), red (socialists and labor), green (environmentalists), and pink (pacifists) at mass protests around the world. They shaped the various networks that mobilized against the US 'war on terror'. They were there when urban autonomists and indigenous groups protested the 'NGOization' of the WSF and its regional spin-offs, when they occupied spaces within the forums to protest their and others' exclusion, and when they self-organized direct actions and meeting spaces simultaneously but 'beyond the WSF'. They have constantly competed in the WSF International Council over whether the council's proper role is a deliberative and representative body or merely a facilitative one which cannot take decisions on the WSF's behalf, as well as on how the forum relates to political parties, government officials, and armed groups. And they are there in the occupied plazas and tent encampments and, in complex and contentious ways, in the MENA rebellions and transitions still underway.

What can be discerned from the above are two dynamics, one centrifugal and the other centripetal: regarding the former dispersive dynamic, disagreements among the three historic leftist tendencies—albeit in hybridized forms—pervade the current left. But as to the latter inclusive dynamic, it is important to notice that the three tendencies *are still all there*—debating, critiquing, conflicting, but also coordinating together—15 years and counting into this cycle: in the shared or parallel physical spaces at social forums, in the virtual spaces of email listserves where they debate and plan inside–outside strategies and future mobilizations, in the intergovernmental summits and street demonstrations coordinating among various blocs and affinity groups, and in the occupations of public squares and parks.

I will briefly take each contemporary strand in turn. Today's equivalent of the Bernsteinian, social democratic reformers denounce corporate power vis-à-vis the state, society, and the environment and work to promote democratic reforms and oversight at the national and international levels of governance. This continues to be the most prosaic, or even hegemonic, tendency, if only because (neo)liberal discourse recognizes its right to exist as a separate but *ur*-political sphere. Liberal scholars and activists hail this tendency as an emergent 'transnational civil society' (Della Porta and Tarrow, 2005; Florini and Simmons, 2000; Keane, 2003; Keck and Sikkink, 1998; Risse, 2000; Smith and Johnston, 2002). Many have argued that civil society's active engagement with international regimes raises the prospects of international declarations being adopted (Keck and Sikkink, 1998, p. 25) and augments the legitimacy and democracy of global governance (Florini and Simmons, 2000; Reinicke, 2000). Wallgren (2009) regards the reformist and globalizing impulse of many Northern activists as constitutive of the liberal discursive regime of 'civil society' wherein: 'The combination of universal ethical commitment and a concern for global challenges and problems turns rather mechanically into a reason for a grand scale of intervention and a positive prejudice towards high-level institution-building'.

The reasons for 'scaling up' are numerous, and reflect the general demands of many so-called first generation, NGO advocacy networks in recent years. Economic globalization forces have overburdened the governance capacity of any single state. Thus civil society is needed to pressure these institutions into becoming more democratic and as participants themselves in constructing democratic processes. And global problems such as climate change, debt, poverty, weapons proliferation, and financial crises demand global solutions and governance regimes that transcend the *realpolitik* logic of state-to-state relations (Habermas, 2006; Held, 1995; Patomäki and Teivainen, 2004; Sehm-Patomäki and Ulvila, 2007; Wallgren, 2009). Most NGOs thus pursue strategies of demanding recognition, rights, resources and reforms from the transnational tangle of informal, quasi-formal, or intergovernmental actors—the legitimacy, authority, and power of which many NGOs at the same time contest.

Yet, by the very act of petitioning, their more radical critics—latter-day Luxemburgians and Bakuninites—argue that the NGO reformers empower these actors at the transnational level while instantiating their own relative marginality in an emergent, stratified global polity. In the current context of multiple and interrelated crises wracking the global economy and taxing the earth's carrying capacity, which have in turn exacerbated inequalities, deprivations, and conflicts, leftist praxis has again radicalized. No longer isolated voices crying out in the wilderness against neoliberal capitalism, the debate has pushed beyond Keynesian and Polanyian-style reforms toward re-visioning and practicing anew radical and utopian projects. These strive to draw lessons from both the failures of past communist experiments and the successes of non-capitalist and non-Western socio-economic arrangements that have persisted over centuries.

Thus, a major rethink—if less so a re-do—of communism for the twenty-first century is underway, centered especially on experiments in 'post-anarchism' conjoined with pre-, post-, and antimodern autonomism and anti- and de-coloniality (see Adamovsky, 2007; Balakrishnan, 2003; Conway, 2007; Day, 2005; Graeber, 2004; Graeber and Grubačić, 2004; Hardt and Negri, 2000, 2004; Holloway, 2005; IIRE, 2005; Juris, 2008; May, 1994; Mignolo, 2009; Newman, 2011; Notes from Nowhere, 2003; Sullivan, 2005; Turbulence Collective, 2007a, b, 2008, 2009; Zibechi, 2010; Žižek, 2009). Marxist geographer David Harvey (2010: 259) asserts:

> While traditional institutionalized communism is as good as dead and buried, there are . . . millions of de facto communists active among us . . . ready to creatively pursue anti-capitalist imperatives. If, as the alternative globalisation movement of the late 1990s declared, 'another world is possible', then why not also say 'another communism is possible'?

This 'other possible communism' owes much of its dynamism to the resurgence of anti-state, anti-colonial, and anti-capitalist anarchism and autonomism. While reanimating the classical debates and dichotomies between revolutionary marxists and anarchists, the resurgence has precipitated a truce and sparked creative hybrids between the two currents; that is to say, a truly leftist dialectic is once again in full swing. Harvey (2010, p. 225) notes that this revival has tended to eschew Leninist strategies of seizing the state in favor of experimenting with networked, federative, affinity-based, social organizational forms aimed at circumventing the state and capital. It has thus brought about 'a convergence of some sort between the Marxist and anarchist traditions that harks back to the broadly collaborative situation between them in the 1860s in Europe'. This has also generated a creative ferment around re-imagining power, the state, sovereignty, democracy, and global governance, as witnessed in the jazz-like fusions of neo- and post-marxist, autonomist, *operaist*, and anarchist praxis.

Yet as the cycle crested in the early 2000s and then ebbed, it has left few lasting changes, much less utopias. Some began to doubt the workability of the horizontalist political ethic after the increasingly hostile responses and criminalization of protests in the wake of the 11 September 2001 attacks, and to question whether spontaneous rebellions, micropolitics, and autonomous experiments could survive, let alone multiply and link up. The confusion over which way forward for the Occupy movement, and the submerging of youthful Arab rebellions under the resurgent power struggles among conservative forces, have raised further doubts along these lines. In this context, 'verticalist' Leninist critiques have begun to ring a bit truer, even in the ears of 'horizontalists', like the perennial warning delivered by French Trotskyist philosopher Daniel Bensaïd (in IIRE, 2005, p. 11) to *Zapatismo* scholar-activist John Holloway: 'Those who thought they could ignore state power and its conquest have often been its victims: they didn't want to take power, so power took them.'

Based on these experiments, reflections, and ongoing dialogues among marxist and anarcho-autonomist tendencies, some inspired by the latter strand have come to provisionally accept the former's call for a degree of internal organization as well as engagement with state power and broader non-state allies (Adamovksy, 2007; De Marcellus, 2009; McLeish, 2009; Turbulence 2007a, b, 2008, 2009). Climate and anti-nuclear activist Tadzio Müller (2010) described this shift as follows:

> Post-autonomous politics, exemplified historically by groups like Ya Basta/Disobbedienti, and most coherently today by the Interventionist Left alliance in Germany comes out of a frustration with autonomous politics as *auto-marginalizzazione* (in Italy and Germany) and as being primarily

about creating islands of difference and freedom in a sea of capitalist sameness and exploitation. This recent post-autonomous tradition wants to focus on intervening into actually existing social conflicts, and to *there* work in such a way that empowers more people to take 'radical' action, breaking the rules of the everyday madness around us. In order to do that, post-autonomous politics have generally adopted a less sub-cultural style (less exclusionary), have focused more on building alliances with non-left-radical groups, on communicating far more openly and in a more 'fashionable' and, within the mainstream, 'understandable' style.

Finally, this contemporary leftist *melange* of post-autonomism and post-marxism has further been facilitated, informed, and challenged by radical activists' deepening familiarity and networking with indigenous movements in places like Bolivia and Ecuador, and more generally the rising tide of native militancy across the Americas. The latter is itself articulating in novel and contentious ways with the 'pink tide' of leftist parties that came to power in Central and South America in recent years. Indigenous communities and rural social movements have played decisive roles, for example, in pushing through radically new constitutions in Ecuador and Bolivia which recognize a 'pluri-national' state that is home to many autonomous nations with distinct economic, political, legal, and cultural forms. In addition to disaggregating the legal fiction of the unitary and sovereign state, these constitutions radicalize the notion of rights by guaranteeing the right to each group's self-determination and, in the case of Bolivia, the rights of mother earth, or *pachamama* (see Mignolo, 2009; Zibechi, 2010).

These developments, which are the culmination of centuries of struggle against Western colonization and capitalism, at once expand, collapse, and transcend the European leftist categories. By moving from resistance to antagonistic engagement with the state and, finally, to attempts at transforming the state into a movement-society (Zibechi, 2010), they have managed to fundamentally challenge the Western unitary state ideal, its indivisible sovereignty, and its limited guarantees of liberal rights. Many communities resisting or in open rebellion today have managed to sustain unique features of social, political, cultural, economic, and ecological systems that pre-date colonialism, capitalism, and the European state form. But rather than promoting their autonomous or hybrid models as universals to be exported *pace* Christianity, liberalism, or Marxism-Leninism, these indigenous and anti-colonial experiments—along with the hybridized governance forms and new categories of rights they are articulating—are rather 'an invitation to organise and re-inscribe communal systems all over the world . . . erased and dismantled by the increasing expansion of the capitalist economy, which the European left has been unable to halt' (Mignolo, 2009, p. 31).

Volume's Approach and Contributions: Critical Globalization Scholarship and Participatory Research Methods

Like the diversity of the global left—and 'more than left'—surveyed above, the nine contributions in this volume span the social movement spectrum. They range from those of organized labor and the salience of class conflict and economic justice (see Bieler; Funke; Reitan), through the 'new' identity-based and post-materialist movements of peace (Reitan), the environment (Reitan and Gibson), feminism (Conway), and indigenous (Powless), to the 'newest' currents in post-autonomy, post-anarchism, and anti- or de-coloniality, informed by post-structural and postcolonial theory (Stierl; Grubačić; Agathangelou). But, again, we will see that these are neither discrete movements nor 'moments' in the evolution of the left, and instead that considerable continuity and commonalities exist among them, including the concern with countering neoliberal globalization/capitalism, dispersing power into more democratic forms, and building inter-movement alliances while retaining intra-movement autonomy.

The contributing authors bring rich and varied histories of engagement with social movements, as well as a diversity of theoretical and methodological approaches to study them. These combined scholar-activist roles allow us to offer critical, insider reflections on diverse movement strands that help comprise the whole of global left activism in the most recent cycle of contention. Our involvement also allows us to shed crucial light on *how* each current works to create a broader movement via networking, debating, cooperating, and campaigning with others in spaces such as the social forums and activist protest sites as well as via the Internet. We aim to illuminate existing as well as potential connections across movements, and thus spotlight avenues for greater cooperation toward strengthening the AGM. We also expose tensions, contradictions, conflicts, missed opportunities, or perceived failures within and between movements. Throughout, the authors have striven to situate each movement historically, within recent globalization trends, and in relation to other movements comprising the AGM.

Turning from empirical to theoretical and methodological contributions, the volume combines a critical globalization studies orientation with participatory research methodologies. Both share a commitment to reflexivity and historicism, de-centering and inter-disciplinarity, and to challenging and transforming hegemonic concentrations of power by giving voice to marginalized and emancipatory visions (Eschle and Maiguashca 2005; Kemmis and McTaggart, 2000; Mittelman, 2005). A number of authors have elaborated on their role as scholar-activist or have reflected on their positionality or standpoint vis-à-vis the struggle they are researching. Though levels of movement participation vary, each author shows an affinity for the egalitarian ethic of Participatory Action Research (PAR), where the scholar's stance is one of empathetic— but also critical—insider who seeks to *accompany* social movement actors toward articulating a consensual 'common sense' which those involved might consider clarifying, legitimate, and useful in their practice.[5] Therefore, in addition to providing detailed case studies of nine key activist networks comprising the AGM, the volume will also serve as a methodological resource to aid further scholar-activist research.[6]

The first three contributions are concerned with more 'traditional' social movement issues based on class, organized labor, economic justice, and countering neoliberal globalization/capitalism. In 'Coalescence of the Global Peace and Justice Movements', Ruth Reitan uses a 'dynamics of contention' approach to trace the *transnational coalescence* process between the post-Seattle, anti-neoliberal movement and anti-war concerns triggered by the 9/11 attacks and the 'war on terror'. She demonstrates the crucial role of key bridge-building organizations in first shifting down to harness nascent activist energies by brokering new ties and reinvigorating old ones, as well as frame-extending between emerging and extant concerns, in order to then scale back up as a broader transnational movement for Global Peace *and* Justice.

'The Global Social Forum Rhizome: A Theoretical Framework' by Peter Nikolaus Funke adapts Deleuze and Guattari's concept to map the WSF process and its implications for the broader global left. While the social forum as rhizome allows for unprecedented connections and has helped temper inter-movement antinomies, he cautions that its logic also limits coalescence and creates a politics unable to get beyond symbolic acts and resistances and toward a common articulation of and movement against capitalism with class as the main organizing principle. Relatedly, Andreas Bieler's '"Workers of the World, Unite"? Globalisation and the Quest for Transnational Solidarity' assesses the possibilities and obstacles facing trade unions in their quest to build transnational, intra- and inter-movement solidarity. Analyzed against the background of structural economic change and the dynamics of capitalism, he compares and contrasts the limited successes of two initiatives which organized labor has launched within the WSF, the ITUC's 'Decent Work, Decent Life' campaign and the Labour and Globalisation Network.

Turning to the so-called 'new social movement' concerns of identity and post-materialist struggles, Reitan's contribution described above serves as a kind of hinge from the more classical concern with economic justice to that of peace. Janet Conway's 'Transnational Feminisms Building Anti-Globalization Solidarities' is similar to Bieler's work on organized labor, in that she compares two transnational feminist networks—the World March of Women and the Articulación Feminista Marcosur, as they seek to build broader alliances within the WSF. She identifies two modalities, 'dialogues across difference' and 'coalition-building', which are both underpinned by discourses of intersectionality and transversality, as remaking the praxis of solidarity as well as transforming feminisms and other social movements in this process.

In 'Climate Change or Social Change? Environmental and Leftist Praxis and Participatory Action Research', Ruth Reitan and Shannon Gibson share findings from their participatory action research on the internal dynamics and debates among the three main climate activist networks mobilizing at the UNFCCC summit in Copenhagen, those of Climate Action Network, Climate Justice Now!, and Climate Justice Action, and embed these interactions within the diverse history of transnational environmental and left praxis. They show how reformist and especially more radical currents are engaging with non- or anti-Western indigenous struggles to forge the contemporary transnational climate movement. Understanding of these interactions is further enriched by Ben Powless's 'An Indigenous Movement to Confront Climate Change'. In it he traces the movement's roots to indigenous calls for human rights within the UN, describes their unique discourses, epistemology, agenda, main concerns, and mode of self-organization, and highlights the nascent relations but still-considerable gulf between indigenous and non-indigenous movements around this issue.

Finally, the 'newest' social movement tendencies of post-autonomy, -anarchy, and -coloniality are also well-represented in this volume. Maurice Stierl's '"No One Is Illegal!" Resistance and the Politics of Discomfort' shows how a Foucauldian understanding of power and resistance illuminates the more situated and cautious expressions of dissent among undocumented migrants, or *sans-papiers*, supported by the German activist network No One Is Illegal. He argues that local and practical resistances nonetheless embody a broader critique of sovereign hypocrisy, violence, and the 'governmentality of documentation'.

In 'Balkanization of Politics, Politics of Balkanization', Andrej Grubačić juxtaposes the historic colonial violence of 'Balkanization from above' with the social and cultural affinities, customs in common resulting from mutual aid and solidarity, and inter-ethnic self-activity which he terms 'Balkanization from below'. He calls for a recuperation of this historical vision of a trans-ethnic, anti-authoritarian, and pluricultural society and project, expressed in local self-government, communal land use, and federative movements, which, like Stierl, he argues has significance far beyond its immediate locale. Finally, in 'The Living and Being of the Streets: Fanon and the Arab Spring', Anna M. Agathangelou stages a conversation with Frantz Fanon about the space and time of revolutions. She searches for his least sovereign—and potentially most revolutionary—*wretched* subject, which Fanon celebrated in the decolonization and anti-slavery struggles of his era, and finds them in the contemporary MENA uprisings. She interprets these rebellions as advancing toward a socialism that may finally put an end to dispossession and slaughter in the name of development. As each of these diverse studies attest, the weaving goes on and on.

Notes

1 But see the edited works of Jackie Smith and her colleagues (Smith, 2011; Smith et al., 2011), Jai Sen and his (Sen, 2011; Sen and Saini, 2005; Sen and Waterman, 2007), Robin Broad (2002), and Cavanagh and Mander (2004).
2 I thank Andrej Grubačić for engaging in the conversation that helped me to clarify this view, and for hosting the 'Radical Past, Radical Futures: Conversations on Contemporary Social Movements' at the California Institute for Integral Studies, Department of Social and Cultural Anthropology, San Francisco on 30 March 2012 where I first presented it.
3 An earlier iteration of this theoretical argument appeared in Reitan (2011). I thank Peter Funke for comments and suggestions for building on that work.
4 And in engaging with and learning from non-and anti-Western struggles, some may eventually chart paths *beyond* the historical limitations and failures of the left.
5 Our use of participatory methods is particularly novel in that most studies to date employing PAR have been local ethnographies, whereas we focus on more complex, transnational and virtual spaces and relations.
6 In this regard, this volume was envisioned as a sequel, of sorts, to the editor's earlier *Global Activism* (Reitan, 2007), which provides detailed case comparisons of four of the main networks mobilizing against the 'neoliberal triumvirate' of the World Bank, IMF, and World Trade Organization, those of the Jubilee 2000 and follow-on anti-debt campaigns, the post-Seattle Our World is Not for Sale network countering free trade agreements, the mass peasant movement Via Campesina, and the anarchistic Zapatista-inspired Peoples' Global Action.

References

Adamovksy, E. (2007) Autonomous politics and its problems, 11 December, http://www.zcommunications.org/autonomous-politics-and-its-problems-by-ezequiel-adamovsky

Albrow, M. & Seckinelgin, K. (2010) *Global Civil Society 2011: Globality and the Absence of Justice* (New York: Palgrave Macmillan).

Bakunin, M. (1996 [1873]) S. Dolgoff, *Bakunin on Anarchism* (Montreal: Black Rose Books).

Balakrishnan, G. (2003) *Debating Empire* (London: Verso).

Bernstein, E. (1993 [1889]) Tudor Henry, *Bernstein: The Precondition of Socialism* (Cambridge: Cambridge University Press).

Bonnell, V. E. (1983) *Roots of Rebellion: Workers' Politics and Organization in St. Petersburg and Moscow, 1900–1914* (Berkeley: University of California Press).

Boswell, T. & Chase-Dunn, C. (2000) *The Spiral of Capitalism and Socialism: Toward Global Democracy* (Boulder, CO: Lynne Rienner).

Broad, R. (2002) *Global Backlash: Citizen Initiatives for a Just World Economy* (Lanham, MD: Rowman & Littlefield).

Cavanagh, J. & Mander, J. (2004) *Alternatives to Economic Globalization: A Better World Is Possible*, 2nd ed. (San Francisco: Berrett-Koehler).

Conway, J. (2007) Transnational feminisms and the World Social Forum: encounters and transformations in anti-gobalization spaces) *Journal of International Women's Studies*, 8, pp. 49–70.

Curran, G. (2007) *21st Century Dissent: Anarchism, Anti-Globalization and Environmentalism* (Basingstoke/New York: Palgrave Macmillan).

Day, R. J. F. (2005) *Gramsci Is Dead: Anarchist Currents in the Newest Social Movements* (London: Pluto Press).

De Marcellus, O. (2009) Muscle and bone) *Turbulence*, 5, p. 30.

Della Porta, D. & Tarrow, S. (eds) (2005) *Transnational Protest and Global Activism* (Lanham, MD: Rowman & Littlefield).

Eschle, C. & Maiguashca, B. (eds) (2005) *Critical Theories, International Relations and 'the Anti-Globalisation Movement': The Politics of Global Resistance* (London: Routledge).

Florini, A. M. & Simmons, P. J. (eds) (2000) *The Third Force: The Rise of Transnational Civil Society* (Tokyo &, Washington DC: Japan Center for International Exchange and Carnegie Endowment for International Peace).

Gould, R. V. (1995) *Insurgent Identities: Class Community and Protest in Paris from 1848 to the Commune* (Chicago: University of Chicago Press).

Graeber, D. (2004) The new anarchists, in T. Mertes (ed.) *A Movement of Movements: Is Another World Really Possible?* (London: Verso) pp. 202–218.

Graeber, D. & Grubačić, A. (2004) Anarchism, or the revolutionary movement of the twenty-first century, *Znet*, 6 January.

Habermas, J. (2006) *The Divided West* (Cambridge: Polity Press).
Hardt, M. & Negri, A. (2000) *Empire* (Cambridge, MA: Harvard University Press).
Hardt, M. & Negri, A. (2004) *Multitude: War and Democracy in the Age of Empire* (New York: Penguin).
Harvey, D. (2010) *The Enigma of Capital: And the Crises of Capitalism* (Oxford: Oxford University Press).
Heirich, M. (1968) *The Beginning: Berkeley 1964* (New York: Columbia University Press).
Held, D. (1995) *Democracy and the Global Order: From the Modern State to Cosmopolitan Governance* (Cambridge: Polity Press).
Holloway, J. (2005) *Change the World Without Taking Power: The Meaning of Revolution Today* (London: Pluto Press).
IIRE [International Institute for Research and Education] (ed.) (2005) Change the world without taking power? . . . or . . . take power to change the world? a debate on strategies on how to build another world, http://www.marxsite.com/ChangeTheWorld.pdf
Jasper, J. M. (1997) *The Art of Moral Protest* (Chicago: University of Chicago Press).
Juris, J. (2008) *Networking Futures: The Movements Against Corporate Globalization* (Durham, NC: Duke University Press).
Keane, J. (2003) *Global Civil Society?* (Cambridge: Cambridge University Press).
Keck, M. E. & Sikkink, K. (1998) *Activists beyond Borders: Advocacy Networks in International Politics* (Ithaca, NY: Cornell University Press).
Kemmis, S. & McTaggart, R. (2000) Participatory action research, in N.K. Denzin & Y.S. Lincoln (eds), *Handbook of Qualitative Research* (London: Sage 2000), pp. 567–606.
Laclau, E. & Mouffe, C. (2001 [1987]) *Hegemony and Socialist Strategy: Towards a Radical Democratic Politics* (London: Verso).
Levitsky, S. R. (2007) Niche activism: constructing a unified movement identity in a heterogeneous organizational field, *Mobilization: An International Quarterly Review*, 12(3), pp. 271–86.
Luxemburg, R. (1973 [1900]) *Reform or Revolution* (New York: Pathfinder Press).
May, T. (1994) *The Political Philosophy of Poststructuralist Anarchism* (University Park: University of Pennsylvania).
McAdam, D. (1982) *Political Process and the Development of Black Insurgency, 1930–1970* (Chicago: University of Chicago Press).
McLeish, P. (2009) From horizontal to diagonal, *Turbulence*, 5 (December), p. 7.
Mignolo, W. (2009) The communal and the decolonial) *Turbulence*, 5, pp. 29–31.
Mittelman, J. (2005) What is a critical globalization studies?, in R.P. Appelbaum & W.I. Robinson (eds), *Critical Globalization Studies* (London: Routledge), pp. 19–32.
Morris, A. D. (1984) *The Origins of the Civil Rights Movement* (New York: Free Press).
Müller, T. (2010) Email correspondence with author, 24 October.
Newman, S. (2011) *The Politics of Postanarchism* (Edinburgh: Edinburgh University Press).
Notes from Nowhere (eds) (2003) *We are Everywhere: The Irresistible Rise of Global Anticapitalism* (London: Verso).
Noël, A. & Thérien, J.-P. (2008) *Left and Right in Global Politics* (Cambridge: Cambridge University Press).
Patomäki, H. & Teivainen, T. (2004) *A Possible World: Democratic Transformation of Global Institutions* (London and New York: Zed Books).
Polanyi, K. (2001 [1944]) *The Great Transformation: The Political and Economic Origins of Our Time* (Boston: Beacon Press).
Reinicke, W. H. (2000) The other world wide web: global public policy networks, *Foreign Policy*, 117, pp. 44–57.
Reitan, R. (2007) *Global Activism* (London: Routledge).
Reitan, R. (2009) The global anti-war movement within and beyond the World Social Forum, *Globalizations*, 6, pp. 509–23.
Reitan, R. (2011) Coordinated power in contemporary leftist activism, in T. Olesen (ed.) *Power and Transnational Activism* (London: Routledge), pp. 51–72.
Risse, T. (2000) The power of norms versus the norms of power: transnational civil society and human rights, in A. M. Florini, P.J. Simmons (eds), *The Third Force: The Rise of Transnational Civil Society* (Tokyo and Washington DC: Japan Center for International Exchange and Carnegie Endowment for International Peace), pp. 177–210.
Sehm-Patomäki, K. & Ulvila, M. (eds) (2007) *Global Political Parties* (London: Zed Books).
Sen, J. (ed.) (2011) *Interrogating Empires* (New Delhi: OpenWord & Daanish Books).
Sen, J. & Saini, M. (eds) (2005) *Are Other Worlds Possible? Talking New Politics* (New Delhi: Zubaan).
Sen, J. & Waterman, P. (eds) (2007) *World Social Forum: Challenging Empires* (Montreal: Black Rose Books).
Smith, J. (2011) *Handbook on World Social Forum Activism* (Boulder: Paradigm).
Smith, J. & Johnston, H. (eds) (2002) *Globalization and Resistance: Transnational Dimensions of Social Movements* (Lanham, MD: Rowman and Littlefield).

Smith, J., Byrd, S., Reese, E. & Smythe, E. (eds) (2011) *Handbook on World Social Forum Activism* (Boulder, CO: Paradigm Publishhers).
Sullivan, S. (2005) 'We are heartbroken and furious!': violence and the (anti-) globalisation movement (s), in C. Eschle & B. Maiguashca (eds), *Critical Theories, International Relations and 'the Anti-Globalisation Movement': The Politics of Global Resistance* (London: Routledge), pp. 174–194.
Tarrow, S. (2005) *The New Transnational Activism* (Cambridge: Cambridge University Press).
Turbulence Collective (2007a) What would it mean to win? *Turbulence*, 1.
Turbulence Collective (2007b) Move into the light, *Turbulence*, 3.
Turbulence Collective (2008) Who will save us from the future? *Turbulence*, 4.
Turbulence Collective (2009) Shifting grounds, *Turbulence*, 5, pp. 4–7.
Wallgren, T. (2009) From Kant and Habermas to Gandhi: the destruction of European democracy and the prospects of a new cosmopolitanism, unpublished paper.
WSF [World Social Forum]. (2008) Strategy debate, http://www.forumsocialmundial.org.br/dinamic.php?pagina=strategy_debate_en
Zibechi, R. (2010) *Dispersing Power: Social Movements as Anti-State Forces* (Edinburgh: AK Press).
Žižek, S. (2009) *First as Tragedy, Then as Farce* (London: Verso).

Coalescence of the Global Peace and Justice Movements

RUTH REITAN

University of Miami, USA

ABSTRACT *This work examines how the Alter-Globalization Movement has sustained a transnational presence throughout the ongoing cycle of contention that began in the mid-1990s, even as priorities, leaders, targets, claims, and frames have continuously evolved. It traces the 'transnational coalescence' process between the post-Seattle, anti-neoliberal movement and anti-war concerns triggered by the 9/11 attacks and George W. Bush's war on terror, and centers on the protest wave that crested in the global day of action against war on 15 February 2003. Rather than simply an exodus—i.e. 'spillover' or 'spillout'—from one movement to another, or a distinct transnational movement arising spontaneously, key bridge-building organizations have proven crucial in shifting down to harness nascent activist energies by brokering new ties and reinvigorating old ones as well as frame-extending between emerging and extant concerns, in order to scale back up as a broader transnational movement for Global Peace and Justice.*

> It is a war that has brought to [the] fore the links between corporate-led globalization and militarization . . . [and] has forced the convergence between the peace movement and the anti-corporate led globalization movement where they have been previously separate. . . . Both movements have been broadened and reinvigorated as a result. A global peace and justice movement is born.
> General Assembly of the Anti-War Movement, World Social Forum (in FGS, 2004)

For nearly two decades, the Alter-Globalization Movement (AGM)—also called Global Justice, Anti-Globalization, or simply the Movement of Movements or Network of Networks—has surged from issue to issue and risen and fallen in strength, pitch, and level of contention. This 'sea' of transnational activism is comprised of a myriad of social movement organizations, coalitions, non-governmental organizations (NGOs), and loosely affiliated activist networks who refuse, resist, rebel, denounce, petition, campaign, and create alternative practices opposed to neoliberal globalization and capitalism, and for greater equality, dignity, democracy, devolution of power, autonomy, sustainable living, peace, and justice at the local, national, and transnational levels and across economic, political, social, cultural, and environmental domains.

Despite this diversity and constant flux, those comprising the AGM have managed to sustain a transnational presence throughout this cycle of contention, even as priorities, issues, leaders, targets, and claims continuously evolve. The cycle can be marked as commencing with the Zapatista uprising in Chiapas, Mexico, against the North American Free Trade Agreement (NAFTA) on 1 January 1994 and spreading quickly through existing and emerging solidarity networks via Internet and print media across the Americas and Europe. Subsequent triggers, or *bellwether* issues, have drawn in activists from Asia and Africa, galvanizing the broader AGM around new threats and opportunities. The movement's 'coming out party' in the popular press and discourse was the 'Battle in Seattle' against the World Trade Organization (WTO) in late 1999. Three years later under a banner of 'global peace and justice', the cycle's wave arguably crested in the 15 February 2003 day of action against the looming war in Iraq that mobilized tens of millions on every continent. This coalescence of anti-neoliberalism and anti-war into one great surge of protest on '2/15' is the empirical focus of this work.

How is it that the AGM can shift among issues while appearing to maintain a transnational presence? Specifically, I seek to answer: what triggers the broader movement's reorientation in emphasis; what kind of activist entity initiates it, and how; what is the relationship between the 'new' and 'old' issues and movements; and at what levels of contention is this reorientation conducted? Toward these ends, following McAdam et al.'s (2001) 'dynamics of contention' approach, below I posit mechanisms that comprise what I call the *transnational coalescence* process. I then illustrate the mechanisms at work in the AGM's reorientation between 2001 and 2004 from the post-Seattle 'global justice' emphasis to 'anti-war' and 'anti-imperialism', triggered by the George W. Bush administration's 'war on terror' in response to the September 11 attacks. Evidence which illuminates these mechanisms is drawn from scholarly research cited throughout, organizational web-based documents, and participant observation and interviews I conducted in Washington, DC, in the early 2000s, with key movement participants from the American Friends Service Committee, AFL-CIO, Public Citizen, Institute for Policy Studies, 50 Years is Enough, and Focus on the Global South (FGS), as well as at European and World Social Forums (see Reitan, 2007, pp. 44–50).

Mechanisms Constituting the Transnational Coalescence Process

To help us understand this phenomenon, I've surveyed several conceptual clusters of social movement literature before selecting one concept from each that arguably subsumes the others, and thus best serves as a mechanism constituting *transnational coalescence*. Figure 1 sketches this process. It entails *bridge-builders* (which incorporates related concepts of *movement crossovers*, *strategic entrepreneurs*, *mesomobilization actors*, *multi-issue groups*, *rooted cosmopolitans*, and *hybridized identities*) who, when faced with a new *bellwether* or *trigger issue*, temporarily *scale down* (i.e. *internalize*, or *loop back*) to the local, national, or macro-regional levels, but with the aim to *scale up* again to the transnational level of contention as a broader movement. To do so, they use various framing tactics while *brokering* new ties and *diffusing* information among existing and new activists, particularly *frame extension*, in order to foster *transnational coalescence* (or *miscibility*—both terms provide a broader framework that may encompass *spillover* and *spillout*) between 'new' and 'old' issues and movements.

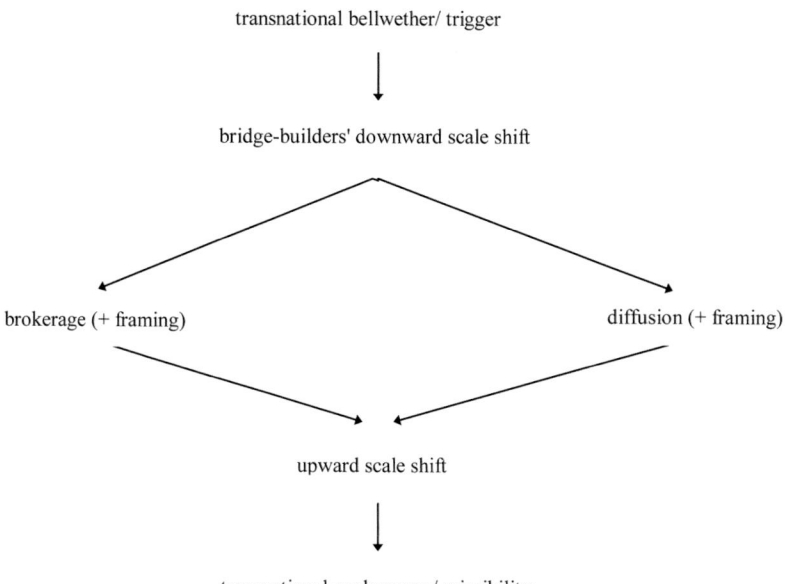

Figure 1. Transnational social movement coalescence (i.e. miscibility) process.

Taking each mechanism in turn, a *bellwether* issue is a commonly perceived, urgent problem that temporarily unites a wide range of activists sharing similar beliefs and concerns (Meyer and Whittier, 1994; Vasi, 2006), and thus *triggering* contention (McAdam et al., 2001; Reitan, 2007). To harness and channel this rather spontaneous reaction, *bridge-builders* (Feree and Roth, 1998) are crucial. This generic term encompasses and pre-dates most related concepts including *movement crossovers*, which Reese et al. (2010) define as a specific kind of bridge-builder, who in the face of a new threat or opportunity, reorient their multi-issue organization, create new ones, shift resources, build coalitions, and coordinate domestic and transnational actions, campaigns, protests, and lobbying. Bridging organizations are usually *multi-issue* groups (Tarrow, 2011) with *hybrid identities* (Rojas and Heaney, 2009) who become *strategic entrepreneurs* (Goss and Heaney, 2010) that 'sample and recombine' ideas and strategy from previous movements in order to constitute themselves and advance their agendas.

Bridge-builders also facilitate movement *scale shift* among levels of contention. They are *mesomobilization actors* (Gerhards and Rucht, 1992) who coordinate micromobilization groups and collect resources for action, while integrating groups by articulating a master frame regarding the triggering event that spurs broader mobilization. Said differently, they are *rooted cosmopolitans* 'whose relations place them beyond their local or national settings without detaching them from locality' (Tarrow, 2005, p. 42). Thus, rather than being root*less* cosmopolitans—or even 'transnational tourists' as sometimes derided (see e.g. Chandler, 2011)—these bridge-builders are among the most committed and seasoned activists, with expertise, leadership experience, and ready access to domestic-level, material and symbolic resources.

This compound concept of 'rooted cosmopolitan' intimates two additional mechanisms related to shifting scale. The first word—rooted—speaks to bridge-builders' *downward scale shift*. Also called *internalization* (Tarrow and McAdam, 2005, p. 364), it is 'the scale shift of foreign or transnational forms of mobilization downward into domestic politics'. Examples include World Social Forum participants creating regional and local forums or—as will be highlighted below—key global justice activists temporarily shifting down to bridge to re-emerging anti-war sentiments. They did so via the *diffusion* of information through existing networks and *brokerage* of relations with new activists or reinvigorating ties with former allies (see McAdam et al., 2001; Reitan, 2007). Both mechanisms require ongoing efforts of *frame alignment*. This is because movement activities, goals, and ideology must be perceived by non-affiliated individuals to be congruent with their own interests, values, and beliefs for successful bridging, and thus alignment, to occur (Tarrow, 2002, p. 235). To foster movement coalescence, the tactic of *frame extension* is most salient. Here bridge-builders extend the boundaries of their existing primary frame in order to encompass interests or points of view that were previously incidental to their objectives, but which are of considerable import to those with whom the organization wishes to broker ties toward joint action.

We turn next to the second mechanism suggested by 'rooted cosmopolitan'. While 'rooted' connotes the downward scale shift just discussed, 'cosmopolitan' describes the intent and immediate actions following that shift, namely to scale back *up* to the macro-regional and then transnational levels. *Upward scale shift* is 'a change in the number and level of coordinated contentious actions leading to broader contention involving a wider range of actors and bridging their claims and identities' (McAdam et al., 2001, p. 331). While scale shift has been theorized as a process itself elsewhere (see Ibid.; Reitan, 2007), here it is used as the final mechanism leading to *transnational movement coalescence*. Coalescence, or miscibility, builds on the work of Ion Bogdan Vasi (2006, 2010; Vasi and Strang, 2009) and describes social movement organizations who, for a time, 'dissolve into' each other via collaborating and mobilizing. Coalescence is said to depend on the level of ideological compatibility and density of interpersonal networks. It may occur quite spontaneously and effortlessly if compatibility and networking are already high, but may also be enhanced by the more active mechanisms of brokerage, diffusion, and framing tactics described above (Vasi and Strang, 2009, p. 1749).[1]

Calling this process *coalescence* rather than the more commonly used *spillover* (Meyer and Whittier, 1994; Rojas and Heaney, 2009; Tarrow and Della Porta, 2005; Van Dyke, 2003) or *spillout* (Hadden and Tarrow, 2007) reflects the growing appreciation among scholars of the dynamic complexity and interrelatedness of contemporary social movements, wherein considerable interdependencies exist, boundaries are blurred, and movements feed back into one another (Rojas and Heaney 2009, p. 4). Turning to our illustrative case of '9/11' to '2/15', while instances of unidirectional, zero-sum, spillover or spillout have likely occurred, here I seek to offer a more agent-driven, holistic, and for activists themselves a more *hopeful* account, by sketching movement coalescence, or miscibility. Organizations that played key, strategic bridge-building roles in the shift down from Global Justice and then up to Global Peace *and* Justice will be highlighted, as will their broad framing tactics employed, which extended the issues of neoliberalism and war into each other.

Global Justice Bridge-Builders Shift Down to Meet Threats and Opportunities of the War on Terror

In many ways, the post-9/11 Global Anti-War Movement (GAWM) appeared to have been 'born transnational': first, a number of key initiators hailed from activist organizations and networks already coordinating across borders against neoliberal globalization. Second, it evolved through a series of transnational meetings held in far-flung locales and under different names, many within the spaces of the World and European Social Forums called the Global Assembly of the Anti-War Movement, but also in the Cairo Conferences, the Jakarta Peace Consensus, the International Solidarity Forum in Tokyo, and the International Strategy Meeting of Anti-War and Anti-Globalisation Movements held in Beirut. Third, in the wake of September 11 and the war on terror, GAWM members' perception of the level at which the threat was posed—and therefore the appropriate scale at which to coordinate action—was also global from inception.

Yet a closer look at the activities of key bridging organizations in the US, the UK, and Asia tells another story, captured by the mechanisms described above. Here we see that when confronted with a rapidly changing domestic and international scenario due to the global trigger or bellwether of war, several multi-issue organizations already mobilizing for global economic justice, among them the American Friends Service Committee (AFSC), scaled down to create the largest US domestic anti-war coalition, United for Peace and Justice (UFPJ). Similarly, the UK's Socialist Workers Party (SWP) and its broader umbrella coalition Globalise Resistance, which had earlier mobilized against the 2001 Genoa G8 meeting and was active in social forums, was instrumental in forging the main UK coalition Stop the War (STW-UK). Further, an Asian Peace Alliance (APA) came together with the help of FGS, a key facilitator of the Our World Is Not for Sale anti-WTO network, who scaled down to the macro-regional level to coordinate responses to war. Figure 2 situates the key bridging organizations discussed in the following sections by region and network involvement.

Together, these examples drawn from North America, Europe, and Asia provide evidence that a global anti-war movement did not emerge spontaneously from transnational spillover (or spill-out) alone, nor independently of the Global Justice Movement or the broader cycle of contention against neoliberal globalization. For it was also forged strategically by key movement bridge-builders through a process of transnational coalescence, requiring scaling down, brokerage, diffusion, and frame extension, in order to scale back up as a broader transnational movement.

This is not to deny that the US-led wars were the catalytic trigger in mobilizing millions in the streets. The sheer numbers that turned out on 15 February 2003, when compared with other global days of action against neoliberal targets, indicates the imminent attack on Iraq in particular was a galvanizing force.[2] It is rather to sketch a fuller and more dynamic picture of these events, by underscoring the importance and types of organizations who assumed key brokerage and diffusion

Location	Global economic justice (i.e. anti-neoliberal) networks & main targets	Key network bridge-building organizations	Scaled down to forge domestic anti-war coalitions	Scaled back up to forge transnational coalitions:
North America/ USA	Mobilization for Global Justice (MGJ) targeting World Bank & IMF	American Friends Service Committee (AFSC)	United for Peace and Justice (UFPJ)	⇒ Anti-war Assemblies within the World Social Forum (WSF) & European Social Forum (ESF); ⇒ Jakarta Peace Consensus; ⇒ Beirut International Strategy Meeting of Anti-War and Anti-Globalisation Movements; ⇒ Occupation Watch; ⇒ No Bases network; ⇒ World Tribunals on Iraq; ⇒ Cairo Anti-War Conferences
Europe/ UK	Globalise Resistance (GR) targeting the G8	UK Socialist Workers Party (SWP-UK)	Stop the War (STW-UK)	
Asia/ Thailand	Our World Is Not for Sale (OWINFS) targeting WTO	Focus on the Global South (FGS)	Asian Peace Alliance (APA)	

Figure 2. Key global justice movement bridge-builders scaling down and then up again to forge anti-war coalitions.

roles. First domestically and then transnationally, these bridge-builders chose dates, framed and organized global action days, and coordinated auxiliary anti-war and anti-imperialist campaigns including Occupation Watch, the World Tribunal on Iraq, and No Bases network. Since many were already key coordinators in the struggles against neoliberal globalization, these bridge-builders worked strategically to birth a Global Peace *and* Justice Movement.

Global Justice Actors Scale Down to the US Domestic Level

After the attacks on New York and Washington, a rapid reorientation of attention and resources occurred from existing transnational targets and claims centered on the World Bank and International Monetary Fund (IMF) toward the US's threats of retaliation in Afghanistan and Iraq and its implications in various countries. This shift is most clearly seen by tracing the dissolution, reformation, and reemergence of coalitions in Washington DC. For months prior to the attacks, a broad umbrella group named the Mobilization for Global Justice (MGJ) had been planning protests against the Bretton Woods institutions' autumn meetings. This coalition already engendered considerable inter-movement coalescence: in addition to groups whose main focus was neoliberal globalization like Global Exchange and 50 Years is Enough, MGJ was comprised of the AFSC (i.e. Quakers), AFL-CIO, Feminist Majority, and Anti-Capitalist Convergence among many others (Gillham and Edwards, 2003; Heaney and Rojas, 2007, 2008, 2011; Maney et al., 2005). MGJ had roots in prior DC campaigns and was invigorated by the 1999 Battle in Seattle and the major transnational network that grew out of it, OWINFS, as well as earlier global campaigns like the anti-debt Jubilee 2000.

Immediately following the attacks, a number of high profile organizations whose central target was *not* the Bretton Woods institutions, including the AFL-CIO, Friends of the Earth, Oxfam, and the Feminist Majority, pulled out of the coalition altogether, providing evidence of spillout. In this uncertain environment, MGJ was dissolved at an emergency spokescouncil meeting days later, which could be seen as demobilization. Yet something else was afoot: a few groups with deep peace movement roots including the AFSC stepped into the breach as bridge-builders. They began brokering new ties, diffusing a reframed call across existing networks, and shifting claims from economic justice to include and emphasize anti-war.

In this way, 'MGJers' with hybridized identities like AFSC, the Religious Working Group, and the Interfaith Service network merely took off their 'economic justice' hats and replaced them with their well-worn anti-war ones. They quickly shifted gears and planned new events in what would have been World Bank/IMF week, transferring permits and encouraging participation in daily silent vigils and the People's March for Peace organized by the Washington Peace Center (WPC). They further brokered ties with former allies not involved in MGJ, such as the Fellowship of Reconciliation, the American Muslim Council, and the Alliance for Jewish Renewal. A latent peace movement—out of and bound up with economic justice—was thus brought back to life, via scaling down, brokerage, and diffusion through pre-existing but dormant relationships and the activation of old schemas in order to frame the new objects and claims post-9/11 (see Gillham and Edwards, 2003).

United For Peace and Justice (UFPJ, 2004a) was founded at a DC meeting in October 2002 by over 70 peace and justice organizations—many of them former MGJ members.[3] Embodying both sides of 'rooted cosmopolitanism', the elected steering committee hailed from major domestic anti-war groups as well as those most active transnationally, including AFSC and Global Exchange's newly formed Code Pink. And demonstrating both domestic movement coalescence and the collective intent to scale back up as a broader movement, a number of groups whose primary target had not been war and militarism but rather neoliberal globalization were also elected, chief among them seasoned MGJ members (UFPJ, 2004b). In the following years, UFPJ has deepened its analysis and thus frame extension toward movement coalescence both domestically and internationally, evidenced in the framing of their ongoing campaign for 'Global Justice' (see UFPJ, 2003).

Global Justice Scale Down in the UK

In Britain, the main peace coalition to emerge was Stop the War UK (STW-UK). Its initiator was Globalise Resistance (GR), an umbrella group which protested the Genoa anti-G8 summit in the summer of 2001. Both GR and STW-UK have been coordinated largely by the Trotskyist SWP (see German and Murray, 2005). Thus the main organization behind the UK coalition was also a longtime—if controversial—bridge-builder active in the anti-neoliberal globalization struggle yet with deep domestic roots via its diffuse party apparatus.

While SWP leadership and rank-and-file played the major role in GR, they successfully brokered wider relations and disseminated information among local and national groups and individuals wanting to mobilize against both neoliberalism and war. SWP/GR quickly reached out to debt relief campaigners, anti-nuclear and environmental activists, trade unions, student groups, and faith-based organizations to frame-extend and foster miscibility among a number of domestic social movements.[4] They called a meeting in London upon the US's declaration of the 'war on terror', which brought together some 2,000 people. Those present agreed to form the umbrella STW-UK (2001) that would allow member groups to develop their own analysis and actions while still providing a vehicle for occasional united actions under the broad banner of 'stop the war'.

To foster domestic coalescence, they called on all peace and labor activists to forge a mass movement under a three-part platform, reasoning that 'any war will simply add to the numbers of innocent dead, cause untold suffering, political and economic instability on a global scale, increase racism and result in attacks on civil liberties'. Party members helped establish a GR website which played both non-relational brokerage and diffusion roles and helped frame-extend among anti-war, anti-militarism, and anti-capitalism. It encouraged already established groups to join the larger umbrella, as well as put individuals in contact with others in their area to form their own Stop the War group. As a result, local affiliates quickly mushroomed across the UK, while pre-existing organizations joined the campaign. In a matter of months 70 STW local groups had self-organized, and nearly as many independent peace, union, cultural, and religious groups and green parties affiliated themselves with the umbrella coalition (Ibid.; German and Murray, 2005).

Members organized a number of innovative actions to attract adherents to their cause and put pressure on Prime Minister Tony Blair's government. These included educational peace conferences, creative political-cultural events such as cinema and street theater, protest camps, information stalls, bicycle protests, 'weapons inspector' demos at a US Air Force base, weekly vigils and pickets, petition drives to bring British troops home, and embassy actions. Their initially successful brokerage leading to greater miscibility culminated in some of the largest demonstrations ever held in London, including an estimated 400,000 on 28 September 2002 and nearly two million on 2/15.

Global Justice Scale Down in Asia

Similarly to the above cases of scale down in the US and UK, in mid-September 2001, FGS, a longtime Global Justice movement bridge-builder, reactivated regional ties with scholars and artists comprising the Asian Regional Exchange for New Alternatives (ARENA). Within weeks of 9/11, they jointly brokered a meeting in Hong Kong for a wide spectrum of Asian actors already mobilizing for economic justice and more traditional anti-war, -bases, and -nuclear issues, thus beginning to foster coalescence at the macro-regional level. This public forum discussed the potential impacts and wider implications for Asians of a US assault on Afghanistan. Those present agreed to found an Asian Peace Alliance (APA) in an effort to strengthen emergent peace networks at the domestic level and articulate a common regional response. Their goal was twofold: 'to address threats to peace in the region, and promote alternative constructs and practices of peace and people's security' (Arena Online, 2001; see also Bello, 2008).

After several months of organizing in their respective localities, the APA was formally launched in Quezon City, Philippines, in August 2002 with an assembly of more than 100 representatives from over 15 Asian countries, as well as representatives from the US and Canada. This first assembly was crucial for diffusing information among those already connected, as well as for brokering new ties. It further provided an opportunity to discuss and arrive at a common frame that would establish their targets and content of claims, both necessary to undertake coordinated action. Their final resolution reflected both their emerging target of the US's war on terror and their frame extension between war, terrorism, and peace and those issues against which many were already mobilizing. At the assembly they also devised an organizational structure to try to effectively build a regional peace movement from the pre-existing, largely national-level ones, with resource injections from global justice groups (APA, 2001).

Their goal, and therefore their vision of peace, entailed not only the immediate claim of stopping the war. It also comprised a transformative vision of constructing a global society based on a cluster of values that extended the definition of peace to include economic justice, equality, and environmental sustainability, and thus fostering movement coalescence. These values were juxtaposed to those they attributed to the US's retaliatory response: they feared the war's destabilizing and negative effects on other Asian countries, the erosion of democracy through US support of repressive local elites, and the creation of a unilateral world order which 'the US alone will use to violate and undo all principles of international law that have been worked out in the last 50 years' (Ibid.). Armed with this collective frame and vision, as the attack on Iraq grew nearer, the APA called on Asians to press their governments to oppose US warmongering and to organize demonstrations across the region.

Bridge-Builders Scale Back Up to Coalesce into a Global Peace and Justice Movement

While the above demonstrates a temporary scale shift down on the part of key bridge-builders from the Global Justice Movement to help organize and mobilize domestic and regional anti-war activity, below we will see the final mechanism in action toward transnational coalescence, upward scale shift. Three transnational meeting spaces were crucial here: (1) the World and European Social Forums, especially the anti-war assemblies convening within them, where STW-UK, FGS, and UFPJ members have all played important bridging roles; (2) the Jakarta Peace Consensus leading to the Beirut International Strategy Meeting of Anti-War and Anti-Globalisation Movements, facilitated by FGS and attended by the others; and (3) the Cairo Anti-War Conferences, where STW-UK has played the most prominent role of the three bridging groups examined here.

We will see, first, that although the lead individuals or groups in each venue have rotated, a key bridge-builder has consistently hailed from the Global Justice Movement, who scaled down to harness the anti-war movement before scaling back up. A second constant in this upward scale shift has been frame extension between peace and economic justice. Third, over time a fluid steering group emerged to coordinate international protests and campaigns, which drew together over 20 representatives from the largest anti-war coalitions and anti-neoliberal networks worldwide (FGS, 2004).[5] All three points provide evidence of transnational coalescence, not simply unidirectional spillover.

Bridging with Asia and the Middle East toward Transnational Peace and Justice Coalescence: Jakarta, Beirut, and Cairo Meetings

Asian bridge-builders, already organizing at the macro-regional level, were quick to scale back up to the broadest transnational level. Their efforts culminated in major meetings in Jakarta and Beirut. In March 2003, FGS's Walden Bello, accompanied by other civil society members and parliamentarians from Southeast and South Asia, led one of several delegations to Baghdad in the weeks prior to the US invasion, to provide international solidarity and attempt to stall the attacks and find a diplomatic resolution. Unable to stop the war, this group called an international meeting in Jakarta in mid-May. In attendance were representatives of peace and justice organizations from some 26 countries and every continent, including several European and American delegates from the emerging STW-UK and UFPJ networks. Here they fostered solidarity and began to craft a multi-pronged anti-war campaign that included global days of protest as well as more sustained efforts leading to Occupation Watch, the No Bases network, and World Tribunals on Iraq (Bello, 2008).

Out of these discussions came the Jakarta Peace Consensus (2003). In it, FGS and other rooted cosmopolitans framed expansively by diagnosing shared threats emanating from war, imperialism, and class and race-based oppression, and from the intergovernmental organizations (IGOs)—namely the IMF, World Bank, and WTO—who concentrate and wield power on behalf of First World elites and their interests. Further, their prognostic framing was for a 'peace based on global justice'. The consensus elaborated principles and aspirations of a:

> genuine internationalism from below . . . based on equality and democracy. . . . We believe that a world free of war, exploitation, inequality, poverty and repression is possible . . . growing [from] movements of youth, women, workers, students, migrants, the unemployed, human rights and peace and justice activists and citizens who are bringing the spirit, energy and work together in the fight for genuine peace based on global justice for all the world's peoples. (Ibid.)

Building on Jakarta, FGS took charge of organizing the next major event, the International Strategy Meeting of Anti-War and Anti-Globalisation Movements in Beirut. The aim was to bridge geographically to anti-war and anti-imperial groups in the Middle East and Arab countries as well as across issues, and thus enhance transnational coalescence into a Global Peace *and* Justice Movement. In September, hundreds came to Beirut from over 50 countries, the majority being Lebanese, Palestinians, Iraqis, Greeks, Egyptians, and Jordanians. There were also numerous activists from India, the Philippines, Japan, Turkey, and the US, the latter represented by UFPJ members including AFSC, Code Pink, and Corpwatch (see ISP, 2004; Reitan, 2009).

A somewhat autonomous bridging initiative to the Middle East that also promoted transnational coalescence was the Cairo Anti-War Conferences. Their driving force in the Global North was the SWP/ STW-UK's John Rees along with the US's more militant umbrella organization ANSWER (Act Now to Stop War and End Racism) and Workers World Party member Elias Rashmawi. Conferences were held annually from 2002 to 2008, and were thus the most sustained effort to establish a space where political parties and armed resistance groups from the Middle East opposed to US-led war and neoliberal globalization could meet their international counterparts. The first Cairo Declaration (2002) declared their intention to found a radical, transnational, anti-war platform, and demonstrated their frame extension efforts from anti-capitalism through anti-imperialism to the anti-war movement: 'The Cairo Meeting is not an isolated event, but an extension of a protracted international struggle against imperialism, from Seattle and Genoa to Lisbon and Florence, to Cordoba and Cairo'.

Locally, the Cairo Conference was funded by Egyptians with business interests in Iraq and was hosted at the Egyptian journalists' union offices by an umbrella group encompassing an array of ideologies called the Egyptian Popular Campaign to Confront U.S. Aggression. It was led by Egypt's banned Muslim Brotherhood party and included other Islamists, Marxists, Nasserists, trade and professional unionists, popular committees, and researchers (Crooke, 2003). The meetings attracted a few hundred delegates annually, including communists and anti-imperialists from Europe and the Americas, UN representatives, anti-colonial heroes, and major opposition parties from across the Arab world (see Beinin, 2008; Reitan, 2009).

Transnational Coalescence and Coordination Within the Social Forums

Consistent with and linked to the above meetings in Jakarta, Beirut, and Cairo, FGS and SWP/ STW-UK activists also served as key alter-globalization to anti-war bridge-builders in the scaling up to World and European Social Forums (ESF). This is evidenced in the many seminars, workshops, plenaries, tribunals, 'terrain' spaces, preparatory assemblies, and WSF International Council and steering group meetings in which these groups have played leading roles. The looming war galvanized European NGOs and social movements' preparations for the first ESF in Florence in November 2002. The forum's organizing committee, on which the SWP/ STW-UK was prominent, acted as a movement crossover by prioritizing the war theme in ESF seminars as well as staging the first mass demonstration in Europe of up to one million on the closing day. The next morning, hundreds of representatives of European organizations and others gathered at the Social Movement Assembly and set 2/15 as the first global day of mobilization against war, a call that was diffused at the WSF that January and via activist list-serves and websites.

The most important meeting to emerge within the social forum spaces to foster transnational coalescence has been the Global Assembly of the Anti-War Movement. At the second ESF in Paris in autumn 2003, hundreds of activists converged to discuss 20 March as the next transnational day of action, which was preferred by US activists and was eventually agreed to at the closing Social Movements Assembly (see Reitan, 2009). At the fourth WSF in Mumbai in January 2004, FGS and STW-UK helped convene the Global Assembly, which was estimated to be the largest and most diverse transnational meeting of peace movements ever held. The Assembly's statement (in FGS, 2004) touched on a number of mechanisms that have constituted the process by which alter-globalization and anti-war coalesced at the transnational level: namely, war as a trigger or bellwether, the work of bridge-builders or crossovers, who reorient their own organizations, shift resources, broker ties and frame-extend from existing issues to new concerns, all in an effort to foster a transnational, coalesced movement.

The breadth of signatories to the Assembly declarations attests to this coalescence, evidencing considerable movement bridging with anti-neoliberal concerns: among them have been the Continental Campaign Against the Free Trade Area of the Americas, Corpwatch, Canadian Polaris Institute, Freedom from Debt Coalition, Jubilee South, and trade unions from Korea, Brazil, Italy, and South Africa. But in addition, transnational peace coordination within the social forums has gone beyond these mass assemblies aimed at planning demonstrations. Building on ideas first discussed in Jakarta, at the fourth WSF in Mumbai, the World Tribunal on Iraq held its first of several international public hearings, called the World Court of Women on U.S. War Crimes (Sokmen, 2008). Also in Mumbai activists held a series of meetings that eventually led to the 2007 launch of the International Network for the Abolition of Foreign Military Bases (or 'No Bases'; see Yeo, 2009).

9/11 Postscript: A Decade On, Movement Coalescence—and the 'Occupation'— Continues

In the years that followed, peace and justice activists (myself among them) have continued to protest the ongoing occupations of Iraq and Afghanistan and to coordinate within the Global Anti-War Assemblies held at social forums and via the Internet. Many have joined the follow-on campaigns and networks mentioned above. Activism, however, did not prevent nor bring an end to these wars and occupations. Indeed, despite official US withdrawal from Iraq in late 2011, thousands remain as private military contractors to defend the largest embassy on earth along with Western strategic and commercial interests. In Afghanistan, the decade-long, Bush-initiated misadventure is starting to be called Barack Obama's Vietnam (Green, 2012). And under the latter US president who heralded so much 'change', unmanned drone strikes there and in neighboring Pakistan have become routine, killing hundreds of civilians along with targeted Al Qaeda and Taliban suspects.

Yet the vocal, coordinated, and sustained dissent has reflected—and likely bolstered—the much broader opposition to the US-led wars in almost every nation. This widespread disapproval by an active minority and more quiescent majority laid bare the so-called 'democratic deficit', especially in those countries that joined the US's 'coalition of the willing'. This is an underappreciated legacy of 9/11, the dynamics and frustrations of which are still coalescing into new modes and movements of resistance and refusal, persistence and transformation. The chasm between the majority's desire for peace and justice and the brazen ways in which governments flouted voices, votes, and protests exposed for a new generation the thin(ning) democratic veneer masking authoritarian and collusive practices of state–corporate regimes.

But if 'the gloves have come off'—as Bush and co. were fond of threatening in those early, heady days—so has Power's mask, sparking a new wave of occupation—this time from below. (Neo)imperial overstretch, coupled with banking, debt, and unemployment crises ricocheting around the Global North later in the decade, have propelled more and more citizens, and especially youth, to draw connections between foreign wars and occupations and domestic impoverishment, repression, and inequality. Majorities of the so-called 'informed publics'[6] across the world have come to distrust their political and economic leaders as an out of touch, corrupt, ruling class— or as the notorious '1%', as the contemporary Occupy Wall Street movement frames them.

In complicated ways, this brazen unmasking of power before the citizenry stirred a kind of indignation that in 2011 galvanized youth especially to go out, seize, and try to hold public spaces (assisted by coordination in virtual space) to demand *real* change—in who governs, how, and in whose interests. The Arab Spring of city-square occupations ignited revolutions, regime reforms, civil wars, and foreign interventions; in Latin America, students staged university occupations and protests (most notably in Chile) to defend the right to public education; anti-austerity protests across southern Europe in summer included general strikes called by trade unions and pitched street battles between precarious youth and 'robo-cops', along with *indignado* encampments throughout Spain; and in autumn, the Occupy movement sprouted—or squatted—in a park near Wall Street and quickly spread across the USA and as far away as Nigeria and the Philippines.

While this work has focused on movement coalescence between economic justice and peace in the wake of 9/11, we can 'spot-test' the robustness of this process 10 years on by asking how our main bridge-building organizations are today engaging with the Occupy movement. As this began in North America—having been called by the Canadian *Adbusters* magazine and responded to with most enthusiasm just south of their border—we'd expect the AFSC to be active, and indeed they have been. The Quaker organization has embraced grassroots occupations while amplifying the peace and nonviolent aspects of this nascent movement against inequality. As of early 2012, AFSC offices in 16 US cities were supporting the 'Occupy Together' movement. They seized the opportunity of the Martin Luther King Jr. national holiday to frame-extend to his legacy of nonviolent civil disobedience. In San Francisco, Quakers launched the 'Occupy Be the Change Pledge' and have set up caucuses around the nation to encourage an ethical, not solely tactical, commitment to nonviolent struggle.[7]

Lending stronger evidence to the robustness of 'movement coalescence' are actions of our illustrative bridging organizations outside the US. In Britain, the SWP has given Occupy London and other encampments considerable coverage in its print and online publications. They've published dozens of pieces in the *Socialist Worker* and *Socialist Review*,[8] wherein they frame Occupy as part of the larger class struggle against the capitalist system and thus amplifying its historical and international connections. And moving from sympathetic media coverage to solidarity and brokering actions, one SWP member joined the London encampment for the duration while others participated in working groups, spoke at the 'Tent City University', and inviting occupiers to address their union branches. The party further brokered ties between the labor movement and Occupy by organizing a trade union solidarity event that issued a statement pledging to defend the London camp in the face of eviction (Leather, 2012).

And turning to Asia, FGS has also appropriated the Occupy frame in its struggle to defend women's health and reproductive rights. FGS senior analyst and now Philippino legislator Bello helped organize an 'Occupy for Reproductive Health' action in late 2011, leading hundreds of advocates in a march on Congress. Inspired by the Occupy Wall Street movement and frustrated by years of delays in national health care reform, they pledged to camp out and hold teach-ins until their demands were met.[9] These examples from Asia, Europe, and North America demonstrate the creative ingenuity with which key bridge-builders have taken up the Occupy mantle to once more foster movement miscibility, by linking existing concerns and mobilizations for peace and economic justice to the newest cries against growing inequality, state–corporate collusion, and attacks on human rights. In the process, the revolution, Occupation, and coalescence among movements will continue.

Notes

1. My decision to use *coalesce* instead of *miscibility* was due the nature of the words themselves: the aim is to trace a process rather than describe a state of being, so a verb—to coalesce—rather than a noun—miscibility—is warranted. Vasi uses the former in defining the latter, and thus the two are used interchangeably throughout this work.
2. For a detailed scholarly treatment of 2/15 based on survey research in eight countries, see Walgrave and Rucht (2010). For a photographic record of the day's events, see Hello NYC (2003).
3. UFPJ's main competitor, ANSWER, emerged three days after the attacks. It is reminiscent in tone, framing, organizational style, targets, and solidarity alliances of more militant anti-war and anti-imperialist movements abroad, including the SWP/GR-Islamist alliance that was forged in the UK, discussed below. For an examination of this fractious relationship, see Heaney and Rojas (2008).

4   Whereas in previous campaigns, faith-based groups would be largely Christian charities, given the targets of the 'war on terror', SWP/GR activists bridged to both mainstream and more militant Muslim organizations, some of which voiced blanket support for Iraqi resistance as well as Hezbollah and Hamas. This proved to be a bridge too far for a number of non-SWP allies and anti-war sympathizers, and caused considerable spillout from GR and eventual demobilization of the peace movement in the UK (see Reitan, 2009).

5   Prominent anti-war members have been Stop the War coalitions from the UK and Greece, the APA, South Africa's Anti-War Coalition, Japan's Peace Boat, the Mexican Serapaz, and India's Coalition for Nuclear Disarmament and Peace. Alter-globalization groups include Global Exchange, Brazil's Movimento dos Sem Terra (MST) and the global Via Campesina it helped establish, the World March of Women against poverty and patriarchy, the South American Hemispheric Social Alliance, Red Mexicana de Acción frente al Libre Comercio, and ATTAC Japan.

6   In the 2011 Edelman Trust Barometer poll of elite citizens in 25 countries (screened by criteria of income and education), trust in their own governments plummeted nearly 10 points from 2010 to 43%, while just over half (56%) trust 'business' and only 38% find corporate CEOs to be 'credible spokespeople'. Disaffection and distrust is even higher in the core economies and democracies: American elites are more disaffected than the international average (exactly one half distrust business), while in Germany, France, and Spain the disaffection rates run to 2/3 and even higher. See Edgecliffe-Johnson (2012).

7   See http://www.afsc.org/friends/occupy-together-occupy-be-change-caucus-launches; and http://www.afsc.org/story/afsc-supports-occupy-organizers-nationwide

8   See http://www.socialistworker.co.uk/topic.php?id=105

9   See http://sexandsensibilities.com/2011/11/22/activists-occupy-for-rh/

References

ANSWER (Act Now to Stop War and End Racism) (2004) About us, http://www.internationalanswer.org/

APA (Asian Peace Alliance) (2001) APA statement against a war on Iraq. http://www.arenaonline.org/details/103816730831637.shtml

Arena Online (2001) Inauguration of Asian Peace Alliance, http://www.arenaonline.org/details/103816730831637.shtml.

Beinin, J. (2008) Underbelly of Egypt's neoliberal agenda, *Middle East Report Online*, 5 April, http://www.merip.org/mero/mero040508.html

Bello, W. (2008) Interview with the author, http://www.as.miami.edu/internationalstudies/pdf/ruthreitan/Bello%20interview%20NIGD%20News%20and%20Notes%20by%20Reitan.pdf

Chandler, D. (2011) Evading the challenge: The limits of Global Activism, in T. Olesen (ed.) *Power and Transnational Activism* (London: Routledge), pp. 34–50.

Crooke, S. (2003) The Cairo Declaration: Is it really a 'great opportunity'? *Workers' Liberty*, 28 January, http://www.workersliberty.org/node/590

Edgecliffe-Johnson, A. (2012) Faith in government plummets, survey says, *Financial Times*, 22 January.

Feree, M. M. & Roth, S. (1998) Gender, class and the intersection between social movements: A strike of West Berlin day care workers, *Gender and Society*, 12(6), pp. 626–648.

First Cairo Declaration (2002) http://www.stopwar.org.uk/article.asp?id=301202

FGS (Focus on the Global South) (2004) A report of the general assembly of the anti-war movement, http://www.focusweb.org/pdf/Anti-War Assembly Report.pdf

Gerhards, J. & Rucht, D. (1992) Mesomobilization: Organizing and framing in two protest campaigns in West Germany, *The American Journal of Sociology*, 98(3), pp. 555–596.

German, L. & Murray, A. (2005) *Stop the War: The Story of Britain's Biggest Mass Movement* (London: Bookmarks).

Gillham, P. & Edwards, B. (2003) Global justice protesters respond to the September 11 terrorist attacks: The impact of an intentional disaster on demonstrations in Washington, DC, in M. F. Myers (ed.) *Beyond September 11: An Account of Post-Disaster Research* (Boulder, CO: University of Colorado), pp. 483–520.

Goss, K. A. & Heaney, M. T. (2010) Organizing women *as women*: hybridity and grassroots collective action in the 21st century, *Perspectives of Politics*, 8(1), pp. 27–52.

Green, M. (2012) The war in Afghanistan: from necessity to atrocity, *Financial Times*, 15 March, p. 7.

Hadden, J. & Tarrow, S. (2007) Spillover or spillout? The global justice movement in the United States after 9/11, *Mobilization: An International Quarterly*, 12(4), pp. 359–376.

Heaney, M. T. & Rojas, F. (2007) Partisans, nonpartisans, and the antiwar movement in the United States, *American Politics Research*, 35(4), pp. 431–464.

Heaney, M. T. & Rojas, F. (2008) Coalition dissolution, mobilization, and network dynamics in the U.S. antiwar movement, *Research in Social Movements, Conflicts and Change*, 28, pp. 39–82.

Heaney, M. T. & Rojas, F. (2011) The partisan dynamics of contention: demobilization of the antiwar movement in the United States, 2007–2009, *Mobilization*, 16(1), pp. 45–64.

Hello NYC (2003) *2/15: The Day the World Said NO to War* (Oakland: AK Press).

ISP (Iraq Solidarity Project) (2004) Alliances and solidarity: Report on Beirut anti-war conference, http://beirut.indymedia.org/ar/2004/10/1800.shtml

Jakarta Peace Consensus (2003) Jakarta peace consensus, http://www.activistmagazine.com/index2.php?option=com_content&do_pdf=1&id=48

Leather, A. (2012) Email correspondence from the SWP National Office to the author, 22 February.

Maney, G. M., Woehrle, L. M. & Coy, P. G. (2005) Harnessing and challenging hegemony: the U.S. peace movement after 9/11, *Sociological Perspectives*, 48(3), pp. 357–381.

Meyer, D. & N. Whittier (1994) Social movement spillover, *Social Problems*, 41(2), pp. 277–297.

McAdam, D., Tarrow, S. & Tilly, C. (2001) *Dynamics of Contention* (Cambridge: Cambridge University Press).

Reese, E., Petit, C. & Meyer, D. S. (2010) Sudden mobilization: movement crossovers, threats, and the surprising rise of the U.S. antiwar movement, in N. Van Dyke & H. J. McCammon (eds) *Strategic Alliances: Coalition Building and Social Movements* (Minneapolis: University of Minnesota Press), pp. 266–291.

Reitan, R. (2007) *Global Activism* (London: Routledge).

Reitan, R. (2009) The global anti-war movement within and beyond the World Social Forum, *Globalizations*, 6(4), pp. 509–523.

Rojas, F. & Heaney, M. T. (2009) Hybrid politics: social movement mobilization in a multi-movement environment, Paper presented at the 104th Annual Meeting of the American Sociological Association, San Francisco, California, 7–11 August.

Sokmen, M. G. (ed.) (2008) *The World Tribunal on Iraq: Making the Case Against War* (Northampton: Olive Branch Press).

STW-UK (Stop the War—United Kingdom) (2001) Aims and constitution, http://stopwar.org.uk/index.php/about/what-we-stand-for

Tarrow, S. (2002) From lumping to splitting: specifying globalization and resistance, in J. Smith & H. Johnston (eds) *Globalization and Resistance: Transnational Dimensions of Social Movements* (Lanham, MD: Rowman & Littlefield), pp. 229–240.

Tarrow, S. (2005) *The New Transnational Activism* (Cambridge University Press), pp. 35–58.

Tarrow, S. (2011) *Power in Movement: Social Movements and Contentious Politics* (Cambridge: Cambridge University Press), pp. 176–95.

Tarrow, S. & Della Porta, D. (2005) *Transnational Protests and Global Activism* (Lanham, MD: Rowman & Littlefield).

Tarrow, S. & McAdam, D. (2005) Scale shift in transnational contention, in D. della Porta & S. Tarrow (eds) *Transnational Protests and Global Activism* (Lanham, MD: Rowman and Littlefield), pp. 121–50.

UFPJ (United for Peace and Justice) (2003) Global justice campaign, http://www.unitedforpeace.org/article.php?sub=36&list=sub

UFPJ (2004a) About United for Peace and Justice, http://www.unitedforpeace.org/article.php?list=type&type=16

UFPJ (2004b) UFPJ national steering committee, http://www.unitedforpeace.org/article.php?id=17571

Vasi, I. B. (2006) The new anti-war protests and miscible mobilizations, *Social Movement Studies*, 5(2), pp. 137–153.

Vasi, I. B. (2010) Brokerage, miscibility and the spread of contention, *Mobilization*, 16(1), pp. 11–24.

Vasi, I. B. & Strang, D. (2009) Civil liberties in America: The diffusion of municipal bill of rights resolutions after the passage of the USA PATRIOT Act, *American Journal of Sociology*, 114, pp. 1716–1764.

Walgrave, S. & Rucht, D. (eds) (2010) *The World Says No to War: Demonstrations against the War on Iraq* (Minneapolis: University of Minnesota Press).

Yeo, A. (2009) Not in anyone's backyard: the emergence and identity of a transnational anti-base network, *International Studies Quarterly*, 53, pp. 571–594.

Ruth Reitan is Assistant Professor in the University of Miami's Department of International Studies, Coral Gables, FL, focusing on international relations theory and transnational social movements. She is author of two books on transnational activism, *Global Activism* (Routledge, 2007) and *The Rise and Decline of an Alliance: Cuba and African American Leaders in the 1960s* (Michigan State University, 1999) and has conducted participatory research at several World and European Social Forums and international protest events.

The Global Social Forum Rhizome: A Theoretical Framework

PETER NIKOLAUS FUNKE
University of South Florida, USA

ABSTRACT *This work draws on Deleuze and Guattari's image of the 'rhizome' to develop a framework for mapping and understanding the global social forum process and its implications for the broader global left. The image of the rhizome is insightful for analytically accentuating the nature and workings, as well as the challenges and contemporary shortcomings, of the social forum process and more generally the broader global movement(s). Thriving on multiplicity and thus lacking a dominant core or main axis, the social forum-as-rhizome emphasizes the multi-connectivity and heterogeneity of this process, which has no central actor, issue, strategy, or ideology, beyond the strong opposition to neoliberalism. While what I call the 'Global Social Forum Rhizome' allows for unprecedented connections as well as tempering and managing inherent antinomies of the alter-globalization movement(s), its logic simultaneously limits the degree of congealed and resilient movement building. In the final analysis, these intrinsic rhizomatic characteristics foster a rather thin articulation of commonalities and convergences, which result in a politics often unable to move beyond mere symbolic acts and resistances and towards organizing, campaigning, and concrete movement building.*

The success of the first World Social Forum (WSF; or 'Forum') in January 2001 in Porto Alegre, Brazil, triggered a dynamic and variegated process. This unprecedented initial gathering of social movements, networks, unions, and nongovernmental and other civil society organizations opposed to neoliberalism gave birth to a decade of world, regional, national, local, and thematic social forums.[1] Based on a peculiar organizational matrix that stresses self-organized, non-hierarchical, open meeting spaces, social forums have been held on all five continents,[2] in various regions (e.g. Maghreb Social Forum, the Mediterranean Social Forum, the Midwest Social Forum (USA), and Southern African Social Forum), multiple national settings (e.g. Brazil, Chile, Denmark, Germany, and US), countless localities (e.g. Berlin, Chicago, Genoa, Houston, Quebec, Rio de Janeiro, and Sydney) and around thematic axes (e.g. a Border Social Forum and Migration Social Forum).

As such, the first Forum in 2001 generated a manifold and heterogeneous 'global social forum process'. For the past decade, leftist groups and movements from around the world have been meeting and discussing, interlinking and strategizing at workshops, panels, testimonies, seminars, or round tables, at cultural events and through on-site marches and rallies. While most of these forums are explicitly based on the WSF Charter of Principles and considered a vital 'part of a process of construction and universalization of the World Social Forum',[3] they are self-organized, autonomous events that do not stand in any hierarchical or subordinate relationship to the WSF and its International Council.[4] Moreover, as social forums are organized in various parts of the world, they take on different dynamics, contingent on time and space. As Janet Conway (2005a, p. 24; see also 2008) points out, '[w]herever the world event is organized, it enacts its own culturally-specific, geographically rooted social movement processes'.

The variegated nature of this process extends to the uneven actualization, expansion, and maturing of social forums. While the process is still thriving in the Americas and modestly growing in Africa, it is in particular the European Social Forum (ESF) that seems to have stalled, as numbers of participants and forums held have fallen off considerably in the last few years. In sum, the global social forum process, characterized by its myriad time- and space-contingent forums on local, national, regional, and global levels, confounds easy legibility and classification—much less actual articulation and coordination.

Analyzing and theorizing social movements and forums is always done from a particular vantage point. 'Theory', as Robert Cox reminds us, 'is always *for* someone and *for* some purpose' (1981, p. 128; emphasis in original). The following is thus an interpretation and argumentation, which imposes representations, concepts, and theories onto the world from a particular perspective—and in this case, from a European, youngish, male, neo-Marxist ethnographer who is sympathetic to many of the alter-globalization movement (AGM) goals, and has engaged in participant observation at various forums including Berlin, European, and World Social Forums.

From these various positionalities, I have developed a framework useful for mapping and understanding this kaleidoscopic global social forum process and its implications for the broader global left. Throughout I have drawn on the growing social forum literature, which includes informative, early compilations (Fisher and Ponniah, 2003), pioneering empirically focused accounts (e.g. Smith et al., 2008, diverse and thick descriptions (e.g. Leite, 2003), insider analyses (e.g. Whitaker, 2007) and macro-conceptualizations (e.g. Pleyers, 2004; Sousa Santos, 2006), including broad ranging, captivating, and insightful edited volumes (Blau and Karides, 2008; Sen et al., 2008). This piece, along with my broader and ongoing research agenda, is informed by and adds to this body of work. Based on years of participant observation at various social forums, including 'virtual ethnography'[5] as well as interviews with activists and organizers, I seek to advance a larger theorization and more comprehensive analytic framework on the social forum phenomenon still missing from much of the extant literature.

Drawing on Gilles Deleuze and Félix Guattari (1980), I suggest that the image of the 'rhizome' assists us in analytically accentuating the nature and workings, as well as the challenges and contemporary shortcomings, of the social forum process, and more generally the broader global movement(s). The WSF seen as rhizome thrives on multiplicity and thus lacks a dominant core or main axis. This view emphasizes the multi-connectivity and heterogeneity of this process. What I am calling the Global Social Forum Rhizome has no central actor, issue, strategy, or ideology, beyond the blanket opposition to neoliberal globalization.

This common opposition, however, suggests a rudimentary system of affinity-based interactions by this nonetheless highly segmented and decentralized organizational form. Like the 'mass of roots' which connect and thus generate a botanical rhizome, the Global Social Forum Rhizome too provides the texture and infrastructure for groups and movements from various parts of the world and of different sizes, scales, issues, and strategic outlooks to interact with any other. In just one example from the WSF, in the forum spaces global environmental networks, German labor unions, Amazonian fisherfolk, and North American human rights groups have learned about and now seek to support one another's struggles. Since the first WSF, they have been connecting and coordinating their efforts related to an aluminum production process that runs from the Brazilian Amazon to Northern Europe (see Funke, 2008, 2012).

The rhizomatic nature of the global social forum process thus allows for the diversity of constitutive groups and movements of the broader alter-globalization movement (AGM) to come together without fear that their autonomy will be compromised. The horizontalist ethos of the forums does not call for participants to agree on programmatic and binding positions, or submit to an overriding or superior struggle, actor, or strategy. The core characteristics of the Global Social Forum Rhizome are aimed at protecting the integrity, uniqueness, and independence of each group and movement, while at the same time providing the *possibility* to articulate and enact linkages, commonalities, and convergences.

The ensuing connections, however, are not without drawbacks, which the concept of the rhizome also helps to analytically unearth, represent, and understand. While the rhizomatic texture arguably allows for unprecedented ties as well as the tempering and managing of the AGM's inherent antinomies, its logic simultaneously limits the degree of congealed and resilient movement building. Thus, the integral characteristics of the rhizome foster a rather thin articulation of commonalities and convergences, which results in a politics that is often unable to move beyond mere symbolic acts and resistances and towards a politics of organizing and concrete movement building.

The logic of the Global Social Forum Rhizome is thus a double-edged sword. As I argue elsewhere, it operates well as a 'resistance relay' for the AGM, generating contacts, linkages, and awareness of the various struggles without encroaching on the independence of groups and movements. Yet, this rhizomatic logic that promotes and protects diversity is at the same time is less able to function as an 'organizational relay' for building a consolidated movement. The latter would arguably require transversal mechanisms and structures that could generate a new synthesis across movements and groups, but which is simultaneously a project that would likely sow derision among today's diverse and autonomous social movements (Funke 2008, forthcoming).

While I will revisit these challenges, I focus in the following on developing the conceptual framework of the Global Social Forum Rhizome. After overviewing the neoliberal context and the protest moments and cycles out of which the WSF emerged, I introduce the concept of the rhizome to structurally map and delineate the WSF and the process it has sparked. I enumerate core characteristics of the Global Social Forum Rhizome and its implications for the broader global movement(s), before closing with future research avenues and praxis-oriented reflections on more resilient movement building.

Neoliberal Capitalism and the Emergence of the World Social Forum

The WSF and the broader social forum process it has triggered across the world emerged from the recent mobilizations and protests against the implementation of global neoliberal restructuring policies that began to consolidate in the 1970s in the Global South. Since then, economic growth strategies have prescribed market driven approaches based on privatization, deregulation and liberalization across the globe (Harvey, 2007 [2005], p. 3). The policies include the commodification of publicly or communally owned industries, services, and resources including water and land as well as the deregulation and liberalization of trade in goods and services. These neoliberalization dynamics have expanded and deepened the scope of the capitalist commodification and profit logic, which increasingly go beyond the strictly economic realm and encroach on cultural, ecological, and formerly public and societal spheres such as education, retirement, and health care.

The transformations of the global political economy are in turn generating modified capital and class relations and are thus restructuring the composition of struggles and movements as well as their practices and strategies (Funke, 2012; Funke et al., 2012). These dynamics have been fragmenting and at the same time broadening the collectivity of progressive groups and movements resisting neoliberalizing capitalism. The center of resistance is no longer predominately comprised of exploitation on factory floors or assembly lines but includes increasing numbers of service sector workers, students, and those oppressed due to gender, race, or sexual orientation.

As such, class has to be reconceptualized to include other experiences and social subjectivities that comprise the current labor–capital conflict (Lorenzano, 1998, pp. 132–3). As I have argued elsewhere in detail, the increasing existence and recognition of these various forms of oppression is nevertheless objectively shaped by neoliberal capitalism and class relations (Funke, 2012). Patriarchy and racism are to a certain extent restricted hierarchies whereas class relations are part of all capitalist formations and social groups, constituting a more basic and common structure of exploitation (Dyer-Witheford, 1999). As I suggest below, failing to identify this shared enemy and thus common struggle against the structuring power of capitalism and class relations, can account for the volatile and voluntaristic nature of the current movement cycle as illustrated most recently by the 'Occupy Wall Street' protests.

In addition to these structural imperatives, the organizational history of the left itself generates the need for novel processes and linkages among this more extensive but also increasingly heterogeneous and splintered grouping. In particular, the failures of state socialist projects have made those on the left 'wary of any group playing a vanguard role in defining the society that the overall global movement should pursue' (Fisher and Ponniah, 2003, p. 13) while somehow recognizing the need to 'articulate a common vision' (Ibid.). As I argue below, rhizomatic organizational constellations are emerging that enable configurations which seek to safeguard heterogeneity and group autonomy while at the same time recognizing the need to bridge and congeal leftist groups and movements into new formations.

Accordingly, new forms of resistance with innovative characteristics have emerged, which influenced the formation of the AGM in general and the WSF in particular (Leite, 2003, p. 41). Specifically, the Zapatista uprising in Chiapas, Mexico that went public and issued their first declaration on the day the North American Free Trade Agreement came into effect on 1

January 1994 and the anti-World Trade Organization protests in Seattle in 1999 arguably provided two of the most direct influences for organizing the first Forum in January of 2001.

While the Seattle protests were important in that they became a symbolic marker in the Global North and thus consolidated the global resistance to neoliberal policies (Burbach, 2001, pp. 23; Leite, 2003, p. 55) it was the Zapatistas with their radically democratic and pluralistic approach that prefigured much of what would become the social forum logic. The Zapatista vision is epitomized in their slogan 'one no and many yeses'. It encapsulates the unified 'no' to neoliberalism while acknowledging the diversity and plurality of alternatives, needs, aspirations, tactics, or ways of living and doing (Midnight Notes, 1998).

This perspective arguably undergirds the social forum principle of collectively rejecting neoliberalism while embracing a diversity of alternative worlds, and thereby allowing for affinity-based linkages and convergences. Moreover, the various International *encuentros* of the Zapatistas with 'the People of the World' taking place since 1996 foreshadowed core organizational dimensions of social forums, such as their emphasis on radical democracy and self-organization as well as autonomy and diversity. That said, it is important, and ironic, to note that, given the WSF Charter's ban on armed groups, the Zapatistas are not allowed to participate in the forum spaces.

In many ways, then, the WSF was 'born Latin', as Isabelle Biagiotti put it (2004, p. 536). Not only because its founders and early participants drew inspiration from the Zapatistas, nor solely because it was an invention of mainly Latin American and to a lesser degree Southern European activists, but also because the Forum recalibrates relations between groups and movements of the Global North and South. Emancipatory efforts during the Cold War including the Third World solidarity movements were arguably characterized by mostly one-way flows of ideas, resources, and solidarity from the richer, stronger First World activists to the poor and allegedly more passive recipients in the Third World. With the rise of the Zapatistas and the WSF phenomena, this relationship has become more reciprocal and egalitarian. Newly shared organizational ideas, practices, and strategies include the emphasis on participatory democracy as a vital part and engine of socio-economic change, the belief that radical change must emerge from below, and the recognition that the multiple facets of exploitation have to be fought everywhere not only in Chiapas or the Niger Delta but equally in Philadelphia and Berlin.[6]

The First World Social Forum

The WSF in name, place, and approach was initially conceived of as a counter-event to the World Economic Forum, which annually brings together global elites in Davos, Switzerland and elsewhere throughout the year (Cassen, 2003). With the crucial political and organizational support by the Brazilian Workers' Party-run state of Rio Grande do Sul and the city of Porto Alegre, the first Forum took place in January of 2001. Under the slogan 'Another World is Possible', roughly 4,000 delegates, 16,000 registered participants from 117 countries, 1,870 journalists (with roughly 400 foreigners), as well as an unknown number of walk-in participants attended. They held 16 plenary sessions, about 400 workshops, and 20 testimonials, as well as numerous autonomous activities simultaneously in the city, such as the World Parliamentary Forum, the Forum of Local Authorities for Social Inclusion, the Intercontinental Youth Camp (with around 2,400 participants), the Indigenous Peoples Camp (with about 700 participants) and many parallel meetings, marches, demonstrations, concerts, cultural activities, and parties.

Since then, the annual WSFs have grown three- to seven-fold, and more importantly for our analysis, the social forum idea and matrix has 'globalized'. In a seemingly paradoxical top-down, or global to local, fashion, countless autonomous regional, national, local and thematic social forums have sprung up, generating a 'global social forum process'. For the local and regional forums that emerged, the 'global birthplace' of the social forum process is significant as it marks the importance of the global political economy for the national and local contexts. From the start in 2001, a central characteristic of social forums has been that '[o]rganizations whose horizons have in the past been limited to the nation, or the locality have found themselves connecting with groups engaged in similar struggles across national borders'.[7]

The Berlin Social Forum in the spring of 2007, for instance, aimed to embed its events in the broader European and global social forum processes. Structuring themes were related to the Group of Eight meeting in Heiligendamm, Germany in the summer of that year. One of its principle themes was simply thus: 'why and how does the G8 summit have anything to do with Berlin.' The idea was, as one organizer put it, to 'bridge the local and the global. G8 politics are fucked up [. . .] and they massively impact Berlin politics.'

Striving to go beyond the more reactive mobilizations and protests at meetings of international financial institutions and elite forums, the first WSF set a pattern and a standard for how movements, networks, organizations, and groups around the world can come together. Hoping to withstand the ebb and flow of protest cycles, many social forums that have been organized on local, national, or regional levels echoed the organizational form of the WSF event. They are self-organized, non-hierarchical, open meeting spaces for discussion, linkages, and convergence of the diversity of left emancipatory groups and movements from around the world that are 'opposed to neo-liberalism and to domination of the world by capital and any form of imperialism' (Principle 1 of the WSF Charter). During these often multi-day events various actors congregate in workshops, testimonies, seminars, press conferences, panel debates, and round tables. These events are often accompanied by a lively cultural program, demonstrations, and protest marches.

As the social forum idea is taken up in different locations and contexts, it adapts and transforms. Janet Conway writes with respect to the WSF in general and the 2007 Forum in Nairobi in particular, 'I have sought to problematize treating the WSF, as event or process, as a single thing, an undifferentiated whole. Instead, I have advocated recognizing the plurality of the spaces, places and differences that constitute the WSF, both as event and as a global process' (2008, p. 69). Forums are time and space dependent and the WSFs in Porto Alegre in 2002 or 2005, in Mumbai in 2004, or 2007 in Nairobi and 2011 in Dakar are not duplicates. The musicological term 'variation' might be helpful in capturing the commonalities and differences when social forums travel across time and space. Like so-called 'Fantasia Variations' where musical material is altered and repeated in a different manner during repetition while the fundamental musical idea is unaltered, social forums are context-dependent and vary greatly while encompassing or 'repeating' core principles.

The remainder of this essay draws on Deleuze and Guattari's conceptualization of the rhizome to develop a framework that aids us in theorizing this diverse global social forum phenomena writ large. The concept of the Global Social Forum Rhizome allows us to map and analyze social forums' core principles, their time and space dependent dynamics as well as the accomplishments, challenges and shortcomings of this rhizomatic logic.

The Global Social Forum Rhizome: Developing a Framework

The above account has already suggested the messy, abounding nature of the global social forum process, interspersed by geographic, temporal, cultural, and sociopolitical differentiations and variations. The following begins to develop the rubric of the 'Global Social Forum Rhizome' to conceptually map and analyze the dynamic texture and praxis of this uneven process as well as its challenges for sustained organizing and movement building. There are two principle ways in which the 'rhizome' is useful for understanding the global social forum process and the AGM in general: as an epistemology and as a theoretical framework. Epistemologically, the rhizome provides a particular way of approaching and studying social forums, while a framework, which is the focus herein, can help us to better understand the global social forum process and its implications.

I appropriate the term 'rhizome' from Deleuze and Guattari (1980) who use it to describe singularities that interact to form a multiplicity: that is to say, a unity that is multiple in itself. '[T]he rhizome connects any point to any other point', the authors write, 'and its traits are not necessarily linked to traits of the same nature [. . .]. The rhizome pertains to a map that must be produced, constructed, a map that is always detachable, connectable, reversible, modifiable, and has multiple entranceways and exits' (Ibid., p. 21). Moreover, like botanical rhizomes, each detached piece can generate a new rhizomatic structure (Ibid., p. 519).

Transposing this rhizomatic image helps to conceptualize the global social forum process. The latter is made up of and constructed by singularities (e.g. groups and networks, but also individual social forums themselves) of various scales (e.g. smaller groups such as individual organizations or unions and global networks such as Via Campesina) that interact on multiple levels (local to global) and through time. The concept of the rhizome thus 'suggests networks of heterogeneous elements that grow in unplanned direction, following the real-life situations they encounter' (Escobar, 2004, p. 352).

Rhizomes need open and unstructured spaces. The global social forum process relies on a politics of open-space and inclusiveness. The only precondition for participation is to abide by the deliberatively vague principles set out in the Charter, which define a social forum as an 'open meeting place for reflective thinking, democratic debate of ideas, formulation of proposals, free exchange of experiences and interlinking for effective action, by groups and movements of civil society that are opposed to neoliberalism and to domination of the world by capital and any form of imperialism'. More specifically, three closely related and reciprocal characteristics of the rhizome are particularly useful for understanding the social forum process: its multi-connectivity, heterogeneity, and multiplicity. Each shall be discussed below.

Multi-Connectivity

Rhizomes are characterized by their connectivity. 'Any point', Deleuze and Guattari (1980, p. 7) write, 'of a rhizome can be connected to anything other, and must be. This is very different from the tree or root, which plots a point, fixes an order'. Unlike a tree structure, with only one path from one particular point to any other point, rhizomes represent non-hierarchical structures where any point can connect to any other point, generating links that can stretch—unevenly and asymmetrically—across spaces, times, scales, issues, or strategies. Again, unlike a tree structure with its 'root node' or starting point and its 'leave nodes' or end points, rhizomatic structures can be entered and exited from any point. Analogously, the social forum process has multiple 'entranceways', is constructed and produced, reversible and modifiable. For example, unlike more circumscribed meetings of trade unions, human rights networks, environmental conferences or indigenous rights forums, the Global Social Forum Rhizome brings together each of these diverse actors and more. The less inclusive meetings of unions or human rights activists are also less likely to generate this degree of contact points. One participant emphasized that organizing a workshop means 'you never know who might show up [. . .]. People that you would otherwise never get at one table [. . . and] people that prior to the forum have not been aware of each other [. . .]. A unionist from Nigeria comes, and one from Thailand and another from Indonesia with which you would not have any contacts through the official channel [. . .]. This possibility to create networks we do not have otherwise.'

Moreover, social forums themselves are rhizomatically connected. They do not stand in hierarchical relations to one another as a kind of 'matryoshka doll'. A local forum—such as the Berlin Social Forum—is not nested in and subordinate to the German Social Forum, which itself does not fold into the ESF, nor the latter into the WSF. Rather, the various levels are interlinking asymmetrically, generating and at the same time using the Global Social Forum Rhizome.

Consequently, participation in social forums does not necessarily overlap. That is to say, some groups and individuals might be active on the WSF level but not on the continental, national, or local level. The potential reasons are manifold. For instance, groups in the Global North that work on development use the WSF event to link up with their partners in the Global South (Brinkmann, 2006). They see little reason for attending, for instance, the ESF or local social forums. 'If church-based aid networks meet with their partners from the developing world at the World Social Forum they have no clue what to do at the European Social Forum', Philip Hersel (2006) from Blue 21, a Berlin-based environmental and development organization, points out. 'On the European level this [aid work] is not really an issue. There are then other church [sponsored . . .] immigration groups for example, who naturally are more interlinked and networked on the European level.' Similarly, local social forum participants often do not have the resources or inclination to participate in continental or world forums. While still other groups such as Friends of the Earth affiliates may attend all levels of forums, as their campaigns span the local to the global. The multi-connectivity of the Global Social Forum Rhizome thus fosters but does not *require* linkages of diverse participants, groups, or networks. This heterogeneity is a second characteristic of rhizomatic structures.

Heterogeneity

The Forum's rhizomatic connections are not only between similar or cascading elements—as in, returning to our botanical image, one finds in tree roots—which anchor the main stem structure which has apical dominance. Rhizomes enable 'things of differing status' (Deleuze and Guattari, 1980, p. 7) to connect. As such, social forums can bring together large actors such as labor unions with smaller collectivities of fishermen; or indigenous groups with direct action networks; or more traditional advocacy organizations with others focusing on the environment, gender inequality, or fair trade. The possibilities for heterogeneous connections are truly endless.

One example of this can be found in the Confederation of German Trade Unions (DGB), the umbrella organization of several trade unions representing roughly seven million members, interacting with environmentalists, local fishermen, peasants, and indigenous groups at the social forums around issues related to Brazilian aluminum The production lines starts in the mining factories of Albras (Alumínio Brasileiro S.A.) and Alunorte (Alumina do Norte do Brasil, S.A.) in the Amazon and leads to the refineries in Belém, where the aluminum oxides are obtained. It is then shipped to the Global North where it is processed into end products. Multiple environmental as well as social problems emerge along this production line.[8]

This nascent, yet heterogeneous, network illustrates how the WSF serves as the contextual environment for these linkages, bringing together the individual and otherwise isolated groups affected by this transnational commodity production chain. Each is impacted, however, not in the same way but rather views the problem from a different angle requiring translational work (ranging from language to cultural issues) and different, but coordinated, responses, which are enhanced by information-sharing among networked partners. The inclusiveness and openness that defines social forums allows for the coming together of these diverse actors, something that a more focused or narrower meeting, like a union conference, an indigenous rights forum, or an environmental convention, would be less likely to accomplish.

Multiplicity

The example of the aluminum production chain brings forth the third core characteristic of the Global Social Forum Rhizome. Rhizomatic structures are marked by their multiplicity. Its constitutive entities, groups, and individual forums are irreducible and 'cease to have any relation to the One [...] image and world' (Deleuze and Guattari, 1980, p. 8). Concomitantly, social forums reject 'the one' and rather embrace the multiplicity that operates without a central actor or political protagonist—a multiplicity and diversity of indivisible actors, where all are essential and have a place.

This multiplicity includes the bringing together of diverse movement traditions (including the labor movement, new social movements, indigenous and peasant movements) and operating levels (ranging from neighborhood groups, city and regional projects to global networks) from the Global North and South. The reciprocal relationship between the rhizomatic infrastructure and its diversity indicates a potentially new kind of political formation. As Conway notes, '[i]t is this extraordinary paradox, that embracing diversity is producing unprecedented coordinated action on global and local scales, that is key to the generative power of the Social Forum and suggestive of a new democratic, decolonized and decolonizing politics on a world scale' (2005b, p. 427).

The rhizome's multiplicity applies similarly to the range of issues, strategies, and alternatives. As such, social forums seek to bring out, embrace, and link a range of different substantive foci (e.g. groups that work on anti-racism, the environment, indigenous lands, labor issues, media democracy, or gender equality), tactics and strategies (e.g. holding counter-summits; organizing demonstrations, nonviolent direct action and (symbolic) property destruction), medium-term objectives (e.g. documenting and reporting; conducting specific welfare enhancing activities and programs; establishing autonomous zones, social and workers centers; building networks and movements), and long-term horizons (e.g. systemic reform or revolution). The social forum thus stands in opposition to what the *Le Monde Diplomatique* editor and ATTAC founder Ignacio Ramonet (1995) has called the 'pensée unique', or the 'single thought' of hegemonic discourse that declares there is no supposed alternative to neoliberalism.

The multiplicity of rhizomatic structures also extends to attempts to alter temporalities. Achim Neumann who is a shop steward with Ver.di, recalls one experience of this kind from the ESF in Athens. There he organized a panel and information stand on Lidl, one of Europe's biggest discount supermarket chains based in Germany, whose labor relations are widely criticized. In Athens, Neumann (2006) recounts, 'many came to us and have asked what is going on? In particular people from Turkey [...] definitely want[ed] to keep ... informed about what is happening because. ... Lidl will also come to Turkey and then we want to be ready for them. So ... they act before they have to react'. This example indicates that rhizomatic structures enable the recognition and operation of these organizers, unionists, and activists on the plane of time. The characteristics of rhizomatic structures that eschew hierarchy and linearity allow Turkish activists to 'overleap time', to engage politically with as of yet unrealized threats by connecting at and through social forums.

Accomplishments and Limitations of the Rhizome

On the basis of the rhizomatic infrastructure with its unique organizational matrix, social forums have arguably been successful in producing awareness, connections, and mobilization around the globe. Put differently, the Global Social Forum Rhizome functions effectively as a 'resistance relay', by acting as a catalyst and generating linkages, mobilizations and convergences of the multi-centered global movement(s) (Funke, 2008). Moreover, social forums have been instrumental in holding the diversity of the global left together. As Ruth Reitan (2011, p. 52) points out, a distinctive characteristic about the 'present moment is the degree to which the global left has *not* fractured into its historical constituent parts of liberalism, Marxism, and anarchism-autonomism'. While the overall weakness of the global left arguably plays a role, the Global Social Forum Rhizome has been a crucial element for this unprecedented degree of contact and 'hanging together' of the various wings of the global left.

Yet while its peculiar organizational structure has buttressed these centripetal dynamics, the rhizomatic matrix and logic of social forums is also riddled with tensions and challenges. The quality and extent of its integrative dynamics are in part generated through the paucity of concrete and coherent goals and strategies. While the organizational limitations of openness and horizontality, diversity and consensus decision-making that define the AGM in general and the Global Social Forum Rhizome in particular prevent a deeper fracturing of the global left, its rhizomatic structure at the same time tends to lead to transient networks that present serious challenges to movement building and long-term viability.

The contemporary rhizomatic logic allows for the convergence and networking of the various constitutive parts of the global left, just as it safeguards groups' and movements' diversity and autonomy. The results, however, tend to produce a politics of resistance that eschews institution and movement building as well as sustained organizing (Epstein, 1991). The image of the rhizome is insightful here as well, as it evokes something that is always in the process of becoming and of growing in unplanned ways. Deleuze and Guattari write that '[a] rhizome doesn't begin and doesn't end, but is always in the middle, between things, interbeing, intermezzo' (1980, p. 519). It suggests an 'unplanned', spontaneous, or at least under-strategized direction. By its very nature, the rhizome lacks 'genetic axis or deep structures', or what Deleuze and Guattari define as the rhizomes' principles of 'cartography and decalcomania' (1980, p. 12) that can bind the AGM in more robust formations.

This 'movement of movement's' iconic diversity in general and the principled safeguarding of participants' autonomy as well as the resulting cacophony present barriers for strategizing and sustained movement building. The contemporary weakening or possibly waning of the AGM might be due to the challenges inherent in such a rhizomatic logic for building resilient, potent movements. The *rhizoma*, the rhizome's 'mass of roots' make it taxing—perhaps even impossible—to work through diversity and difference toward achieving some new and higher synthesis.

For sustained organizing and movement building it needs some form of leadership and degree of hierarchy—or rather 'heterarchy' as I will suggest in the conclusion. That is to say, generating a process of 'becoming other together' needs mechanisms for decision-making that approach differences not as absolutes but rather as something 'to work through [. . . toward] coming up with a new synthesis' (Nunes, 2006, p. 305). As I argued above and elsewhere (Funke, 2012), it is in particular the sidestepping of the structuring power of capitalism and class which has thus far prevented a new synthesis from being developed, and contributes to the transient nature and current weakening of the Global Social Forum Rhizome and the AGM. For it is the revolving of gendered and racial structures of domination around the principles of commodification and profit that gives capital and class relations its singular force (Dyer-Witheford, 1999).

Conclusion

This work suggested that the image of the Global Social Forum Rhizome provides us with a larger theorization and more comprehensive analytic framework on the social forum phenomenon. The concept of the rhizome allows us to theorize the constructedness, reversibility, and transformability of the global social forum process and its constitutive dynamics of multi-connectivity, heterogeneity, and multiplicity. While this theoretical approach aids us in understanding the forums' accomplishments, it at the same time brings out inherent challenges and shortcomings. In particular, the versatility, malleability, or structureless-ness of the Global Social Forum Rhizome, which allows for bringing together the diversity of the AGMs and groups, is also, as this piece suggested, limiting more resilient and sustained movement building dynamics. By way of conclusion, I want to suggest avenues for future research and movement praxis.

The global social forum process and its rhizomatic nature may be an instantiation of an emerging new stage in left movement politics, which I have called elsewhere the 'Rhizomatic Left' (Funke, 2012). This terminology is helpful for theorizing the current Left along with its organizational form and dynamic interaction principles. In ideal-typical terms, the term Rhizomatic Left captures and can thus be set apart from the Old Left and New Left. While the Old Left was hierarchically organized and made up of homogeneous elements that 'grew in planned' directions on a class basis, the New Left was made up of heterogeneous parts and issues and a prefigurative dynamic for a cultural revolution. The Rhizomatic Left, on the other hand, is consciously seeking connections between Old and New Left on the basis of a rhizomatic logic that unfolds on the shared background of opposing neoliberalism while stressing the singularities in the plural unity of the Left and allowing for time- and space-dependent transformability and adaptability. The notion of the Rhizomatic Left can thus mark the diversity of the Left writ large since 'rhizome' denotes a heterogeneous multiplicity, allowing us to map the various strands of the global left, ranging from more prefigurative movement based 'shoots' and 'roots' which arguably dominate at social forums to the statist left of, for instance, the progressive governments in Latin America.

The logic of this Rhizomatic Left in general and the social forums in particular also generates challenges and limitations, which warrant further analysis. Here, I want to suggest two factors, which might help us to understand current weaknesses and shortcomings: the absence of a unifying dimension or transversal axis and an orthodox understanding of its organizational model. For the former, Raymond Williams's (1989) and later David Harvey's concept of 'militant particularism' is insightful. Movements begin as particularized struggles in specific settings, places, and communities. The notion of militant particularism stresses that inherent characteristics, such as knowledge, practices, skills, and imaginaries, need to be generalized to overcome particularity and be employed across a 'spectrum of specific situations and singular struggles' (Harvey, 1996, p. 33). I submit that despite the diversity of oppressions, each is also shaped by the capitalist mode of production and is thus situated in the context of capitalist forces and relations that produce it (Gimenez, 2005, p. 20). As such, all other structures of oppression (patriarchy, racism, etc.) stand in *relation* to capital and class relations. Hence, global capitalist and class structures establish the respective material conditions of possibilities for the various groups and movements that participate in social forums and make up the broader Left. A renewed emphasis on capital and class relations is not to argue that gender- or race-based oppression can be reduced to the former, nor does it imply that structures of domination should not be resisted where ever they occur. However, it does suggest that oppositional and resistance movements that fight for women's rights or racial equality reach limits without engaging capitalism, and conversely, that these movements could find common ground with other struggles of workers and the unemployed.

A second factor that limits the degree of congealed and resilient movement building resides in the contemporary organizational model for movement politics that informs social forums and the global movements more generally. The social forum process as well as the global AGM have been inspired by the Zapatistas and their allegedly purely horizontalist, consensus-based, grassroots and democratic practices. While this is certainly a pivotal part of Zapatismo, a second, dialectically linked dimension, I maintain, has been largely ignored: namely, the Zapatistas' successful fusing of the more hierarchical, movement-building approach of the Fuerzas de Liberación Nacional with the horizontal, grassroots and radical democratic approach of the indigenous communities. This, I suggest, generates a new synthesis, which I call 'heterarchy'.

Heterarchy describes the 'the relation of elements to one another when they are unranked or when they possess the potential for being ranked in a number of different ways' (Ehrenreich et al., 1995, p. 3). The notion of heterarchy allows going beyond the dichotomy of hierarchy vs. horizontality. Heterarchy suggests that elements and their issues can be valued differently, depending on the context and perceived needs of the moment. This innovative organizational principle was largely sidelined in favor of horizontality in the AGM and the social forum process in particular, and thus leading to a purist politics of 'form over function', which rarely goes beyond networking or 'protest swarming'. Thus, the Global Social Forum Rhizome has come to espouse a rather romantic notion of change, while renouncing some of the very tools that are necessary to bring about that change. It is my argument that we must reclaim this forgotten principle of heterarchy that lies at the heart of Zapatismo praxis if we are to innovate new ways of moving forward within the social forums toward a stronger and more resilient 'movement of movements'.

Acknowledgements

I wish to thank Todd Wolfson for helpful suggestions on an earlier version of this article as well as the two anonymous reviewers for insightful and constructive comments and Ruth Reitan for her invaluable substantive suggestions and editorial guidance. Moreover, I would like to acknowledge the support of the University of South Florida's Research and Development Grant.

Notes

1 To date, eight centralized WSFs have been organized with four forums in Porto Alegre (Brazil) in 2001, 2002, 2003, and 2005 and one each in Mumbai (India) in 2004, Nairobi (Kenya) in 2007, Belém (Brazil) in 2009, and Dakar (Senegal) in 2011, in addition to one polycentric WSF in 2006 at three different locations—Bamako (Mali), Caracas (Venezuela), and Karachi (Pakistan)—and two decentralized WSFs where various forums or activities took place around the globe, in 2008 and again in 2010.
2 Starting with the first European Social Forum (ESF) in Florence (2002), the first Asian Social Forum in Hyderabad (2003), the first Social Forum of the Americas in Quito (2004), and the first African Social Forum in Conakry (2004).

The ESFs have drawn the largest number of participants: Florence in 2002: 60,000; Paris in 2003: 70,000; London in 2004: 50,000; Athens in 2006: 35,000.
3   http://www.forumsocialmundial.org.br/dinamic/main.php?id_menu=11&cd_language=2
4   The International Council (IC) is the permanent body of the WSF in which over 150 movements and organizations are represented. The IC assumes operational responsibility for the WSF.
5   Virtual ethnography is part of the 'toolbox' of multi-sited ethnography, which goes beyond a particular bounded field site. It is a methodological approach to study networked forms, including ethnographies of virtual, Internet-based environments, texts groups and communities and their use of information technology as well as the practices which make those uses of the internet meaningful in various contexts (see Hine, 2000).
6   On the transition from 'Third World solidarity' to 'global solidarity' to encompass a more reciprocal North–South relationship, see Olesen (2004).
7   http://www.tni.org/detail_page.phtml?&text10=newpol-docs_eurotopia&menu=11f
8   Funke (forthcoming).

References

Biagiotti, I. (2004) The World Social Forums: a paradoxical application of participatory Doctrine, *International Social Science Journal*, 56(182), pp. 529–540.

Blau, J. & Karides, M. (eds) (2008) *The World and US Social Forums: A Better World is Possible and Necessary* (New York: Lexington Books).

Brinkmann, M. (2006) Coordinator of political education department of the Confederation of German Trade Unions. Interview with author, Frankfurt, Germany, 12 September.

Burbach, R. (2001) *Globalization and Postmodern Politics: From Zapatistas to High Tech Robber Barons* (London: Pluto Press).

Cassen, B. (2003) On the attack, *New Left Review*, 19 January/February, pp. 41–60.

Conway, J. (2005a) The empire, the movement, and the politics of scale: considering the World Social Forum. Paper prepared for 'Towards a Political Economy of Scale: Studies in the Political Economy Conference', York University, 3–5 February, http://www.openspaceforum.net/twiki/tiki-read_article.php?articleId=159.

Conway, J. (2005b) Social forums, social movements and social change: a response to Peter Marcuse on the subject of the World Social Forum, *International Journal of Urban and Regional Research*, 29(2), pp. 425–428.

Conway, J. (2008) Reading Nairobi: place, space, and difference at the 2007 World Social Forum, *Societies Without Borders*, 3, pp. 48–71.

Cox, R. (1981) Social forces, states and world orders: beyond international relations theory, *Millennium: Journal of International Studies*, 10(2), pp. 126–155.

Deleuze, G. & Guattari, F. (1980) *A Thousand Plateaus: Capitalism and Schizophrenia* (Paris: Minuit).

Dyer-Witheford, N. (1999) *Cyber-Marx: Cycles and Circuits of Struggle in High-Technology Capitalism* (Chicago: University of Illinois).

Ehrenreich, R., Crumley, M., Carole, L. & Levy, J. E. (eds) (1995) *Heterarchy and the Analysis of Complex Societies* (Chapel Hill, NC: University of North Carolina Press).

Epstein, B. (1991) *Political Protest and Cultural Revolution: Nonviolent Direct Action in the 1970s and 1980s* (Berkeley: University of California Press).

Escobar, A. (2004) Other worlds are (already) possible: Self-organisation, complexity, and post-capitalist cultures, in J. Sen, A. Anand, A. Escobar & P. Waterman (eds) *The World Social Forum: Challenging Empires* (New Delhi: Viveka), pp. 122–129.

Fisher, W. F. & Ponniah, T. (eds) (2003) *Another World is Possible: Popular Alternatives to Globalization at the World Social Forum* (London: Zed Books).

Funke, P. N. (2008) The World Social Forum: social forums as resistance relays, *New Political Science: A Journal of Politics and Culture*, 30(4), pp. 449–474.

Funke, P. N. (2012) The rhizomatic left and neoliberal capitalism: theoretical interventions on contemporary social movements in the global north, *International Critical Thought*, 2(1), pp. 30–41.

Funke, P. N. (forthcoming) The World Social Forum As Resistance Relay: Building a Global Movement?

Funke, P. N., Robé, C. & Wolfson, T. (2012) Suturing working class subjectivities: media mobilizing project and the role of media in building a class-based social movement, *tripleC Cognition, Communication, Co-operation*, 10(1), pp. 16–29.

Gimenez, M. E. (2005) Capitalism and the oppression of women: Marx revisited, *Science and Society*, 69, pp. 11–32.

Harvey, D. (1996) *Justice, Nature and the Geography of Difference* (New York: Blackwell).
Harvey, D. (2007 [2005]) *A Brief History of Neoliberalism* (New York: Oxford University Press).
Hersel, P. (2006) Blue 21, Interview with author, Berlin, 25 August.
Hine, C. (2000) *Virtual Ethnography* (Thousand Oaks, CA: Sage Publications).
Leite, J. C. (2003) *The World Social Forum: Strategies of Resistance* (Chicago: Haymarket Books).
Lorenzano, L. (1998) Zapatismo: recomposition of labour, radical democracy and revolutionary project, in J. Holloway & E. Pelaez (eds) *Zapatista! Reinventing Revolution in Mexico* (London: Pluto Press), pp. 126–158.
Midnight Notes (1998) One no many yeses, in *Introduction to Midnight Notes 12* (Leeds: Autonomedia).
Neumann, A. (2006) Ver.di trade union, ESF participant and workshop organizer, interview with author, Berlin, 27 June.
Nunes, R. (2006) Nothing is what democracy looks like: openness, horizontality and the movements of movements, in D. Harvie, K. Milburn, B. Trott & D. Watts (eds) *Shut them Down! The G8, Gleneagles 2005 and the Movement of Movements* (Leeds: Dissent! and New York: Autonomedia), pp. 299–319.
Olesen, T. (2004) From third world solidarity to global solidarity? *Third World Quarterly*, 25(1), pp. 255–267.
Pleyers, G. (2004) The social forum as an ideal model of convergence, *International Social Science Journal*, 56(182), pp. 507–517.
Ramonet, I. (1995) La pensée unique, *Le Monde Diplomatique*, January, http://www.monde-diplomatique.fr/1995/01/RAMONET/1144.
Reitan, R. (2011) Coordinated power in contemporary leftist activism, in T. Olesen (ed.) *Power and Transnational Activism* (London: Routledge), pp. 51–72.
Sen, J., Anand, A., Escobar, A. & Waterman, P. (eds) (2008) *The World Social Forum: Challenging Empires* (London: Black Rose Books).
Smith, J., Karides, M., Becker, M., Brunelle, D., Chase-Dunn, C., della Porta, D., Garcza, R. I., Juris, J., Reese, E., Smith, P. & Vazquez, R. (eds) (2008) *Global Democracy and the World Social Forum* (Boulder, CO: Paradigm Publishers).
Sousa Santos, B. (2006) *The Rise of the Global Left: The World Social Forum and Beyond* (London: Zed Books).
Whitaker, F. (2007) *Das Weltsozialforum: Offener Raum für eine andere Welt* (Hamburg: VSA Verlag).
Williams, R. (1989) *Resources of Hope: Culture, Democracy, Socialism* (London: Verso).

'Workers of the World, Unite'? Globalisation and the Quest for Transnational Solidarity

ANDREAS BIELER

University of Nottingham, UK

ABSTRACT *As a result of the transnational organisation of production across borders and an increasing informalisation of work, trade unions find it ever more difficult to represent the interests of their members and broader society. This work assesses both the possibilities and obstacles for trade unions to build transnational, intra-, and inter-movement solidarity. The agency of labour is analysed against the background of structural change in the global economy as well as the fundamental dynamics of capitalism. Two main strategies initiated within the World Social Forum spaces are explored: those of 'Decent Work, Decent Life' headed by the International Trade Union Confederation (ITUC) and related organisations and focusing on side agreements to free trade treaties, and initiatives by the Labour and Globalisation Network to increase cooperation with social movements.*

Introduction

Since the call by Marx and Engels (1848)—'Workers of the world, unite!'—the quest for transnational solidarity among workers across borders has been an unaccomplished task. In 1914, workers en masse went to war against each other on behalf of their respective countries. During the Cold War, trade unions were divided along ideological lines. Today too workers continue to compete with each other through lower wages in, for example, so-called national 'solidarity pacts' with employers, while exploitation is intensifying at the global level around neoliberal restructuring. My aim is to analyse the reasons behind the difficulties of transnational solidarity among different national labour movements as well as the possibilities for overcoming them. Trade unions as the institutional expression of workers will be investigated, but so will be other organisations, which represent parts of the labour movement.

Unlike mainstream institutionalist and pluralist policy-making approaches that downplay the importance of the underlying social relations of production when analysing trade unions (see Bieler, 2011, pp. 165–6) this study takes a historical materialist approach whereby social class forces are seen as the key actors as engendered by the production process (e.g. Morton, 2007). This then requires not only a focus on the agency of labour, but especially on the underlying dynamics of the capitalist social relations of production. Importantly, though, the focus here does not externalise or marginalise social movements. Their struggles against exploitation are also understood as part of the broader class struggle.

Moreover, it takes a nuanced approach to production structures, viewing them as only determining in the first instance, following Stuart Hall (1996, p. 44): 'The economic provides the repertoire of categories which will be used in thought. What the economic cannot do is (a) to provide the contents of the particular thoughts of particular social classes or groups at any specific time; or (b) to fix or guarantee for all time which ideas will be made use of by which classes.' Whether a class moves from a 'class-in-itself' resulting from people's position within production to a 'class-for-itself' and is able to develop a common class consciousness is an open question and a result of struggle. It is in this struggle that a whole range of compatible discourses may combine resistance against exploitation in the workplace with resistance against discrimination on gender or racial grounds with active strategies for the protection of the environment, and so forth.

The historical materialist approach, put forward here, is part of a broader post-positivist, critical theory group of approaches. This implies a normative commitment to contribute to an emancipatory project (Cox, 1981). My purpose, thus, is to contribute positively towards reflections on how transnational solidarity can be fostered in order to resist neoliberal globalisation and restructuring. Part of the empirical material collected results from participant observation at meetings of trade unions and social movements committed to resistance. Nevertheless, despite my normative commitments, the limits of such an academic endeavour must also be acknowledged. The purpose cannot be to 'tell' labour and other movement actors which strategy they should pursue. At best, my work can assist in clarifying some possibilities for action as a result of analysing labour's current strategies. Critical theorists are not 'organic intellectuals', defined by Antonio Gramsci as a 'strata of intellectuals which give [a social group] homogeneity and an awareness of its own function not only in the economic but also in the social and political fields' (Gramsci, 1971, p. 5). Only those intellectuals who actively organise and mobilise workers in concrete struggles are organic representatives of a particular social group and can be called 'organic intellectuals' in the Gramscian sense.

The next section will delineate the wider structural setting of capitalism. This includes an analysis of the key dynamics behind capitalist expansion and the more recent structural changes in the global economy related to neoliberal globalisation and the implications for labour. The second section will then focus on the agency of labour. Two different strategies are analysed, the campaign for Decent Work, Decent Life, led by the ITUC, on the one hand, and the Labour and Globalisation Network on the other. It will be shown that both have proven largely unsuccessful thus far at establishing solid or broad-ranging relationships of transnational solidarity. That said, the conclusion will highlight a few concrete examples of successful initiatives of transnational solidarity. It will be argued that while grand strategies have not yielded many positive results to date, there are a whole range of initiatives underway which at least demonstrate that, despite the structural conditions of capitalism, transnational solidarity is *possible*, and thus give some cause for hope.

The Structuring Conditions of Global Capitalism

Capitalist social relations of production are characterised by the private ownership of the means of production and 'free' wage labour. Because employers have to reproduce themselves through the market, they operate in direct competition with each other towards a constant increase in profit levels. 'There is only one basic driving force which compels capital in general to step up capital accumulation, extraction of surplus value and exploitation of labour, and feverishly to look for profits, over and above average profits: this is competition' (Mandel, 1970, pp. 26–7).

The inner logic of capitalism in this relentless search for higher rates of profits, however, also implies that there is an inner tendency towards crisis, the second core dynamic of capitalist accumulation. While the constant search for higher profits through the introduction of new machinery and technology into the production process may be a logical thing to do for the individual capitalist, for capitalism as a whole it is disastrous. In other words, if all capitalists attempt to produce more goods at cheaper prices and with fewer workers, then eventually there will be a lack of demand for their products resulting in a crisis of overproduction. 'Individual capitalists, in short, necessarily act in such a way as to de-stabilize capitalism' (Harvey, 2006, p. 188).

In times of crisis, capital has several possible options. As Marx and Engels wrote in 1848, 'how does the bourgeoisie surmount these crises? On the one hand through the enforced destruction of a mass of productive forces; on the other through the capture of new markets and a more thoroughgoing exploitation of old ones' (Marx and Engels, 1998 [1848], p. 18). First, devaluation in the form of the partial destruction of production capacities, be it through inflation, unemployment, or underused machines, will bring development back down to a level from where it can start afresh (Harvey, 2006, p. 196). Second, capital can intensify the exploitation of the existing workforce (Mandel, 1975b, p. 25). Measures here include longer working days without additional pay, lower wages and cutbacks in labour-related costs, and the like. Third, capital attempts to secure new markets and locations for cheaper production costs abroad in competition with other capitalists. Hence, there is a general expansive outward dynamic of capitalism (Mandel, 1975a, p. 47). Through such a 'spatial fix', capitalist crises of overproduction or over-accumulation, in the words of David Harvey, are contained within a particular geographical area by a further expansion of capitalist production. 'The tendency towards overaccumulation within the region remains unchecked, but devaluation is avoided by successive and ever grander "outer transformation"' (Harvey, 2006, p. 427).

Importantly, this geographical expansion of capitalism proceeds in an uneven but combined way, as first conceptualised by Leon Trotsky (2007 [1929], pp. 132–7). Development is combined in that outward expansion results in industrialisation elsewhere, but it is uneven in that the core gains more than the periphery and that the gap increases between both (Bieler, forthcoming). As Mandel (1975a, pp. 71–2) argues, 'on the world market, the labour of a country with a higher productivity of labour is valued as more intensive, so that the product of one day's work in such a nation is exchanged for the product of more than a day's work in an underdeveloped country'. And it is these processes of uneven and combined development that put workers in such different positions within the global social relations of production. Workers in advanced industrial countries with higher rates of productivity have to some extent benefited from the privileged position of their country in the overall situation of unequal exchange (Mandel, 1970, p. 25), thus creating a major obstacle for transnational labour solidarity.

Structural change related to globalisation since the early 1970s has further shaped the structuring conditions for agency by labour. In response to a crisis of overproduction, capital has abandoned the post-World War II class compromise embodied in the Keynesian welfare state in developed countries. The related restructuring was driven by neoliberalism, which has to be understood as a project by capital to restore class power (Harvey, 2006, p. 29). Several main developments can be related to neoliberal globalisation from the perspective of labour movements (Bieler et al., 2010, pp. 249–53).

First, globalisation has led to an increasing transnationalisation of production, with the production of many goods being organised across borders. Outflows of FDI rose from US$88 billion in 1986 to US$1187 billion in 2000 as peak year (Bieler, 2006, p. 50). A period of recession caused a decline in FDI flows from 2001 to 2003, but four years of consecutive growth led to a new all-time high of FDI outflows of US$1996.5 billion in 2007 (UN, 2008, p. 253). Overall, there were close to 80,000 transnational corporations (TNCs) with roughly the same number of foreign affiliates in 2007 (Ibid., p. 212). Empirical indicators of the increasing organisation of production across borders also include 'the phenomenal increase in cross-border mergers and acquisitions; the increasing transnational interlocking of boards of directorates; the increasingly transnational ownership of capital shares; the spread of cross-border strategic alliances of all sorts; and the increasing salience of transnational peak business associations' (Robinson, 2008, p. 30). As a result, workers in different countries and varying national contexts, both in the North and in the South, have been thrust into unprecedented competition with each other in these transnational production sectors. All too often unions locally at the factory level and nationally in centralised negotiations are confronted with the threat that unless they agree on concessions, employers will transfer production units and jobs to locations with lower labour costs (Bieler et al., 2008, p. 272). In short, trade unions predominantly organised at the national level are no longer able to fulfil their basic task of keeping wages out of capitalist competition.

Second, the increasing transnationalisation of production, which implies a 'centralization of command and control of the global economy in transnational capital' (Robinson, 2004, p. 15), has gone hand in hand with greater decentralisation and fragmentation of the production process itself through processes of outsourcing along the production chain. Thus, transnational production, under the direction of TNCs, is increasingly organised in global commodity chains (GCCs) (Robinson, 2008, p. 27). These GCCs, too, have made it more difficult for trade unions to organise the workforce. It is challenging to organise transnational production workers within one company, but it is even more difficult to organise diverse and dispersed workers along a GCC characterised by a multitude of employers. What is clear yet again is that the traditional, national-level organisation of labour movements with their predominant focus on negotiating with governments and national business associations is ill-suited for responding to these new circumstances.

This reorganisation of the production process around transnational outsourcing and centralisation of decision-making as part of globalisation has led to an increasing casualisation and informalisation of the economy—the third major consequence of globalisation—in which permanent, full-time employment contracts have to a large extent become a thing of the past. This is especially the case in developing countries, which had never been in a position to establish a large industrial sector with permanent and secure employment. Nevertheless, informalisation more and more also affects developed countries in the North, where employers are on the offensive and demand a flexibilisation of the labour market with the argument that it is necessary in order to retain competitiveness (Bieler et al., 2008, pp. 266–7). Indeed, 'it is no longer accurate today', Dan Gallin (2001, p. 228) rightly avers, 'to describe the informal sector as "atypical"'. Traditionally, trade unions were strongest in industrial sectors with large companies. Many workers in one and the same location were easier to organise. But the combined informalisation of the labour market with the rise of the service sector industry has made the organisation of workers increasingly difficult for trade unions. With the exception of some Nordic countries such as Finland, Norway, and Sweden, a decline in membership is the general trend.

Globalisation, finally, has not only led to an intensification of exploitation in the workplace. Exploitation has also increasingly been extended into the sphere of social reproduction. This includes financial cutbacks, the introduction of competition principles as well as outright privatisation of traditional public sectors such as education and health services. It also implies an intensified exploitation of the environment. Resistance to globalisation, therefore, also includes resistance to these other forms of exploitation on the part of progressive social movements—and thus, potential allies—as well as on the part of reactionary, nationalistic groups (van der Pijl, 1998, pp. 46–8).

Returning to the earlier discussion of combined and uneven development, it is important to bear in mind that the impact of these general structural conditions of global capitalism in the current phase of neoliberal globalisation on individuals, production sectors, and geographical locations varies considerably, in line with the underlying dynamics of core–periphery development (Novelli and Ferus-Comelo, 2009). Moreover, the impact will also be variegated depending on the presence or absence of resistance put forward against restructuring. History has amply shown that workers are not simply the victims in these processes of uneven development. The geography of capitalism is the result of class struggle, and resistance strategies by workers have a direct impact on the outcome (Herod, 2006, pp. 158–60). Hence, the agency of labour matters. It is to organised labour's recent attempts at transnational solidarity-building that I will now turn.

The Agency of Labour in Neoliberal Globalisation[1]

The World Social Forums (WSF) and regional social forums have been key sites for trade unions over the last decade to forge closer cooperation with each other as well as with NGOs and broader social movement actors. At the WSF in Nairobi in 2007, where the author participated, labour movement actors launched two distinct strategies—the Decent Work, Decent Life initiative by the main official international organisation of workers the ITUC along with several allied NGOs, and the Labour and Globalisation Network by a range of less traditional or more radical trade unions and social movements. What follows is an analysis of these as key examples of initiatives within and outside the established international trade union structures in an attempt to identify and clarify possibilities for, and obstacles to, enhancing transnational solidarity.

Decent Work, Decent Life Initiative

This campaign is supported by an alliance consisting of the ITUC, the European Trade Union Confederation (ETUC), and several NGOs such as Solidar with close links to established trade unions. Their goal is to achieve 'decent work' for all, consisting of 'equal access to employment, living wages, social protection, freedom from exploitation and union rights' (ITUC, 2007a). This initiative is directed against the rationale of neoliberal economics as practised by international organisations such as the IMF or WTO. The campaign believes that globalisation has led to higher levels of economic growth, even social progress, but that the distribution of these benefits has to be re-organised so that everybody can participate. 'Decent work' and its focus on employment, workers' rights, social protection, and social dialogue with employers and state institutions plus international organisations is regarded as the way to achieve a 'fairer form of globalisation' (ITUC, 2007b). Decent work, it is argued, must become a part of trade agreements and the agenda of international organisations (Solidar, 2007). Since 2008, the ITUC has organised the World Day for Decent Work on 7 October, when it asks its affiliates worldwide to stage events in support of this campaign.[2] As such, however, it is a 'largely symbolic' event (Hennebert and Bourque, 2011, p. 156).

In many respects, the Decent Work, Decent Life initiative by the ITUC mirrors and transposes the traditional strategy of Northern trade unions in the post-war era, which obtained concessions for workers in tripartite negotiations with employers and the state. Initiatives like this, as Peter Waterman (2008, p. 252) observes, are simply raising 'the old notion of "social partnership" with capital and state from the national to the global level'. One can understand why organised labour would attempt such a transposition. For this mid-twentieth century strategy was clearly successful. Workers participated in the increasing wealth thanks to almost guaranteed full employment and continuingly rising real wage levels. An ever more expansive welfare state provided additional benefits in relation to housing, health, education, and other social provisions.

Nevertheless, under current twenty-first century conditions, this strategy is questionable for a number of reasons. First, while successful across the 'First World', these arrangements were never extended nor enjoyed in a meaningful way by workers in the 'Third World'. Northern industry and agriculture were protected against imports from developing countries, and bold modernisation strategies following formal independence ended often in failure. Considering that global capitalism has been characterised by uneven development as discussed above, it is clear why this extension was not possible in the halcyon days of the 'grand compromise'. Increasing wealth and development in the North depended on the appropriation of 'surplus value' from the South in relationships of unequal exchange. And so it is, in a more complex way, today: social clauses attached to international treaties can at best cover the sector of formal contract employment. The increasing informal sector is, however, outside their reach.

Second, the Northern strategy of tripartite negotiations with employers' associations and governments was based on high unionisation levels and strong employers' associations, able to impose agreements on their members. These conditions do not exist at the international level. Although the ITUC represents 175 million workers in 151 countries and territories and has 305 national affiliates,[3] unionisation levels are the lowest in many decades, with the exception of some Nordic countries mentioned above. If we consider the increasing informalisation of the economy and trade unions' problems in organising these sectors (see above), this conclusion is even starker. Equally, there is no suitable bargaining counterpart for trade unions at the global level. International associations of employers are neither in a position nor willing to enforce agreements with trade unions onto private companies.

Third, the advances made by labour in developed countries after World War II depended on friendly parties in government. In many respects, social democratic labour parties and trade unions had emerged in tandem as two arms of the same movement during the nineteenth century that would assume powerful positions in the twentieth century. These partnerships have increasingly been strained at the national level with social democratic parties also adopting a strategy of neoliberal restructuring (Upchurch et al., 2009). More significantly, these positive conditions never existed internationally. At the global level, governance institutions such as the WTO or IMF are often driving neoliberal policies, which are increasingly spread and often enforced across the world. Even within the European Union (EU), often regarded as a suitable international arena for tripartism, the European Commission, as one of the main counterparts for trade unions is not comparable to post-war social democratic governments. If at all, it is the Commission that is behind the drive of neoliberal restructuring by propagating a discourse and policies promoting competitiveness (Bieler, 2006, p. 180). In short, the necessary political counterpart for the Decent Work, Decent Life initiative is missing at the global level.

Finally, and most importantly, we need to remember the historical preconditions of the establishment of tripartite institutions and the welfare state after World War II. It was only when labour could match the power of capital as a result of full employment and successful struggles that the latter were prepared to set up bipartite and tripartite institutions and agree to collective bargaining and an expansive welfare state combined with tight national regulations of the market. This was 'facilitated' by the regime-type competition of the Cold War and the fact that communism seemed to be a real alternative (Wahl, 2011, pp. 20–42). In short, trade union strength vis-à-vis capital came first and was often ascertained in long and hard industrial conflicts. Negotiations and tripartite institutions followed, when capital found itself pressed into making concessions. Against the current backdrop of the transnationalisation and informalisation of production, weakened and fractured national-level trade unions have unsurprisingly been unable to match the structural power of capital at the global level, necessary to force the latter into anything close to the compromises and concessions won in the immediate post-war years.

Another unsurprising feature of the Decent Work, Decent Life campaign is its alleged Northern bias leading to tensions and open conflict within the ITUC itself. Reflecting on the ITUC's World Congress in 2010 in Vancouver, Canada, Bongni Masuku, the International Secretary of the South African trade union COSATU, levelled a stinging attack. Accusing the big four Northern unions—AFL-CIO (USA), DGB (Germany), TUC (Britain), and RENGO (Japan)—of domination, Masuku averred that the ITUC would defend the current system and safeguard the interests of capital. He stated that 'despite much talk about trade union independence, the dominant affiliates of the ITUC are not independent of their ruling classes, even if they organisationally seem to be, but they are politically tied to the ruling establishment, hence their vociferous defence of the system' (Masuku, 2010, p. 64). Ultimately, it is the working classes of the Global South who are affected worst by 'the viciousness of the global system' and who go largely unrepresented within the ITUC (Ibid.).

There is some evidence of transnational solidarity expressed within the organisation by Northern trade unions providing funding for labour activities in the Global South around the notion of 'development cooperation'. Nevertheless, 'most of this solidarity activity appears to be on a North-South axis and in a North-South direction' and, thus, reproduces 'top-down, North-South, patron-client relations' (Waterman, 2008, p. 254). In short, there are clear differences within the global labour movement as institutionalised within the ITUC. This too comes as little surprise, considering the uneven nature of global capitalism, described above, and the very different positions workers and labour movements find themselves in. 'The rise in social inequalities and the structural inequity in terms of global wealth distribution have not in any way lessened the disparity of interests between workers in the North and those in the South' (Hennebert and Bourque, 2011, p. 157).

The above critiques evidence that, strategically, Southern labour movements increasingly question the use of the ITUC in the representation of their concerns. Transforming this organisation will be arduous and slow-going. The main emphasis, argues Masuku (2010, p. 65) and many other Southern activists, should instead be placed on organising within the Global South as well as developing a South–South strategy in the interest of Southern workers through new institutions such as the Southern Initiative on Globalisation and Trade Union Rights.[4] To conclude, then, the

Decent Work, Decent Life initiative is unlikely to develop into a general strategy for the global labour movement. If at all, it reflects, replicates and even exacerbates the underlying structural tensions.

Labour and Globalisation Network

As discussed above, increased commercialisation and commodification in the sphere of social reproduction is part and parcel of neoliberal globalisation. The potential cooperation between trade unions, as representatives of various working class fractions, and social movements, organising those progressive forces that resist neoliberal restructuring of the sphere of social reproduction, can therefore also be understood as an expanded form of class struggle. Cooperation of this type increases what Beverly Silver (2003, p. 13) calls trade unions' association power. Combining this power with industrial action would then, in turn, pool structural and association power. The Labour and Globalisation Network attempts precisely this.

Founding organisations at the WSF in Nairobi in 2007 included Transform! Italia, the New Trade Union Initiative of India, the Norwegian Municipal Workers' Union, the French union Solidaires, the Italian metalworkers' union FIOM, and StreetNet International. Their 'Proposal for a Labour Network on and in the World Social Forum Process' (printed in Waterman, 2007) specifies their objectives to include giving labour issues and workers' rights more visibility within the WSF, developing a permanent exchange of information and experiences, and developing a new transnational capacity for action. The Labour and Globalisation Network takes the issue of power resources in society as its starting point and argues that intensified cooperation with other social movements would be the best way forward to broaden the social basis of resistance.

Organising the informal sector, however, requires a new definition of 'worker', beyond the direct employee–employer relationship. 'As this relationship is being replaced by a variety of more diffuse and indirect but nonetheless dependent relationships in the process of production, trade union organising can no longer focus primarily on the employment relationship' (Gallin, 2001, p. 233). Network member StreetNet International is a good example of a non-union organisation mobilising new types of workers in the informal economy.[5] Localised groups who are directly organising street vendors, market vendors, and/or hawkers can affiliate with StreetNet International. The goal is to exchange information on how to best organise people on the peripheries of the labour market so that they can represent their interests in the most effective way through local, national and international campaigns. Coordinating members especially from Africa, Latin America, and Asia makes StreetNet International a truly transnational organisation.[6]

Like founding member StreetNet International, the broader Labour and Globalisation Network embraces this expanded definition of worker and workplace. Those taking part understand that to remain relevant, trade unions must open up to issues far beyond the factory, to defend rights such as the universal access to clean water, which may then become a joint platform for action with social movements working in this area (Bieler et al., 2008, pp. 283–4). This network recognises that trade union campaigns need to combine more organically resistance to exploitation in the workplace with that in the sphere of social reproduction and the environment. Labour must incorporate anti-sexist and anti-racist discourses in the formation of an expanded notion of 'class' consciousness, which in turn has the potential to transform trade unions and other participating organisations themselves.

Another network member, the French trade union confederation Solidaires, represents one such forward-thinking labour organisation.[7] Committed to radical action, it attempts to organise international links outside the structures of established unions. Additionally, it has significant experience of cooperating with other social movements around issues and struggles of social reproduction. This has included the so-called '*sans*'—or 'those without'—groups such as the *sans-employ* (unemployed), the *sans-abri* (homeless), and the *sans-papiers* (undocumented immigrants) (Solidaires, 2002; see Stierl, this volume).

In a way, both StreetNet International and Solidaires reflect what Waterman (2001, p. 12) refers to as 'social movement unionism' or 'new social unionism'; that is, a new form of organisation which surpasses 'existing models of "economic", "political" or "political-economic" unionism by addressing itself to all forms of work, by taking on sociocultural forms and by addressing itself to civil society'. I further concur with Waterman (2012, p. 26) that the use of the Internet and social media more generally are essential in the development of this new type of labour movement, where cyberspace is 'a privileged terrain for an emancipatory global labour movement and the study thereof'.

Compared to the ITUC, the Labour and Globalisation Network has been more successful in expanding its membership, in exchanging information through a large email list, as well as in putting labour issues on the social forum agenda. For example, the network sponsored a whole range of events at the European Social Forum in Malmö, Sweden, in September 2008, where this author was a participant. That said, what has so far eluded both organisations vis-à-vis their initiatives within the WSF has been enhancing transnational capacity for action—a critique that is often made by other groups against the Forum model and ethos (see e.g. Reitan, 2009; Teivainen, 2011, pp. 183–7). To attempt to circumvent this perceived social forum weakness, several key members of the Network decided in Malmö to call for an annual Social Conference in Europe.[8]

The first joint conference was held in Brussels in March 2011. Participants attempted to go beyond the social forum scenario. Unlike at the social forums, membership was not open. Instead, Network members carefully selected who they believed to be similarly minded participating organisations, including trade unions such as Solidaires and the Norwegian Municipal Workers' Union, as well as social movements such as the Seattle to Brussels Network, Transform! and the European Anti-Poverty Network. Debate was to be part of the meeting, but the overall objective was to move beyond the 'talk shop' strictures of the social forum toward agreeing to launch joint actions with a focus on promoting alternatives.

Toward these more ambitious ends, five working parties were asked on the first day to establish three to four priorities for action. Seventeen action themes and areas for actions resulted from these deliberations and were presented to all participants on the second day. Nevertheless, when it came time to whittle this list down to just four to five priorities that all present would then support and agree on joint action, the discussion quickly stalled. More debate was needed, many delegates decried. Draft papers must be reflected upon further. Additional meetings to deepen the discussions would be necessary and welcome, but without them, nobody wanted to commit themselves or their organisation to any kind of joint activity.[9]

This does not mean to say that the two-day conference was a failure. Discussions were deepened, analyses sharpened, and solidarity relationships strengthened. The main objective, however, to move from discussion towards joint action was not accomplished. The picture that emerged was of a more diverse and fragmented 'movement of the movements' than the Network's planners had imagined. Presumed 'like-mindedness' proved insufficient under further probing to move forward. In the end, a press release was published, outlining their opposition to a neoliberal Europe and affirming the importance of deepening their joint analysis toward the development of a common vision[10]—an outcome not unlike those at the WSF. The

Labour and Globalisation Network had, for the moment, reached its limits of transnational solidarity and action.

Obstacles that may have prevented this particular initiative's success are the ones that commonly impede cooperation between trade unions and social movements: unions too often regard movements as potential competitors in international organisations and a threat to their special or privileged status, be it macro-regionally within the EU multi-sector social dialogue with European employers or internationally within the International Labour Organisation (ILO) (Standing, 2008, p. 373). Moreover, unions also argue that social movements lack representative democratic structures and internal accountability. Thus it is unclear for whom and how many they actually speak (Bieler and Morton, 2004, pp. 314–16).

But unless organised labour can find ways to overcome their distrust and accept social movement actors as equal partners in struggle, efforts at cooperation between them will continue to produce results similar to those we have seen so far. To underscore this point, at the First Joint Social Conference in Europe, NGOs and social movements complained that discussions were dominated by trade union issues and a focus on workers, rather than dealing more broadly with social rights. Nor did the dangers posed by climate change and rampant industrialism feature sufficiently in the discussions, according to social movement actors.[11]

These perennial misgivings on the part of trade unions against would-be social movement allies fail to recognise that the main emphasis of many so-called 'new social movements' is 'with empowerment through information, ideas, images, values' rather than constructing representational or interest-based organisations (Waterman, 2001, p. 23). Labour activists should better recognise that 'social movement' is an umbrella concept for a whole range of very different organisations and groups, some of whom they will have greater affinities with, some of whom they will have less. Some movements are organised around human rights, women's issues, or the rights of indigenous groups—all potentially overlapping interests and identities with workers' struggles. Some of the 'newest' social movements actually have union-like characteristics and constituencies, and are mutual-interest-based organisations of informal sector workers. Others have a broad membership base among under-privileged groups of society coupled with remarkably democratic and participatory structures, while others still are more professionalised, top-down structured NGOs.

Thus the challenge for organised labour is to search for strategic allies among all this diversity with whom to forge concrete and discrete campaigns. Viewed from the other side, social movement actors themselves could make greater efforts to broaden their framing of particular issues. In just one example, they could conceptualise their struggle against cutbacks in the government health services as a one against wider neoliberal forces, and thus seek out trade union alliances.

In sum, neither the Decent Work, Decent Life strategy nor the Labour and Globalisation Network approaches have provided a definitive strategic example as to the best way to foster transnational solidarity toward more effective resistance to neoliberal globalisation. One lesson we could draw from the examination of both is that a one-size-fits-all approach may not be suitable in today's complex terrain of struggle. Hence, in the concluding section, a few additional examples will be highlighted, which could be replicated or built upon to foster greater intra-and inter-movement labour alliances and transnational solidarity.

What Future Strategies for Labour?

It is important to remember that the challenges resulting from neoliberal globalisation are decidedly different across sectors and geographical locations and that they, consequently, require varied and multi-pronged responses (Lindberg, 2010). Transnational manufacturing is often singled out as the paradigmatic case of globalisation. In response to the organisation of production across borders, it is argued, trade unions should follow and also organise transnationally in order to close the 'globalisation gap'. And indeed, in instances of transnational production, international sectoral trade union organisations may be the appropriate institutional framework forward. Thus some form of the Decent Work, Decent Life initiative could be useful to ensure comparable conditions across borders in this respect.

The European Metalworkers' Federation (EMF), for example, has been at least partly successful at coordinating national-level collective bargaining rounds at the European level, wherein it calls on its national member federations to demand wage increases according to the formula productivity increase plus inflation. The aim is to avoid competition between different national labour movements trying to underbid each other through wage concessions (Schulten, 2005).

GCCs too are not necessarily beyond a labour strategy of resistance. Jeroen Merk (2010) analyses the apparel industry in South-East Asia with its highly fragmented global commodity chain, buyer-driven by large retail TNCs. The strategy adopted by the Asian Floor Wage (AFW) campaign has been to calculate minimum levels for decent wages in each country that are sufficient to provide basic necessities like food, housing, and water. The goal here too is to prevent wage competition. Fundamental to the campaign is the right to organise and a focus on the agency of trade unions. It also aims to build solidarity linkages with workers along the supply chain, active in transport and logistics, warehouses and retail trade, as well as to involve consumer groups. Thus, they attempt to establish solidarity between workers along the GCC and between workers and social movements representing consumers of branded articles.

And yet, transnational production sectors are ultimately also those sectors in which workers are brought into direct competition with each other. Valeria Pulignano (2007) shows how European trade unions managed to negotiate a framework agreement with General Motors in 2004, which established that there should be no forced redundancies and no closures of European plants. Unfortunately, this has not 'eliminated the employer's effort to play workers off against each other in local negotiations' (Ibid., p. 152). For international framework agreements, signed by global union federations, often lack the necessary cross-border organising campaigns to be truly effective (Stevis and Boswell, 2007).

Hence, perhaps it is public sector workers, who are not competing with each other but face similar threats of privatisation, which are ultimately better placed to cooperate across borders. These are also under attack, as the privatisation of public companies regularly means job losses and less favourable working conditions for remaining employees, as well as an end to the universal provision of these services to wider society. Here, consistent with the underlying ideas of the Labour and Globalisation Network, it is often cooperation with social movements, organising the users of these services, which may be the best survival strategy.

In Norway, for example, the Campaign for the Welfare State has succeeded in forging a large alliance between trade unions and social movements in support of the welfare state (Wahl, 2010). Another example is EMCALI, the public provider of water, electricity, and telecommunications in the Colombian city of Cali (Novelli, 2010). When it was due to be privatised, the trade union organising the workers within this company could rely on the strong support of the local community to resist privatisation effectively. While workers twice staged occupations of a high-profile building in the city, local community members turned out in large numbers to form a protective barrier around the building. Such worker–society cooperation is not, of course, automatic. Following these examples trade unions would do well to recognise the wider social interests they are defending far beyond the workplace in order to gain this much-needed support at the local, national, and especially transnational levels.

Current efforts by the European Federation of Public Services Unions (EPSU) and the Public Services International together with a whole range of NGOs and social movements to ensure people's rights to access clean water constitutes such a broader campaign of transnational solidarity.[12] Campaigns of this type do not necessarily have to choose between working within or outside formal international organisations as the struggle for official recognition for and by domestic and informal workers demonstrates. Here, domestic workers' groups together with trade unions including the International Union of Food Workers successfully advocated for the ILO to adopt the Convention and Recommendation on Decent Work for Domestic Workers in June 2011.[13]

Many more examples of organised labour looking and reaching above and beyond its immediate constituency, workplace, and political arena are necessary in the contemporary environment, and should be studied sympathetically and critically by scholars. Today's truly globalised capitalist system requires more than ever the heeding of the Manifesto's parting call from over a quarter of a millennia ago: In the twenty-first century, workers of the world must continually seek ways to unite with broad swaths of society, now clustered into diverse and transnationalising social movements.

Acknowledgements

I am grateful to participants in research seminars at Tübingen University on 29 June 2011 and at Sussex University on 31 October 2011, two anonymous reviewers, Elif Uzgören, and Ruth Reitan for comments on earlier drafts.

Notes

1. For a critical overview of recent literature on trade unions' role in the global economy, the so-called 'New Global Labour Studies', see Waterman (2012).
2. See http://www.ituc-csi.org/world-day-for-decent-work.html.
3. See http://www.ituc-csi.org/.
4. See http://www.sigtur.com/. Unevenness is also visible in the Global South itself. Some have argued, for example, that COSATU increasingly only represents a privileged core labour force rather than all workers across the formal and informal sectors in South Africa (Pillay, 2008).
5. See http://www.streetnet.org.za/.
6. For an overview of other successful examples of organising informal workers and the potential involvement of trade unions, see Bonner and Spooner (2011).
7. See http://www.solidaires.org/.
8. Based on discussions at the Labour Assembly on 20 September 2008 and at the Trade Union Assembly on 21 September 2008 at the European Social Forum in Malmö. Participant observations by the author.
9. First Joint Social Conference, Brussels/Belgium on 10 and 11 March 2011, Day 2. Participant observations by the author.
10. See http://www.jointsocialconference.eu/var/www/cne/www.jointsocialconference.eu/IMG/pdf/2011_-_jsc_-_en_-_press_release.pdf.
11. First Joint Social Conference, Brussels/Belgium on 10 and 11 March 2011, Day 2. Participant observations by the author.
12. See http://www.epsu.org/a/7647.
13. See WIEGO, http://wiego.org/informal-economy/campaign-domestic-workers-convention.

References

Bieler, A. (2006) *The Struggle for a Social Europe: Trade Unions and EMU in Times of Global Restructuring* (Manchester: Manchester University Press).
Bieler, A. (2011) Labour, new social movements and the resistance to neo-liberal restructuring in Europe, *New Political Economy*, 16(2), pp. 163–183.
Bieler, A. (forthcoming) The EU, Global Europe and processes of uneven and combined development: the problem of transnational labour solidarity, *Review of International Studies*.
Bieler, A. & Morton, A. D. (2004) 'Another Europe is Possible'? Labour and social movements at the European Social Forum, *Globalizations*, 1(2), pp. 303–325.
Bieler, A., Lindberg, I. & Pillay, D. (2008) What future strategy for the global working class? The need for a new historical subject, in A. Bieler, I. Lindberg & D. Pillay (eds) *Labour and the Challenges of Globalization: What Prospects for Transnational Solidarity?* (London: Pluto Press), pp. 264–285.
Bieler, A., Lindberg, I. & Sauerborn, W. (2010) After thirty years of deadlock: labour's possible strategies in the new global order, *Globalizations*, 7(1–2), pp. 247–260.
Bonner, C. & Spooner, D. (2011) Organizing in the informal economy: a challenge for trade unions, *International Politics and Society*, 2, pp. 87–105.
Cox, R. W. (1981) Social forces, states and world orders: beyond international relations theory, *Millennium: Journal of International Studies*, 10(2), pp. 126–155.
Gallin, D. (2001) Propositions on trade unions and informal employment in times of globalisation, in P. Waterman & J. Wills (eds) *Place, Space and the New Labour Internationalisms* (Oxford: Blackwell), pp. 227–245.
Gramsci, A. (1971) *Selections from the Prison Notebooks*, edited and translated by Q. Hoare & G. Nowell Smith (London: Lawrence and Wishart).
Hall, S. (1996) The problem of ideology: Marxism without guarantees, in D. Morley & K.-H. Chen (eds) *Stuart Hall: Critical Dialogues in Cultural Studies* (London: Routledge), pp. 25–46.
Harvey, D. (2006) *The Limits to Capital*, updated edition (London: Verso).
Hennebert, M.-A. & Bourque, R. (2011) The international trade union confederation (ITUC): insights from the second world congress, *Global Labour Journal*, 2(2), pp. 154–159, http://digitalcommons.mcmaster.ca/globallabour/vol2/iss2/6/.
Herod, A. (2006) Trotsky's omission: labour's role in combined and uneven development, in H. Radice & B. Dunn (eds) *100 Years of Permanent Revolution: Results and Prospects* (London: Pluto Press), pp. 152–165.
ITUC (2007a) Decent work campaign launched in Nairobi, http://www.ituc-csi.org/spip.php?article583
ITUC (2007b) WSF 2007: unions out in force to demand decent work, http://www.ituc-csi.org/spip.php?article599
Lindberg, I. (2010) Varieties of solidarity: an analysis of cases of worker action across borders, in A. Bieler & I. Lindberg (eds) *Global Restructuring, Labour and the Challenges for Transnational Solidarity* (London: Routledge), pp. 206–219.
Mandel, E. (1970) The laws of uneven development, *New Left Review I*, 59, pp. 19–38.
Mandel, E. (1975a) *Late Capitalism* (London: NLB).
Mandel, E. (1975b) The industrial cycle in late capitalism, *New Left Review I*, 90, pp. 3–25.
Marx, K. & Engels, F. (1998 [1848]) Manifesto of the communist party, in M. Cowling (ed.) (1998) *The Communist Manifesto: New Interpretations* (Edinburgh: Edinburgh University Press), pp. 14–37.
Masuku, B. (2010) ITUC world congress and ILO conference outcomes: spaces for real change or illusions of a dream permanently deferred, *The Shopsteward*, 19(4), http://www.cosatu.org.za/docs/shopsteward/2010/sept.pdf
Merk, J. (2010) Cross-border wage struggles in the global garment industry: the campaign for an Asia floor wage, in A. Bieler & I. Lindberg (eds) *Global Restructuring, Labour and the Challenges for Transnational Solidarity* (London: Routledge), pp. 116–130.
Morton, A. D. (2007) *Unravelling Gramsci: Hegemony and Passive Revolution in the Global Political Economy* (London: Pluto Press).
Novelli, M. (2010) Thinking through transnational solidarity: The case of SINTREAMCALI in Colombia, in A. Bieler & I. Lindberg (eds) *Global Restructuring, Labour and the Challenges for Transnational Solidarity* (London: Routledge), pp. 147–161.
Novelli, M. & Ferus-Comelo, A. (2009) Globalisation, neoliberalism and labour', in M. Novelli & A. Ferus-Comelo (eds) *Globalization, Knowledge and Labour: Education for Solidarity within Spaces of Resistance* (London: Routledge), pp. 5–20.
Pillay, D. (2008) Globalisation and the informalisation of labour: the case of South Africa, in A. Bieler, I. Lindberg & D. Pillay (eds) *Labour and the Challenges of Globalization: What prospects for Transnational Solidarity?* (London: Pluto Press), pp. 45–64.

Pulignano, V. (2007) Going national or European? Local trade union politics within transnational business contexts in Europe, in K. Bronfenbrenner (ed.) *Global Unions: Challenging Transnational Capital Through Cross-Border Campaigns* (Ithaca, NY: Cornell University Press), pp. 137–154.

Reitan, R. (2009) The global anti-war movement within and beyond the World Social Forum, *Globalizations*, 6(4), pp. 509–523.

Robinson, W. I. (2004) *A Theory of Global Capitalism: Production, Class, and State in a Transnational World* (Baltimore: John Hopkins University Press).

Robinson, W. I. (2008) *Latin America and Global Capitalism: A Critical Globalization Perspective* (Baltimore: Johns Hopkins University).

Schulten, T. (2005) Foundations and perspectives of trade union wage policy, in E. Hein, T. Niechoj, T. Schuten & A. Truger (eds) *Macroeconomic Policy Coordination in Europe and the Role of the Trade Unions* (Brussels: ETUI), pp. 263–292.

Silver, B. J. (2003) *Forces of Labor: Workers' Movements and Globalization since 1870* (Cambridge: Cambridge University Press).

Solidaires (2002) *Qu'est-ce que SUD Solidaires* (Paris: L'Archipel).

Solidar (2007) Nairobi update: migration and development debated in the context of decent work, http://www.solidar.org/Document.asp?DocID=5116&tod=19832

Standing, G. (2008) The ILO: an agency for globalization? *Development and Change*, 39(3), pp. 355–384.

Stevis, D. & Boswell, T. (2007) International framework agreements: opportunities and challenges for global unionism, in K. Bronfenbrenner (ed.) *Global Unions: Challenging Transnational Capital Through Cross-Border Campaigns* (Ithaca, NY: Cornell University Press), pp. 174–194.

Teivainen, T. (2011) Global democratization without hierarchy or leadership? The World Social Forum in the capitalist world, in S. Gill (ed.) *Global Crises and the Crisis of Global Leadership* (Cambridge: Cambridge University Press), pp. 181–198.

Trotsky, L. (2007 [1929]) The permanent revolution, in L. Trotsky (2007) *The Permanent Revolution & Results and Prospects. With Introductions by Michael Löwy* (London: Socialist Resistance), pp. 111–256.

UN (2008) *World Investment Report 2008: Transnational Corporations and the Infrastructure Challenge* (Geneva/New York: United Nations).

Upchurch, M., Taylor, G. & Mathers, A. (2009) *The Crisis of Social Democratic Trade Unionism in Western Europe: Prospects for Alternatives* (Aldershot: Ashgate).

van der Pijl, K. (1998) *Transnational Classes and International Relations* (London: Routledge).

Wahl, A. (2010) How new social alliances changed politics in Norway, in A. Bieler & I. Lindberg (eds) *Global Restructuring, Labour and the Challenges for Transnational Solidarity* (London: Routledge), pp. 165–176.

Wahl, A. (2011) *The Rise and Fall of the Welfare State* (London: Pluto Press).

Waterman, P. (2001) Trade union internationalism in the age of Seattle, in P. Waterman & J. Wills (eds) *Place, Space and the New Labour Internationalisms* (Oxford: Blackwell), pp. 8–32.

Waterman, P. (2007) Labour at the World Social Forum, Nairobi, January 20–25, 2007: reviving and reinventing the labour movement as a sword of justice, http://www.openspaceforum.net/twiki/tiki-read_article.php?articleId=334

Waterman, P. (2008) A trade union internationalism for the 21st century: meeting the challenges from above, below and beyond, in A. Bieler, I. Lindberg & D. Pillay (eds) *Labour and the Challenges of Globalization: What Prospects for Transnational Solidarity?* (London: Pluto Press), pp. 248–263.

Waterman, P. (2012) An emancipatory global labour studies is necessary! On rethinking the global labour movement in the hour of furnaces, *IISH Research Paper*, 49, http://www.iisg.nl/publications/respap49.pdf

Transnational Feminisms Building Anti-Globalization Solidarities

JANET CONWAY

Brock University, St Catharines, Ontario, Canada

ABSTRACT *This is a comparative study of two transnational feminist networks at the World Social Forum and their distinct patterns of alliance-building with non-feminist entities on the anti-globalization terrain. The work identifies two distinct modalities, that of 'dialogues across difference' and 'coalition-building'. Both are underpinned by discourses of intersectionality and transversality and feminist approaches to coalition-building across difference developed in the 1980s and now being brought to bear on the broader social field of anti-globalization struggle. I argue that practices and theories of solidarity are being remade in this new context with attendant transformations for feminisms and social movements more generally.*

Introduction

Feminism is among the most globalized of social movements that converged in the anti-globalization manifestations of the turn of the twenty-first century. Its practitioners are some of the most experienced in building transnational coalitions and working across myriad forms of difference and inequality among women, including class, race, sexual orientation, religion, and nation. This experience has given rise to sophisticated theories and practices of feminist solidarity that have diffused through the worldwide women's movement. In the current context of intense contact and collaboration on the anti-globalization terrain[1] among formerly relatively discrete and/or geographically distant social movements, these feminist theories and practices are being brought to bear on inter-movement dialogues, cross-sectoral campaigns, and long-term alliance-building with non-feminist others. Such practices are premised on movements' retaining their historical specificity and political autonomy while also becoming more porous to the concerns of others with whom they wish to cultivate affinity.

These practices are stretching social movements' self-understandings in new and unexpected ways. In building alliances with non-feminist and mixed-gender social movements within the wider social field of anti-globalization struggle, feminist activists are calling upon and reformulating practices and theories of solidarity. Throughout the 1980s and 1990s these practices grew out of negotiating differences, conflicts, and inequalities among *women's* movements worldwide under the contested sign of 'global feminism'. For heuristic purposes, we could consider the shift presently underway in feminist practice as one from being primarily oriented to building *intra-movement* solidarities among diverse feminist and/or women's movements in the name of feminism to *inter-movement* solidarities with non-feminist, mixed-gender, and often male-dominated movements. These feminist legacies are, moreover, demonstrably saturating the anti-globalization terrain far beyond the borders of specifically feminist movements.

The anti-globalization field of struggle is one of historically unprecedented contact among diverse movements on a global scale. Here, the World Social Forum (WSF) is a particularly privileged site, for it supports a complex continuum of practices of inter-movement solidarity that vary in scope, quality and intensity and are marked by a range of dynamics of solidarity—including altruistic, reciprocal, and 'identity'-based (Reitan, 2007). This continuum ranges from discursive acts of recognition that valorize other struggles, endorsement of the claims and campaigns of others, one-off collaborative actions or co-sponsored events, occasional dialogue, jointly crafted campaigns or coalition-based mobilizations to long-term, relatively stable, cross-sectoral, and multi-issue alliances.

The comparative study undertaken here of two transnational feminist networks within the WSF is grounded in 10 years of fieldwork on various aspects of the Forum process and to which I bring 20 years of experience in feminist and other social movements in Canada and in cross-sectoral, social justice coalitions. My contribution is threefold: an empirically grounded, analytic mapping of contemporary, transnational feminist practices of solidarity on the anti-globalization terrain; a theoretical understanding of solidarity as it is being remade on this terrain, drawing specifically on feminist resources; and a rethinking of attendant understandings of social movements and their transformations under these conditions.

I will argue that while both networks under study are committed to the idea of inter-movement alliances and draw on feminist discourses of multiplicity, intersectionality, and transversality, their approaches differ significantly in orientation and effect. Further, these differences can be understood in terms of their distinct political histories, institutionalizations, and enactments of (intra-movement) feminist solidarity. And finally, that these contemporary practices of inter-movement solidarity by feminists upon the anti-globalization terrain rely on and also stretch theories of solidarity and coalition-building across difference among women articulated in the last decades of the twentieth century, while also extending them into the anti-globalization milieu.

Transnational Feminist Theorizations of Solidarity

To understand the specificity of the feminist debates about solidarity and to appreciate their particular contribution in the present, it is important to locate them in a larger historical context, which is the transnationalization of feminism over the last 40 years, facilitated largely (although not exclusively) by the United Nations.

This historical process can be dated from the UN's declaration of an International Women's Year in 1975 through to the Declaration on the Elimination of Violence against Women at the UN conference in Beijing in 1995. This 20-year period was punctuated by a series of UN-sponsored international women's conferences which brought women's movements from different world regions into contact with one another for the first time. Regional preparatory processes and the emergence of parallel NGO conferences involved many thousands of women activists beyond the ranks of the official, government-sponsored delegations. The occasion of the UN conferences and the resources for organizing that they made available helped propel the proliferation of women's groups around the world, the global circulation of feminist discourses, and the transnationalization of feminist organizing.

Sonia Alvarez (1998, 2009) documented this process and its effects on Latin American feminisms, a study which aids in our understanding the transnational feminisms in the WSF process. For while these conferences were historically unprecedented and enabling experiences, they were at the same time intensely conflictual, as Alvarez' analysis of the Latin American feminist encuentros also demonstrates. One particularly important fault-line shaping global debates from the 1980s onward was that drawn between 'Western' and 'Third World' feminisms. Western feminism, meaning the liberal feminism predominating in white middle-class women's movements, emanated primarily from the US and was influencing the aid and development institutions and their policy prescriptions in Third World societies. This dominant form of feminism was increasingly being confronted by women's movements from the global South on two counts: as ethnocentric in its assumption that all women shared a similar condition of oppression under patriarchy, and as imperialistic in its project for global sisterhood based on women's putatively common identity.

In her seminal essay 'Under Western Eyes' (1991), Chandra Talpade Mohanty argued that hegemonic feminism reduced the explanation of women's oppression globally to gender hierarchies within the family. It projected a false homogeneity about women's diverse realities and in particular erased the specificity of Third World contexts and the agency of Third World women. She further argued that feminists needed to critically situate themselves and their critiques in geopolitical power relations, particularly in the histories and legacies of colonialism in order to avoid reproducing oppressive power relations in the name of transnational solidarity.

In a parallel fashion, movements of racialized women, particularly in the Americas, were challenging the hegemonic feminism of middle-class white-dominated women's movements and forging antiracist feminist politics premised on a multiplicity of oppressions and the intersections of race, class, and gender, among other axes of social differentiation and inequality. Through the 1980s, 'US Third World feminism' was the site of ground-breaking political and theoretical work on coalition-building across difference, on epistemologies for coalition politics and the new subjectivities produced in and through these politics (Haraway, 1991; Harding, 1992; Hill Collins, 2000; Sandoval, 2000; Yuval-Davis, 1997). From these twin processes, 'transnational feminism' emerged as a distinct theoretical and political perspective in feminist studies, beyond its being a simple descriptor for the praxis of transnational feminist networks (Desai, 2008, p. 39; Mohanty, 2003, p. 124; see also Grewal and Kaplan, 1994).

In this perspective, concrete struggles for survival rather than putatively common oppression or shared identity is seen as the more reliable basis for solidarity, and 'coalition' rather than 'unity' is the preferred political goal (Mohanty, 2003, p. 117, citing Reagon, 1983). For marginalized communities struggling for survival, a tactical 'politics of identity', grounded in a common historical experience of oppression and struggle, remains central to consolidating those movements. Crucially, it is also a precondition for coalition politics with others around broader agendas. Both are interdependent and complementary forms of activism (Hill Collins, 2000, p. 67; see also Eschle and Maiguashca, 2010, pp. 159ff). Coalitions as a political and organizational form are premised simultaneously on recognition of social diversity, political pluralism, and organizational autonomy, coupled with the possibility of concrete collaboration across difference.

The above suggests that coalition-building in the face of difference and inequality requires *transversal politics*. 'Transversal dialogue should be based on the principles of rooting and shifting—that is—being centered in one's own experience while being empathetic to the differential positioning of the partners' (Hill Collins, 2000, p. 245; citing Yuval-Davis, 1997, p. 88). Coalition partners remain rooted in their own particular group histories but, through deep listening and dialogue, may shift or expand out from their immediate experience and viewpoints. Such coalition politics is by necessity grounded in an epistemology of partial, positional, and situated knowledges and represents a rupture with the search for hegemonic knowledge in oppositional politics. As Sandoval (2000, pp. 59–60) observes:

> [W]hat U.S. third world feminism thus demanded was a new subjectivity, a political revision that denied any one ideology as the final answer, while instead positing a tactical subjectivity with the capacity to de- and recenter, given the forms of power to be moved . . . The 'truth' of differential social movement is composed of manifold positions for truth.

According to Sandoval (Ibid., p. 63), this mode of resistance exemplifies a new form of historical consciousness that is itself the product of recent decolonizing historical events in which the search for a hegemonic oppositional knowledge has given way to what she calls 'differential consciousness'. Differential consciousness is the basis for 'differential social movement'. Sandoval names this process the 'methodology of the oppressed'. She suggests that decolonizing processes of the late twentieth century have destabilized Western subjectivities such that they also have been rendered more porous to others and are thus also more capable of differential consciousness.

Conditions for dialogical solidarity must be painstakingly constructed and continually and reflexively deepened. In order to craft non-colonizing dialogues across varieties of difference and inequality, Mohanty (2003, p. 125) argues that activists must grapple with 'genealogies of difference'. This requires fluency in one another's histories of oppression and struggle that goes beyond simple affirmations of diversity and pluralism. The point of analyzing difference is that:

> differences can be historically specified and understood as part of larger political processes and systems. The central issue, then, is not one of merely 'acknowledging' difference; rather the most difficult question concerns the kind of difference that is acknowledged and engaged. Difference seen as benign variation (diversity), for instance, rather than as conflict, struggle or the threat of disruption, bypasses power as well as history to suggest a harmonious, empty pluralism. (Ibid., p. 193)

Solidarity in this view becomes a political and ethical horizon that has to be struggled for. For Mohanty, solidarity is grounded in 'mutuality, accountability, and the recognition of common interests' which make relationships among diverse communities and groups possible. Instead of presuming an 'enforced commonality of oppression', Mohanty's notion of solidarity stresses the volitional and ethical choice that groups make to struggle together. Thus, understanding and respecting diversity and difference are central undertakings that cannot be circumvented in the rush to forge strategic alliances.

Transnational Feminist Networks Building Alliances at the World Social Forum

To discuss feminist practices of solidarity and alliance-building on the anti-globalization terrain of the WSF, I focus largely on Articulación Feminista Marcosur (or 'Articulación') and the World March of Women (or 'the March'). Each is a major transnational network in that each is composed of a number of constituent feminist groups based in different countries. The Articulación is a regional-scale transnational network based in Latin America, comprised of nine networks in eight countries, mostly in the Southern Cone, while the March can justifiably be called global, with 6,000 groups active in 163 countries and present on all continents. Each is preoccupied with strengthening feminist solidarities as well as constructing alliances as feminists with other movements, and both are using the WSF to pursue these two priorities.

As feminists operating in the male-dominated spaces of the WSF, their efforts are broadly convergent. They cooperate on the WSF's International Council where they bring long-standing feminist concerns about process, inclusion, and participation in organizational practices and governance and where they continually contest the gendered power dynamics in the WSF. Both draw on discourses developed over several decades of transnational feminist politics in strongly asserting the multiplicity of struggles and appealing to analytics of intersectionality in their alliance-building. Beyond these commonalities however, the two networks evince distinct political cultures, priorities, and alliance strategies that are rooted in different political histories and positionalities in the transnational feminist field. In the WSF, each is a leading member of two distinct clusters of allied feminist groups whose initiatives proceed along largely parallel rather than intersecting paths.

Articulación Feminista Marcosur

Articulación Feminista Marcosur is a Latin American feminist initiative, a 'space for feminist intervention in the global arena' born as a response to the limitations and contradictions of the UN-focused transnational feminism of the 1990s.[2] The Articulación has been known for its strong defense of sexual and reproductive rights and for the visibilization of these issues in the global justice milieu. As feminists, they insist on the centrality of the politics of the body in order to make visible suppressed aspects of the struggles against neoliberalism, militarism, and fundamentalism (Vargas, 2007).

In the 2002 WSF, these feminists spearheaded a major Campaign Against Fundamentalisms, linking economic neoliberalism with rising ethnic and religious fundamentalisms. Cardboard masks depicting giant lips were sported by thousands of participants in the WSF's many street demonstrations. The accompanying slogan was 'your mouth is fundamental against fundamentalisms'. In a single symbol, the masks captured the realities of people silenced by fundamentalisms, people who could speak but are afraid to, and those who raise their voices in protest. This mobilization reappeared in the 2003 and 2005 WSFs in Porto Alegre, 2004 in Mumbai, and 2007 in Nairobi. They increasingly involved other feminist networks including the Association of Women in Development (AWID) and the Women's International Coalition for Economic Justice (WICEJ). Alliance partner Carol Barton (in Duddy, 2004) of WICEJ commented: 'We see it as a very powerful campaign for bridging differences in what have sometimes been different universes within global feminist organizing. It addresses issues around women's rights to control their bodies and their lives as well as women's economic and social rights. It has brought these two strands together.'

In 2003 the Articulación gathered 120 feminists from a dozen networks based primarily in Latin America in a pre-WSF strategy meeting. Concerned about the marginality of feminist voices in the WSF, participants agreed on the importance both of carrying feminist perspectives into global movements for social change and of feminists assuming greater leadership roles, particularly at the WSF. Those present saw feminist analyses on the intersections of race, class, gender, sexuality, nation, and so on, as critical contributions to global social justice movements, including the movement against neoliberalism. Likewise, in their foregrounding of fundamentalism, militarism, and patriarchy, feminist analyses and politics had much to contribute to the discourses of more narrowly economic justice movements.

Subsequently, 'Building Solidarities: Feminist Dialogues' was organized prior to the 2004 WSF in Mumbai. Hosted by the Indian National Network of Autonomous Women's Groups, it took place over two days, involved 140 women, and successfully broadened regional diversity relative to the 2003 feminist encounter in Brazil. For the feminist organizations and networks beyond South Asia, the WSF in Mumbai was an occasion to build knowledge of and relationships with the feminisms of the host region (Barton in Duddy, 2004).

At this meeting, the Articulación Feminista Marcosur was among the leading groups, which also included Development Alternatives with Women for a New Era-South East Asia (DAWN), the African Women's Development and Communication Network (FEMNET), INFORM Human Rights Documentation Centre (Sri Lanka), ISIS International, the National Network of Autonomous Women's Groups (India), and the WICEJ. These seven groups went on to constitute the Co-ordinating Group of the Feminist Dialogues, which was reprised in 2005 in Porto Alegre and in again in 2007 in Nairobi. By 2006, the founding seven networks had been joined by five more.[3]

The Feminist Dialogues have been celebrated by some participants as a unique forum for self-identified feminists to explore sensitive issues in the global women's movement. These include: dynamics flowing from North–South inequalities; competing foci of struggle between, for example, reproductive rights, violence against women, or economic justice; differing assessments of the most efficacious institutional venues, scales of activity, and sociocultural terrains for feminist work; debates over the efficacy of human rights perspectives and strategies; and varying positions about whether and how to engage with religion in different cultural settings. The Dialogues are also seen as an opportunity to advance feminist understandings of the linkages among neoliberalism, fundamentalisms, neoconservatism, communalism, and militarism in the present conjuncture and what this means for women's rights and feminist strategies (Barton in Duddy, 2004).

The Feminist Dialogues have been built explicitly on the discourses of transnational feminism discussed above, their analytics of multiple identities and intersecting oppressions, and their focus on alliance-building among self-identified feminists and already constituted transnational feminist networks, with their particular modalities. However, while the Feminist Dialogues seem more concerned with building intra-movement feminist solidarities than inter-movement anti-globalization alliances, they were founded explicitly as a critique and response to the marginalization of women and feminism in the WSF and should thus be understood as a feminist intervention on this larger terrain (Conway 2007, 2010; Desai, 2008, pp. 49ff). In the words of their organizers, the Feminist Dialogues also signal a 'return to movement activism' for feminists who had spent the preceding decades in policy-making arenas (Gandhi and Shah 2006b, p. 5).

The Articulación Feminista Marcosur has seen the WSF primarily as a space for encounter and dialogue across difference among the movements, which they argue is a long-term process and central to efforts for democratization (Celiberti and Vargas, 2003; Vargas, 2004). Articulación feminists recognize the tensions and contradictions arising from the different priorities, discourses, and logics of the various movements and thus resist reducing the function of the WSF to building campaigns or political convergence across movements. As Articulación member Lilian Celiberti (in Vargas, 2004, p. 230) argues: 'neither organizational centralisation nor an agenda of mobilisation can shorten the distance that must be walked to further the dialogue between the diverse priorities that movements have'.

Coming from this position, Articulación and its allies in the Feminist Dialogues have been at the center of efforts to build discursive relations across movements by instigating a series of dialogues in the WSF spaces beginning in Mumbai in 2004 (Gandhi and Shah, 2006a). These events followed a feminist dialogic method: they involved speakers from several significant movements which, in Mumbai, included women's rights, sexuality rights, labor rights, and dalit rights/racial justice. Each was first asked to speak to how their movement had incorporated class, gender, race, and sexuality questions, the dilemmas and problems they had confronted in doing so, and the strategies they had employed to advance these concerns. Then activists from the other movements were invited to respond. A second speaker from the original movement was next asked to comment, refute, or clarify. This proceeded through four moderated rounds.

This format was repeated in subsequent years in Porto Alegre in 2005, Nairobi in 2007, and Belém in 2009 (Gandhi and Shah, 2006a; Shah, 2005). Such inter-movement dialogues are critical in fostering intelligibility across difference. They are practices of dialogical solidarity across issues, sectors, and regions, although it must be noted that they proceed largely in the terms set by their feminist organizers, notably through analytical discourses of intersectionality (Conway, 2011; Desai, 2005).

Nandita Gandhi and Nandita Shah, two organizers of these inter-movement dialogues, see this initiative as contributing to the evolving methodology of the WSF that seeks to promote exchange among diverse visions and struggles. They are also, however, aware of the inherent tensions and contradictions in the movements' attempts simultaneously to recognize social differentiation while avoiding essentialized identities. Reminiscent of the above discussion of a tactical politics of identity remaining an important precondition for cross-sectoral coalitions, and indicating how activists are grappling with the implications of claims about multiple and intersecting identities, they write:

> social movement activists who have to strike a balance between pragmatism, theorization and strategy agree to a rejection of sweeping categorizations [meaning essentialized identities] but usually retain the concept of categories itself. However, most have not sufficiently come to grips with the politics of differences and the notion of conflicting identities ... This was the underlying motivation behind the organizing of the 'Inter-Movement Dialogues' as a methodology for a collective reflection on inter category and intra category approaches to deepen our theory and build bridges across movements. (Gandhi and Shah 2006a, p. 73)

The World March of Women

The origins of the World March of Women lie in the organizing of a 10-day, women-led mass march in 1994 to protest deepening poverty in Québec. The March was so successful, both as a movement-building mobilization and as a pressure campaign, that Québec feminists introduced the idea of a world march at a workshop at the UN conference in Beijing in 1995. The World March was constituted by a series of actions orchestrated by local and national scale committees around the world and unified by a shared platform of demands focused both on poverty and myriad forms of violence against women. Localized but coordinated activities began on 8 March 2000 (International Women's Day) and continued over the next eight months, culminating at the United Nations headquarters on 17 October 2000 (International Day for the Elimination of Poverty) in which a petition with over 500,000 signatures was delivered. Six hundred groups from 163 countries participated. By 2003, 5,500 women's groups were participating and by 2005, over 6,000 (Dufour, 2005, pp. 2, 6; WMW, 2004, p. 234).

In 2005, the March launched its second global-scale initiative, the Women's Global Charter for Humanity. Through an elaborate year-long process of articulation and negotiation among its members, the March sought to generate a positive, collective, global vision for the world they were seeking to build, rooted in the 17 demands of the 2000 World March Platform (WMW, 2003b). The Charter was directed at governments and international institutions (UN, IMF, World Bank, WTO) as well as toward the March's allied movements and local communities (WMW, 2003b, p. 3). A world relay of the Charter, in which it was handed from one women's group to another, 'from one world region to another, one country to another, and one village to another' (WMW, 2003c, p. 2) traversed political borders, bio-regional boundaries, and cultural differences. It began on 8 March 2005 in Brazil and ended in Burkina Faso on 17 October 2005 with stops in 53 countries and territories. The round-the-world journey of the Charter concluded with '24 hours of global feminist solidarity', a rolling sequence of one-hour actions beginning in Oceania and following the sun westward around the globe.

The March represents a different kind of feminist transnationalism from that of many other transnational feminist networks who have been heavily shaped by their socialization within the UN processes, resulting in their 'NGO-ization', strong focus on policy advocacy, and its resulting cultures of expertise. Resisting this trend toward professionalization and institutional reformism, the March has built a global network of place-based, grassroots feminist groups, privileging the agency of poor and working-class women. It recognizes the diversity of women's priorities, discourses, and modes of activism—including their varied positionalities with respect to 'feminism'. It respects the autonomy of local groups, while negotiating their differences in the construction of a collective identity, political vision, and capacity to organize and intervene on a global scale.

From its origin, the March has been interested in mass movement building—not just among women and feminists but cross-sectorally with mixed- and non-feminist movements alike with whom it could construct political alliances against neoliberalism. The March in Quebec and subsequently the World March forged campaign alliances with unions, churches, and other non-feminist entities and has included in its membership women's groups primarily identified with other sectors.

Its global actions every five years extend and consolidate feminist solidarities while producing instruments and building capacity for more effective feminist intervention in cross-sectoral alliances and vis-à-vis hegemonic processes and institutions. In the diversity of its constituent groups in terms of sectors, scales and modes of activism, in its reliance on 'contentious politics' more than lobbying, and in its articulation to the anti-globalization mobilizations, the March represents novel developments in the field of transnational feminist politics (Conway, 2007, 2008; Dufour and Giraud, 2007; Giraud and Dufour, 2010).

Moreover, the March positions itself as a critique and alternative to the kind of international feminism that developed around the UN—particularly the latter's privileging of urban policy experts and lobbyists and the 'body politics' of sexuality and reproduction over 'popular feminist' struggles for land, water, food, and work. The March resists a hierarchy of primary vs. secondary, or specific vs. general issues in constituting feminist agendas even as they insist that 'feminist' concerns about sexual and reproductive rights or violence against women cannot be separated from or made secondary to the 'anti-globalization' agenda.

Furthermore, for the March, building alliances with non-feminist others is central to its understanding of itself and its struggle to change the world. Thus, over the last decade, the March has become a prominent presence in transnational spaces of social protest, from anti-G8 and -G20 protests, to convergences against the WTO and the war in Iraq, to the world and regional social forums. The March's commitment to grassroots mobilization, street action, and the claiming of public space resonates with many other expressions of anti-globalization activism especially among youth, and also characterizes its presence in the WSF. In the Forum spaces, the World March regularly seeks to educate, mobilize, and expand its base among grassroots women's groups. The March also regularly mounts events in collaboration with other feminist networks, such as Agencia Latino Americano de Información (ALAI), Red Latinoamericano Mujeres Transformando la Economía (REMTE—Network of Women Transforming the Economy), South-South LGBT Dialogue, and Women of Via Campesina.

The March sees the WSF as a privileged space for building alliances with other anti-globalization social movements. Compared to our earlier case of the Articulación Feminista Marcosur, they approach the WSF more pragmatically and instrumentally as a 'convergence space', rather than as a place for encounter. The March has been a major actor in establishing the World Network of Social Movements in 2003 which organizes joint events, meets in a giant assembly at each WSF, and formulates common declarations. This ongoing contact and collaboration has facilitated bilateral alliances between the March and specific partners such as the Committee to Abolish Third World Debt, Focus on the Global South, and Via Campesina—some of which are 'strategic', while others are 'tactical'. The former are based on a long-term joint vision and are oriented toward a converging agenda and common actions, while the latter are more issue-specific or conjunctural (WMW, 2008b).

The most impressive strategic partnership to date is with Via Campesina. The mammoth peasant network invited the March to co-organize the Nyéleni Food Sovereignty Forum in Mali in 2007, from which they conceived a work plan on food sovereignty in conjunction with Friends of the Earth International and the World Forum of Fisher People (WMW, 2008a, p. 40, 2008b) Another outgrowth of this long-term relationship was the 2008 launching by Via Campesina of a major campaign to stop violence against women farmers.

The March is engaged in building a global-scale, counter-hegemonic politics in which the work of alliance-building is central and in which they are a strong, autonomous feminist presence and power. The March is, however, acutely aware of the risks inherent in this collaborative inter-movement work. These include: neglecting their own network's development in favor of investing in coalition work; becoming burdened with the care work of maintaining inter-movement relations; and displacing central feminist concerns, such as reproductive rights or combating violence against women (WMW, 2008b).

The work of alliance-building is thus long-term, resource-intensive, replete with risks and costs, and requiring of multiple, sector- and place-specific approaches. The March is also aware that this work challenges and stretches its own unique identity as it expands its agenda in response to its partners in struggle (WMW 2008a, p. 34ff). In the process, some fear the March may lose its *raison d'être* (Dufour, 2012). Alliance-building in the anti-globalization milieu thus remakes feminists and feminisms even as the March—and their counterparts in Articulación—seek to remake anti-globalization movements: 'As feminists of the WMW, we want the analysis of patriarchy to be etched at the very heart of the questioning of neoliberalism and imperialism' (WMW, 2007).

Feminist Strategies of Cross-Movement Solidarity- and Alliance-Building

As we see from the foregoing, there are plural transnational feminisms operating on the anti-globalization terrain, which pursue their own distinct strategies both for constructing feminist solidarities and building alliances with non-feminist others. The alliance-forming initiatives of the Articulación and the March with non-feminist movements proceed in different modalities and at different levels of intensity. For heuristic purposes, these distinct approaches to inter-movement solidarity can be understood as one which favors 'dialogue across difference' versus one prioritizing 'coalition-building', with the former describing the main approach of the Articulación and its allies, and the latter denoting the preferred practices of the World March of Women.

The dialogue across difference approach associated with the Articulación privileges communicative practices. It aims at building mutual intelligibility and recognition grounded in an acknowledgment of the multiplicity of oppressions and proceeds through an analytic of their intersectionality. This can produce a kind of discursive solidarity in which movements begin to incorporate the language, analytic categories and frames, and core concerns of other movements into their own discourses. It can also prompt critical awareness within movements of their own respective shortcomings, biases and blind spots—a precondition for the 'work of translation' (Santos, 2005).

The March's coalition-building approach, on the other hand, is oriented to sustained collaboration with specific partners on concrete issues of mutual concern. Collaborative practices and intensities vary depending on the partner, issue of concern, timing, and geographic context. While coalition work obviously also relies on dialogue and the negotiation of difference, these conversations arise in the context of and as means to sustained practical collaboration, not as ends in themselves as we find in the former orientation. For the March, for example, such dialogues involve a fuller range of activist partners and practices, in which the March conceives of itself as a feminist partner but does not set the rules of engagement. The March consciously and consistently engages in dialogue in the interstitial spaces of the anti-globalization movement with the aim of building trust and partnerships in practice with *non-feminist* but broadly emancipatory movements. This strategy, over time, has seeded new feminist fronts in predominantly non-feminist movements and cross-sectoral networks, yet is clearly not without its own costs and risks.

Without claiming to definitively 'explain' these different approaches to inter-movement solidarity seen in the March and Articulación, I suggest that they stem from the distinct histories, social compositions, and institutionalizations of these feminisms, as well as from their different approaches to intra-feminist solidarities. While both strands of feminist practice are significantly internationalized, predominantly South–South networks, and strongly rooted in Latin America, the Articulación and its allies in the Feminist Dialogues are more conversant and comfortable with transnational feminist practices and alliances developed around the UN through the 1980s and 1990s. These involve NGO networks led by highly educated, urban, professional, and relatively affluent women, with histories and experience in sectoral policy advocacy, who employ academic legal and policy discourses circulating internationally to advance women's rights.

In contrast, the March has sought to build an alternative feminist internationalism, grounded in localized, grassroots struggles of women without regard for whether they self-identify as feminist and with a high regard for localized difference and autonomy. Moreover, from its origins, the March emerged though a popular, feminist-led but cross-sectoral mobilization against neoliberalism and thus understands and frames its struggle for systemic and emancipatory social transformation as necessarily proceeding in alliance with other such struggles. These different histories and orientations produce distinct present-day patterns, including in their approaches to inter-movement solidarity.

Further, the varying degrees of institutionalization of both networks also shape their inter-movement alliances. Unlike transnational feminist networks such as Articulación and those involved in the Feminist Dialogues, the March's *raison d'être* is mass mobilization. Thus it exists as a powerful, broad-based, and autonomous movement in and beyond the WSF, rather than as a loose network of groups that periodically collaborate on the occasion of the WSF. And *in* the context of collaborating on the anti-globalization terrain of the WSF, the March functions as an autonomous feminist power, pushing for the integration of feminist struggles against patriarchy into all the major movements and in every aspect of the social forum itself (Burrows, 2005; WMW, 2004). Whereas the Feminist Dialogues seek to intervene in the more amorphous and ephemeral spaces of the WSF events and through its constituent members—the leading one being Articulación—maintain a more sustained advocacy and presence in the WSF's International Council.

Whether of low or high intensity, practices of inter-movement solidarity by feminists in the anti-globalization milieu assume the irreducible diversity of social subjects and struggles and thus maintain a permanent commitment to multiplicity, pluralism, and difference. This stance requires a fundamental respect for *sui generis* social movements' dynamic ongoing processes of self-(re)definition, and the maintenance of autonomy. Highly intensive and sustained alliances do not assume, however, that boundaries between movements are or should be dissolved. Yet at the same time, they recognize that collective identities are not fixed even as some axes of social differentiation are more enduring and significant across time and place. The bases for social mobilization shift. Boundaries can and do blur and change as movements become more porous to one another's concerns—but the plurality of movements and their politically salient identities remains.

Conclusion: Feminist Theorizations of Solidarity on the Anti-Globalization Terrain

Central to transnational feminist politics is the recognition of a multiplicity of identities and oppressions, the search for ways to understand their intersection, and in so doing, the building of more inclusive and effective movements with more expansive and transformative visions and powers. Feminists have learned the hard way that there is no one transhistorical 'patriarchy' that produces a common oppression among women, let alone a unified political subject called 'women', nor a unitary feminist politics.

These political confrontations produced new norms for transnational feminist practice and are the foundation of new theories of solidarity. Thinking *through* and working across difference, feminists evince concrete know-how of intra-feminist coalition politics, which they bring to the 'movement of movements' and to the WSF. Analytically, feminists have theorized the interactive and intersectional character of domination based on the mutually reinforcing dynamics of oppressions based on gender, race, ethnicity, sexuality, and class, among other axes of social hierarchy and differentiation.

In the wake of four decades of feminist collaboration across distance and difference, gender relations have come to be understood as intersecting with myriad other forms of hierarchy and axes of identity. Consequently, the struggle for the democratization of these relations is now seen as integrated and aligned with the whole range of movements for equality, rights, and democratization (Vargas, 2003a, p. 918). While feminists can be credited for advancing social movement praxis along these lines, feminist movements and subjectivities have also been transformed in the process in variable and uneven ways. Across the board, these changes have rendered them more porous to other feminisms as well as to other equality-seeking movements, relative both to earlier historical moments and to the porosity of other movements to their 'others'. This more open stance defines the major transnational feminist networks active at the WSF and their approaches to coalition politics, although the balance between 'rooting' and 'shifting' varies among different feminisms.

In the WSF, these theoretical orientations also find diverse practical expression beyond narrowly feminist politics. The language of shared opposition in the WSF has been enlarged to include explicit recognition of a multiplicity of oppressions, of struggles, and of political subjects. In some contexts, notably in Mumbai in 2004, the WSF has been noticeably transformed as a result (Barria and Nelson, 2008, pp. 39–40). Feminist attention to intersectionality has produced more complicated theorizations of neoliberalism itself as a sexist, racist, and homophobic project with uneven effects on human populations beyond those of class, region, or nation, in which the oppression of women and exploitation of their labor is deeply implicated. Feminists have also productively analyzed neoliberalism as a form of fundamentalism, thus linking it with other reactionary social movements and connecting struggles for gender justice against social conservatism with those for economic justice against liberal regimes. These discourses are in circulation in the WSF, although are very unevenly taken up by non-feminist movements.

However, beyond these discursive and analytical breakthroughs, practicing a politics of solidarity premised *abstractly* on intersectionality is a highly uncertain and unsatisfying affair. As Desai (2008, p. 52) writes about the inter-movement dialogues:

> [I]f this session was an indicator of coalition politics, it did not seem very promising. Solidarities with other movements have become the hegemonic movement strategy. But as the intermovement sessions at the forum in 2004 and 2005 showed, movements haven't done the serious work: namely the work of rearticulating their visions to integrate other visions; reorganizing their movements to include others; and rethinking strategies to address issues of all inequalities, such as inequalities of class, race, gender, and sexuality, among others.

This recalls Mohanty's caution about benign acknowledgements of diversity that fail to seriously engage difference in specific contexts of struggle. Although rhetorics of multiplicity and diversity abound in the WSF and among many of its constituent movements, ongoing political and epistemic marginality of women, racialized, indigenous, and other subaltern movements remains evident (Conway, 2012).

A more robust and productive route to coalition-building informed by insights of intersectionality I find in the Word March's practice of sustained engagement with particular partners on particular issues. Their approach is more pragmatic and less theoretically-driven, and is thus more partial and specific than the inter-movement dialogues in terms of the intersections it is engaging at any one time. This more circumscribed endeavor perhaps accounts for its relative success. Solidarities of this kind are built through sustained, experimental, often contradictory and painstaking practice. Furthermore, in its orientations to alliance-building, the March admits to itself and its partners its own partiality, the incompleteness of its own agenda, as well as openness to its own broadening and even self-transformation. In the process, new feminist subjectivities are being produced within the March and beyond it, characterized by the new historical consciousness identified by Sandoval: 'differential consciousness' as the basis for differential social movement.

Flowing from both the recognition of multiplicity of oppressions and the analytic of intersectionality is the *praxis of transversality*. Notions of transversality advanced by feminists at the WSF are congruent with while moving beyond Yuval-Davis's classic definition of the rooting and shifting dynamics required of movements in coalition politics. The feminist commitment to transversality in the context of the WSF is similarly based on standpoint epistemologies. That is, distinct knowledges emerge from particular social locations and that those of the historically marginalized should be privileged in constructing any emancipatory politics claiming to act on their behalf. However, feminists in the WSF argue further that a politics of transversality holds that women and feminists, along with all historically marginalized voices, should be envisioning and addressing *the whole of* a transformative agenda, rather than be limited, or limiting themselves, to historically assigned silos of supposedly discrete issues (Mtetwa, 2005, pp. 134–7). Transversal politics here is more about the *transversality of knowledges* produced by different historically marginalized subjectivities across different domains, rather than transformative dispositions required by those subjectivities, although the two are obviously related.

The feminist networks explored herein all endorse this more developed notion of transversality. They further view the commitment to the transversality of historically marginalized voices including women's as *the* methodology of the WSF (WMW, 2008c, p. 6). It is seen as a process that will, if deepened, promote the emergence of new subjects and new questions (Vargas, 2003b, p. 40). Latin American feminists link this commitment explicitly to the WSF's agenda of overcoming *pensamientos únicos*, among which they include androcentric and ethnocentric forms of thought (León, 2005, p. 13), along with neoliberal and other fundamentalisms.[4] In the view of these feminists, such transversal politics entails a 'complexification' and expansion of the anti-globalization movement's agenda along with positive visions of alter-globalization. But a transversal politics on the anti-globalization terrain with non-feminist others also threatens/promises to expand and render more complex existing feminist agendas. The March's practices of coalition-building are a fuller putting into practice of this politics and a more explicit embrace of the transformative effects of transversal praxis on themselves and for feminism more generally.

For feminists, the commitment to transversality is both a political practice and an epistemological principle but, emergent within it, is also a vision of another sociality, another social ordering, founded on an alternative regime of truth. This alternative regime is grounded in the valorization of the knowledges produced by marginalized subjectivities and their mutual transformations through deep, sustained, democratic, and solidaristic encounter. It is pluralist but not relativist in that it is informed by historical struggles against discrimination. And it is not naive about the operation of power and inequality, including on the putatively egalitarian ground of encounter among emancipatory movements. Through the cauldron of practice on the anti-globalization terrain, feminist theorizations of solidarities of difference are being stretched, refined, and reformulated to nourish an emergent alternative vision of sociality. The anti-globalization terrain of the early twenty-first century may indeed prove to be as creative a period of ferment for feminist theory and practice as was the eruption of Third World feminisms in the last decades of the twentieth century.

Acknowledgement

The author thanks Dominique Masson, Pascale Dufour, and two anonymous reviewers for their invaluable comments on earlier drafts of this paper.

Notes

1. I am using the term 'anti-globalization terrain' to invoke the idea of a transnational social field rather than a discrete movement that can be conceived as separate from the transnational feminisms under discussion.
2. By the mid-1990s, the rising tides of both neoliberalism and religious conservatism were making the UN far less hospitable for feminist policy initiatives. At the same time, many feminists were increasingly skeptical about the efficacy of international agreements in concretely improving the lives of women.
3. These were: Akina Mama wa Africa; CLADEM; REDLAC; Women Living Under Muslim Laws; WIDE.
4. *Pensamientos únicos* refers to unitary modes of thought that exclude the possibility of alternatives. In the discourses of the WSF, neoliberalism is the paradigmatic form of unitary thought against which the slogan 'another world is possible' is directed. The WSF Charter and its supporters oppose all such forms of hegemonic knowledge through a through-going affirmation of multiplicity—a formulation convergent with Sandoval's notion of differential consciousness and differential social movement.

References

Alvarez, S. E. (1998) Latin American feminisms 'go global': trends of the 1990s and challenges of the new millennium, in S. E. Alvarez, E. Dagnino & A. Escobar (eds) *Cultures of Politics, Politics of Cultures: Re-Visioning Latin American Social Movements* (Boulder, CO: Westview Press), pp. 293–324.

Alvarez, S. E. (2009) Beyond NGO-ization? Reflections from Latin America, *Development*, 52(2), pp. 175–184.

Barria, S. & Nelson, O. J. (2008) *Main Debates Around the WSF 2004 in Mumbai*. Critical Engagement No. 4 (New Delhi, India: CACIM).

Burrows, N. (2005) World peace is possible, in I. León (ed.), M. del Pilar Vega Garcia (trans.) *Women in Resistance: Experiences, Visions and Proposals* (Quito: Agencia Latino Americana de Informacion), pp. 117–124.

Celiberti, L. & Vargas, V. (2003) Feministas en el foro, *Revista Estudo Feministas*, 11(2), pp. 586–598.

Conway, J. (2007) Transnational feminisms and the World Social Forum: encounters and transformations in anti-globalization spaces, *Journal of International Women's Studies*, 8(3), pp. 49–70.

Conway, J. (2008) Geographies of transnational feminism: place and scale in the spatial politics of the World March of Women, *Social Politics*, 15(2), pp. 207–231.

Conway, J. (2010) Troubling transnational feminism(s) at the World Social Forum, in P. Dufour, D. Masson & D. Caouette (eds) *Solidarities Without Borders: Transnationalizing Women's Movements* (Vancouver: University of British Columbia Press), pp. 139–159.

Conway, J. (2011) Cosmopolitan or colonial? The World Social Forum as 'contact zone', *Third World Quarterly*, 32(2), pp. 217–236.

Conway, J. M. (2012) *Edges of Global Justice: The World Social Forum and Its 'Others'* (London: Routledge).

Desai, M. (2005) Transnationalism: the face of feminist politics post-Beijing, *International Social Science Journal*, 184, pp. 319–330.

Desai, M. (2008) *Gender and the Politics of Possibilities: Rethinking Globalization* (Lanham, MD: Rowman & Littlefield).

Duddy, J. (2004) How is a gendered perspective being placed on the agenda of the 2004 World Social Forum? an interview with Carol Barton, Women's International Coalition for Economic Justice (WICEJ), *Association for Women's Rights in Development*, http://www.awid.org/Library/How-is-a-gendered-perspective-being-placed-on-the-agenda-of-the-2004-World

Dufour, P. (2005), The World March of Women: first Quebec, then the world?, Paper presented at conference on 'Claiming Citizenship in the Americas', Canada Research Chair in Citizenship and Governance, University of Montreal, 27 May, http://www.cccg.umontreal.ca/pdf/Dufour%20rev%202.pdf

Dufour, P. (2012) Personal communication.

Dufour, P. & Giraud, I. (2007) When the transnationalization of solidarities continues: the case of the World March of Women between 2000 and 2006—a collective identity-building approach, *Mobilization: An International Quarterly Review*, 12(3), pp. 307–322.

Eschle, C. & Maiguashca, B. (2010) *Making Feminist Sense of the Global Justice Movement* (Lanham, MD: Rowman & Littlefield).

Gandhi, N. & Shah, N. (2006a) Inter movement dialogues: breaking barriers, building bridges, *Development*, 49(1), pp. 72–76.

Gandhi, N. & Shah, N. (2006b) An interactive space for feminisms, Paper submitted to *Samyukta: A Journal of Women's Studies*.

Giraud, I. & Dufour, P. (2010) *Dix Ans de Solidarité Planétaire: Perspectives Sociologiques sur la Marche Mondiale Des Femmes* (Montréal: Les éditions du remue-ménage).

Grewal, I. & Kaplan, C. (1994) *Scattered Hegemonies: Postmodernity and Transnational Feminist Practices* (Minneapolis: University of Minnesota Press).

Haraway, D. (1991) Situated knowledges: the science question in feminism and the privilege of partial perspective, in *Simians, Cyborgs and Women: The Reinvention of Nature* (London: Routledge), pp. 183–201.

Harding, S. (1992) Subjectivity, experience and knowledge: an epistemology from/for rainbow coalition politics, in J. Nederveen Pieterse (ed.) *Emancipations, Modern and Postmodern* (London: Sage), pp. 175–193.

Hill Collins, P. (2000) *Black Feminist Thought: Knowledge, Consciousness, and the Politics of Empowerment*, 2nd ed. (London: Routledge).

León, I. (2005) World Social Forum: discussions and gestures of diversity, in I. León (ed.), M. del Pilar Vega Garcia (trans.) *Women in Resistance: Experiences, Visions and Proposals* (Quito: Agencia Latino Americano de Información), pp. 9–24.

Mohanty, C. T. (1991) Under western eyes: feminist scholarship and colonial discourses, in C. T. Mohanty, A. Russo & L. Torres (eds) *Third World Women and the Politics of Feminism* (Bloomington: Indiana University Press), pp. 51–80.

Mohanty, C. T. (2003) *Feminism Without Borders: Decolonizing Theory, Practicing Solidarity* (Durham, NC: Duke University Press).

Mtetwa, P. (2005) Diverse women in the construction of 'another world', in I. León (ed.), M. del Pilar Vega Garcia (trans.) *Women in Resistance: Experiences, Visions and Proposals* (Quito: Agencia Latino Americano de Información), pp. 133–139.

Reagon, B. J. (1983) Coalition politics: turning the century, in B. Smith (ed.) *Home Girls: A Black Feminist Anthology* (New York: Kitchen Table, Women of Color Press), pp. 343–355.

Reitan, R. (2007) *Global Activism* (London: Routledge).

Sandoval, C. (2000) *Methodology of the Oppressed* (Minneapolis: University of Minnesota Press).

Santos, B. & de, S. (2005) The future of the World Social Forum: the work of translation, *Development*, 48(2), pp. 15–22.

Shah, S. (2005) *A Dialogue Between Movements Held at the World Social Forum (WSF) in Porto Alegre, Brazil on the 28th January 2005: A Report* (Mumbai: Akshara—a Women's Resource Centre).

Vargas, V. (2003a) Feminism, globalization and the global justice and solidarity movement, *Cultural Studies*, 17(6), pp. 905–920.

Vargas, V. (2003b) *Globalizacion y Foro Social Mundial: Retos de los Feminismos en el Nuevo Milenio* (Lima: Centro de la Mujer Peruana Flora Tristan).

Vargas, V. (2004) WSF 3 and tensions in the construction of global alternative thinking, in J. Sen, A. Anand, A. Escobar & P. Waterman (eds) *Challenging Empires* (New Delhi: Viveka Foundation), pp. 228–232.

Vargas, V. (2007) Personal communication with author.

WMW (World March of Women) (2003a) *World March of Women Newsletter*, 6(1), February, http://www.worldmarchofwomen.org/bulletin_liaison/2003/fr/

WMW (2003b) *World March of Women Newsletter*, 6(2), May.

WMW (2003c) *World March of Women,* Report of 4th International Meeting in New Delhi, March 18–22, 2003.

WMW (2004) Perspective of women of the World March of Women: declaration at the 2003 World Social Forum, in J. Sen, A. Anand, A. Escobar & P. Waterman (eds) *Challenging Empires* (New Delhi: Viveka Foundation), pp. 233–234.

WMW (2007) The World March of Women and the World Social Forum—Evaluation of the current situation—September 2007, http://www.worldmarchofwomen.org/alliances_mondialisation/cmicfolder.2005-03-02.3713067089/cmicarticle.2007-11-13.2494214198/en

WMW (2008a) *The World March of Women 1998–2008: A Decade of International Feminist Struggle*, http://www.worldmarchofwomen.org/publications/libro1998-2008/en/

WMW (2008b) Information on alliances policy, document prepared for the 'debate on alliances', Paper presented at the 7th international meeting, Galicia, 14–21 October, http://www.worldmarchofwomen.org/alliances_mondialisation/cmicfolder.2005-03-02.3713067089/alliances2008/en

WMW (2008c) Where change is needed: the World March of Women and the debate on WSF's future, http://www.e-joussour.net/en/node/663

Yuval-Davis, N. (1997) *Gender and Nation* (Thousand Oaks, CA: Sage).

Climate Change or Social Change? Environmental and Leftist Praxis and Participatory Action Research

RUTH REITAN* & SHANNON GIBSON**

*University of Miami, USA
**University of Southern California, USA

ABSTRACT *This work seeks to advance and synthesize leftist political and environmental theory and enhance historical and contemporary understanding of environmental activism, especially related to the movement to halt climate change. We share findings from our participatory action research (PAR) on the internal dynamics and debates among the three main climate activist networks mobilizing at the United Nations Framework Convention on Climate Change meetings in Copenhagen in 2009, those of the reformist Climate Action Network (CAN), the more marxian-inspired Climate Justice Now! (CJN), and the autonomist and anarchistic Climate Justice Action (CJA). We elucidate how leftist reformist and especially the more radical currents are engaging with non- or anti-Western indigenous praxis to forge the contemporary transnational environmental movement.*

> Philosophers have only interpreted the world.... The point, however, is to change it.
>
> Karl Marx (1845)

The transnational movement to protect the environment is diverse, divided, and yet still interconnected. It has evolved over more than a century to now claim adherents in all regions of the world as it broadens its network and expands its agenda (Dalton, 1994; Diani, 2003; Rootes, 2007, p. 617). Sympathetic scholars have hailed it a pioneering global social movement (Wapner, 1996) and potentially transformative for postindustrial societies on a par with working class struggles of yesteryear (Touraine et al., 1983). Skeptics, meanwhile, question whether we can speak of a coherent 'environmental movement' at all (Doherty, 2002; Eyerman and Jamison, 1991) much less a global or transnational one (Rootes, 2007, p. 632). Our contribution to this debate is threefold. First, we aim to advance and synthesize leftist political and environmental theory. Second, we do so by adapting a fairly unorthodox methodology in the study of social movements—Participatory Action Research (PAR)—to enhance our historical and contemporary understanding of environmental activism. Third, we focus specifically on this movement's recent transnational manifestations and coordination to halt climate change.

This work is divided into two parts. In the initial theoretical and historical section, we contextualize environmental praxis within the three main lineages of leftist thought (i.e. reformist social democracy, revolutionary marxism,[1] and radical anarchism and autonomism), and then nest it within the broader Alter-Globalization—or Global Justice—Movement (AGM). This advances our argument that not only is it appropriate to speak of a transnational environmental, or green, movement, but further, that *climate change* has become a key galvanizing, or *bellwether*, issue for the broader global left and AGM. In the second section we ground our theoretical assertions in a rich description of contemporary environmental activism, drawn from our engagement as scholars and activists adapting a PAR approach. We share findings on the internal dynamics and debates among the three main climate activist networks mobilizing at the United Nations Framework Convention on Climate Change (UNFCCC) meetings in Copenhagen held in December 2009. In doing so we elucidate how leftist reformist and especially more radical currents have begun to articulate with non-/anti-Western indigenous praxis. By first pulling the lens out and back to view the movement theoretically and historically, we hope to present a fuller and also sharper image of transnational environmental praxis gained by a close engagement with contentious movement actors in motion.

Three Strands of Leftist Praxis in the Historic and Contemporary Environmental Movement

The history of the environmental movement is arguably as old as the modern left and, although each has a distinct lineage, they've grown increasingly entwined in both theory and action. Two themes will be developed here: first, while considered among the most successful of the identity-based and post-materialist 'new social movements' emerging in the 1960s and 1970s (Touraine et al., 1983), the green movement nevertheless is bound up with classical, or 'old', concerns of the politics of equality, production, and distribution, in addition to sharing strong affinities with so-called 'newest social movements' (Day, 2005) of post-anarchism and autonomy. And while this reflects how environmentalism in recent decades has come to be viewed as predominantly a progressive issue,[2] given its critique of humanity's harmful impacts on the earth, it has always posed a challenge—at times tacit, and others overt—to the left's anthropocentric and developmentalist commitments to instrumental rationality, freedom and emancipation, economic prosperity, and technological progress (Rootes, 2007, p. 634; Yearley, 1994).

Many ideological strands have evolved so as to preclude any single vision from uniting this movement. It is common to speak of its successive 'waves'—conservation, preservation, reform environmentalism, ecologism—though all currents remain salient (Mertig et al., 2002; Rootes, 2007). Much scholarly literature is dedicated to classifying the multiple and oftentimes conflicting goals, tactics, and organizational structures of its many collective actors (Carter, 2007; Dryzek, 1997; Rootes, 2007; Wapner, 1996). In its diversity, however, traces of the three broad tendencies of the modern left—namely liberal reformism, marxian revolution, and anarcho-autonomist radicalism[3]—can be discerned.

The movement's main historical tension lies between those who see economic growth and development as beneficial (or at least inevitable) and thus should be harnessed to protect the environment, versus those who view these projects as unsustainable and dangerous for human and other species' long-term survival. The two strands emerging in the early twentieth century of conservation versus preservation pitted an anthropocentric perspective of the earth's bounty as resources to be managed by wise stewards for human enjoyment and gain against eco-, or bio-, centric views of 'wild' nature as inherently valuable irrespective of human needs or profitability (see Brulle, 2000; Rootes, 2007). As concerns mounted over environmental degradation wrought by industrialism, international trade and transport, population growth, and nuclear power and weaponry in the post World War II era, so did calls for greater international coordination to address these issues (Wapner, 1996). This culminated in the first United Nations Conference on the Human Environment convened in 1972 in Stockholm, around which a cluster of policy-oriented, nationally based environmental organizations strove to become international interlocutors and lobbyists.

Both in their domestic and now the international arenas, it is this reformist wing of environmental thought and action that has been widely recognized as among the most successful movements of the twentieth century (Curran, 2007, p. 100; Touraine et al., 1983; Wapner, 1996). Its policy-oriented discourse and organizations have come to dominate the field of environmentalism in recent decades (Rootes 2007, pp. 612–13). This tendency is tightly bound up with, although often critical of, the agenda articulated within intergovernmental forums. Chief among them is the annual UNFCCC negotiations to stabilize greenhouse gas emissions, initiated at the UN Conference on the Environment and Development (UNCED), or Rio Earth Summit in 1992, and whose 15th Conference of Parties (COP15) in 2009 was our research site. Though diverse in their own right, reformers tend to support efforts toward sustainable development, ecological modernization, and state- and market-based solutions. Organizations most engaged with this debate are well-resourced, Northern NGOs, who petition and lobby governments within the UN treaty system to adopt technological, market, and regulatory responses to address climate change. As reformists, they do not fundamentally challenge the dominant economic or development model, the global governance system, or 'civil society's' place within it (Curran, 2007; Gibson, 2011; Reitan, 2011; Rootes, 2007; Wapner, 1996).

While the above sets the parameters for policy and much popular discourse at the domestic and international levels, the more radical and anti-systemic wing of the green movement, known as ecologism, first emerged in the 1970s as the 'fourth wave'. Our case below will show, however, that ecologism has morphed and surged again in what could be called a 'fifth wave', galvanized by the myriad threats posed by climate change.[4] Today's ecologism combines elements of post-anarchism and autonomism with neo-marxist claims against environmental racism and for climate 'justice': specifically, its adherents call for reparations for historical injustices of colonialism and underdevelopment along with demands for equitable distribution of environmental risks.[5] Furthermore, the radical and revolutionary strands of the left engaged in climate activism are also increasingly entwined with and informed by non- and anti-Western praxis from diverse indigenous struggles (see Mignolo, 2010; Powless, this volume; Zibechi, 2010). They view environmental degradation as a direct outgrowth of state-militarism, corporate rapaciousness, and capitalist expansion, and, more fundamentally, the growth-oriented development and industrial model of the last two centuries that was pursued by all states, whether Western liberal democratic, Soviet-style communist, or Third World developmentalist. And given the mounting frustrations over the official talks and market-based solutions that have yielded little concrete measures to stem climate change, both anti-state and anti-capitalist ideas are again gaining a wider audience.

Although often derided by more orthodox forms of marxism (see Curran, 2007, p. 124; Rootes, 2007, p. 620), the radical wing of the green movement has long been enmeshed with and a source of inspiration for communitarian marxism and anarchism. Giorel Curran (2007, p. 99) describes their relationship as 'mutual accommodation', embodied in the varieties of anarcho-ecologism including Murray Bookchin's (2005) social ecology, eco-socialism, eco-marxism, eco-feminism, and deep ecology (Curran, 2007, p. 109). The latter emerged from a profound sense of crisis in the industrialized West, and seeks to transform relations between humans and nature from hierarchical domination to 'organismic democracy' (Merchant, 1992, pp. 1, 86). Deep ecology founder Arne Naess (1973, p. 95) himself drew attention to its anarchistic ethos of 'diversity, complexity, autonomy, decentralization, symbiosis, egalitarianism, and classlessness'. Naess's philosophy thus presents the most fundamental challenge to modernity's anthropocentric and developmentalist assumptions, and to the traditional left writ large, while remaining rooted within the anarchist tradition. As such, deep ecology provides the philosophical bridge to the breadth of resurgent indigenous praxis.

Returning to revolutionary marxism, despite the hybrids referred to above, historically, mainstream marxism and socialism have been viewed as incongruent with and even antagonistic to deep ecology, eco-anarchism, and indigenous worldviews. This is what animates the so-called 'red-green' debate (Curran, 2007, p. 124; Weston, 1986, p. 5). While diverse, eco-socialists have tended to maintain their anthropocentric and economistic approaches and focus on capitalism's degradation of nature and the unequal distribution of contamination along class lines (see Eckersley, 1992; O'Connor, 1988; Pepper, 1993). Yet in recent years, Curran (2007) notes that eco-socialists and eco-marxists, to varying degrees, have attenuated their positions to become more open to ecological, anarchist, and indigenous conceptions of humanity's relationship to the planet—an assertion that is corroborated by our engaged research with the more radical wings of the climate justice movement at the COP15. These tendencies are showing greater sensitivity to the ways that environmental risks are distributed across and within countries and alarm over the global effects of industrialism and economic growth.[6]

Encouraging this convergence between 'red' and 'green' strands is the mounting concern over climate change. In the last two decades, this issue has been recognized by governments, citizens, the private sector, and activists alike as among the most daunting challenges of our time. The Intergovernmental Panel on Climate Change (IPCC, 2007) details the growing scientific consensus on its anthropogenic causes and likely catastrophic effects if mitigation efforts prove unsuccessful and average global temperatures exceed 2°C over the pre-industrial average. Likely consequences entail erratic and extreme weather, increased rainfall and flooding in some areas and severe drought and desertification in others, rising ocean temperatures leading to acidification and stronger hurricanes, glacial melting causing sea levels to rise and the flooding of coastal areas, and the migration and dying off of numerous plant and animal species. And though beyond the scope of most natural scientific studies, it is the social, political and cultural upheavals wrought by these changes that are of central concern to social movement activists and policymakers alike.

In attempting to address these formidable challenges, the IPCC, the UNFCCC, its member parties, and the mainstream media tend to frame the climate crisis as a scientific problem and budgetary liability, and then debate the issues and proposed solutions based on their technical and economic feasibility. Yet many activists argue that other actors and experiences should be prioritized: namely, those who are the most vulnerable to—and already suffering—its effects, especially in the Global South, where they are not only the least able to adapt to these changes, but also the least culpable in creating the threat in the first place. The disparities between North and South, rich and poor, powerful and disenfranchised inherent in the current climate crisis render this issue not only ripe for technical and policy-oriented dispute;[7] they also provoke social movements' indignation and demands for recompense, restitution, and reparation. Indeed, longtime environmental activists have been quick to draw connections between industrialization, globalization, colonialism, climate change, and global power and wealth inequities (Brand et al., 2009; Rootes, 2007).

Thus, we can discern all three leftist tendencies of reform, revolution, and radicalism embedded in diverse calls for environmental—and more recently climate—*justice*, which draws together struggles against environmental degradation and racism with claims for economic, social, ethnic, and gender justice. This broad-based, amorphous struggle also articulates with indigenous peoples and their allies across the Americas demanding recognition as vulnerable populations and a voice in UN negotiations (see Powless, this volume). It also draws in Southern-based movements and organizations like Via Campesina, Third World Network, and Focus on the Global South and their grassroots Northern allies who now compete with professionalized NGO advocates to demand that the communities most affected speak for themselves in global environmental negotiations, and mobilize to effect or even halt the negotiations and implementation of what they denounce as false solutions (see Gibson, 2011).

The lack of progress in over 15 years of talks and in actual emission reductions has spurred many veteran movement actors to radicalize their critiques and tactics. Meanwhile, the integration of market-based, flexible mechanisms and carbon trading under the Kyoto Protocol, which is the current legally binding global treaty on climate change, has raised the ire of those engaged in anti-capitalist struggles, and thus provided a bridge to draw them into the struggle as well. And the introduction of proposals for what activists deride as 'techno fixes', ranging from genetically engineered, mono-crop tree plantations to industrial weather modification, has invigorated and reengaged the fringes of bio- and eco-centric ecologists which had been in abeyance (Bosso, 2000; Eyerman and Jamison, 1991; Jamison, 2001). Finally, the stark juxtaposition of the 'democratic, consensus-based United Nations' image with the reality of power struggles, backroom deals, and the closing down of non-state access to UNFCCC meetings have further thrown into question the UN's democratic credentials and thus legitimacy, triggering frustrated reactions from a large swath of the reformist to anti-systemic left (Gibson, 2011; Hadden, 2011).

Defining a Climate Justice Movement

As the above demonstrates, several overlapping and entwining interests are evident within climate (justice) activism specifically, the broader environmental movement of which it is the most recent manifestation and bellwether issue, and the AGM at large.[8] To comprehend this relationship, we find it most useful to adopt Mario Diani's (2003, p. 1; see also Rootes, 2007, p. 610) consensual definition of social movements as 'complex and highly heterogeneous network structures' resembling strings of loosely connected events across time and space, comprised of individual and collective actors linked together in interactive webs of exchanges that range from formal to informal, direct to mediated, centralized to decentralized, and cooperative to hostile. In light of this definition, we argue that climate activism is, on the one hand, part and parcel of the AGM, yet, on the other, still distinct from it. For example, in attendance at COP15 in Copenhagen were single-issue environmentalists and multi-issue justice and rights-based organizations, hierarchical and horizontal groups, reformists and radicals, and seasoned veterans who had been coming since the first COP (Conference of the Parties) to those who were mobilized for the first time.

In our view, then, climate activism, the green movement, and the larger AGM are co-constitutive of one another. They are 'miscible movements' (Reitan, this volume; Vasi, 2006) or ever-shifting constellations of networked, social movement organizations and individual activists, sometimes overlapping and converging and at others pulling apart or acting separately. Thus, rather than attempting in advance to define or demarcate—and thus reify—the 'climate justice movement', we instead take seriously its emergent, amorphous, and living nature. Our view is consistent with scholars who emphasize movement complexity, diversity, fluidity, and dynamism, that is, *the process and flow of movement* (i.e. Chesters and Welsh, 2006; Diani, 2003; McAdam et al., 2001; Melucci, 1984; Reitan, 2007; Rootes, 2007; Zibechi, 2010), rather than viewing them as strategic actors with stable identities and determinable population borders.

Yet as Rootes (2007, p. 610) astutely recognizes, 'An environmental movement is identical neither with ... organizations ... nor with episodes of ... protest.... It is only when such organizations (and other actors) are networked one with another and engaged in collective action that an environmental movement can sensibly be identified'. Indeed, only a few years ago scholars detected such a high degree of institutionalization (Doherty, 2002; Eyerman and Jamison, 1991) on the one hand, and fragmentation (Bosso, 2000; Jamison, 2001; Rootes, 2007) on the other, to question whether we may conceive of an environmental movement at all. Thus climate change has served as a galvanizing force for what had become a rather dispersed and routinized set of actors, just as the UNFCCC treaty process and COP summit meetings have provided a transnational target, timeline, and periodic convergence space where networking, collective action, and identity can all be bolstered. In our own engaged research then, we consider the 'environmental movement' to comprise, at any particular time, those activists who participate in mobilization and organizational spaces we and others assess to be key sites of convergence and contestation, both physical and virtual (i.e. Internet-based). Thus the sector of the green movement—which can be called the climate justice movement—studied herein includes those individuals, organizations, and networks who were actively engaged in the physical and virtual sites leading up to and during the COP15, where the authors undertook participatory action research.

Participatory Action Research Methodology at the COP15

Given our ontological view of climate activism, and the AGM more broadly, as constantly evolving in form, functions, participants, and discourses, concordant epistemological and methodological stances must accompany it. We agree with Graeme Chesters and Ian Welsh (2006, pp. 1, 101) that:

> Sociologically this is not a movement that can be engaged with using the standard tool box.... To capture the dynamics ..., one must literally be adrift within the network, engaging with movement actors in material and immaterial spaces and sensitised to the emergence of qualities that are irreducible to the sum of the parts of that network.

We thus have adapted a PAR approach in our relationship to climate activism and the broader AGM. Within international relations theory, PAR is closely linked to and informed by feminist approaches emphasizing hermeneutic, conversational, and dialogic methods of understanding power and transformational possibilities emanating from societies' margins, such as Christine Sylvester's (1994) 'empathetic cooperation' yielding what Donna Haraway (1988) and J. Anne Tickner (1997) call 'situated knowledge'. Rather than maintaining a sharp subject–

object distinction, the appropriate ethos for PAR is fundamentally *relational* (Kemmis and McTaggart, 2000, p. 579).

We therefore set out to 'embed' ourselves within the networks and organizations mobilizing around the climate conferences not solely as academics and researchers, but also as activists and *compañeras* via *accompaniment*.[9] The research goal is to illuminate existing along with potential connections across the broad tendencies of climate activism in order to spotlight avenues for greater cooperation or coordination of struggles to protect the life and health of the earth. At the same time, we look for tensions, contradictions, and unintended consequences that arise from certain actions or stances taken within and between network actors. Both aims are consistent with the role of empathetic insider who accompanies other activists and helps articulate a new 'common sense' that those involved would consider authentic, integrative, clarifying, and useful for practice (see Fals Borda and Rahman, 1991; Kemmis and McTaggart, 2000).

Mobilization and meeting spaces leading up to and during the COP15 have provided us with rich milieus in which to observe, interact with, comprehend, and accompany the various ideological strands converging and diverging within the climate justice movement. Our PAR process has entailed a wide range of methods, including theory-driven participant observation of protests and coordination meetings, semi-structured interviews and informal conversations, email listserv monitoring, as well as often spontaneous, volunteer accompaniment roles (including information-disseminator, message-carrier, relationship broker, guide to meetings, media-team supporter, translator, interpreter, blogger, note-taker, meeting facilitator, report-back speaker, witnessing and reporting preventive arrests and police brutality, character voucher, jail solidarity, protest organizer, and mass march runner). The two authors combine a breadth of knowledge of and engagement with AGM activists over time with considerable depth from close engagement with climate activism in recent years: one has been involved with numerous AGM networks for over a decade, including the Washington, DC-based Mobilization for Global Justice and numerous World and European Social Forums (see Reitan, 2007); while the other has been closely following climate activism since 2008, and particularly the radicalization process of some of its participants, in her doctoral and now post-doctoral research (Gibson, 2011).

For the current study, we began our joint participatory research in 2009 during the lead-up to COP15 at the WSF in Belém, Brazil, followed by one of us attending the G20 meeting in Pittsburgh, US. Activities included attendance of and participation in more than 20 global and North American COP15 mobilization meetings and various working group sessions (i.e. media, strategy, action, framing, and logistics). During COP15 itself, in an effort to provide a broader account of the various sectors of the movement, the authors' PAR sites and roles were divided: one focused on 'outside' activist protests, marches, planning meetings, cultural and social events, and educational and informational sessions at the large, parallel, meeting space of the Klimaforum. The other gained accreditation as an official NGO observer with Global Justice Ecology Project (GJEP), a US-based environmental justice organization and key facilitator and actor within the Climate Justice Now! (CJN) and Climate Justice Action (CJA) networks. In this role she monitored and participated in 'inside' informational and planning sessions, media work, and protests by accredited NGOs and their state allies in the official summit site of the Bella Center.

This inside–outside division proved especially valuable as the negotiations wore on, when the UNFCCC began to restrict civil society participation in the Bella Center. This pushed some of the most professionalized NGO insiders *outside* and into the Klimaforum, where they could be observed by the 'outside' researcher, while the 'insider' remained as one of relatively few who continued to be issued new badges for entry. Our inside–outside team served a further, spontaneous accompaniment role during the Reclaim Power March on 16 December: In the face of preventive and ongoing arrests of key organizers, the researchers' SMS contact became the most direct—and possibly only remaining in the event—line of communication between the inside group of NGOs and delegates attempting a walk-out and the outside coordinators of the march trying to breach the Bella Center perimeter fence and police line in order to hold the People's Assembly for Climate Justice.

Observation field notes were taken at multiple mobilization, action, media and cross-network coordination and information-sharing meetings as well as at protests both inside and outside the conference center. Semi-structured interviews were performed at various locations (both at research sites and via Skype) throughout 2008–2010 by one of us.[10] For the case below, first-hand evidence was drawn mainly from our own participant observation, dialogue, and accompaniment roles with other activists. Given the nature and content of these discussions as well as our desire to maintain rapport, trust, and discretion, most of these conversations were informal and understood to be off the record. We consider it our task as participatory action researchers to attempt to synthesize what we saw, heard, discovered in dialogue, and felt during the COP15, into a 'common-sense' understanding of network relations and dynamics—but while also taking responsibility for any conjectures or errors made. Finally, the listservs affiliated with the networks were monitored during this same period. Emails pertaining to international meetings and conference calls, ideological debates, and cross-network discussions on framing and protest strategies were analyzed.

Taken together, these observations, field notes, conversations, interviews, accompaniment roles, and email content analysis conducted from 2008–2009 comprise our primary evidence, and helped shape our theoretical arguments articulated above, in a recursive spiral. We'll next turn to present evidence drawn from our PAR approach and informed by our theorizing, of the climate justice movement as being constituted by dynamic interactions among various actors and tendencies embedded in the three historic leftist strands, as well non- and anti-Western, indigenous praxis.

Pulling Liberal Reformism 'Left' toward Anti-Systemic and Indigenous Strands

The two main networks in which NGOs played key coordinating roles in the lead-up to the 2009 UNFCCC negotiations were the Climate Action Network (CAN) and Climate Justice Now! (CJN). Given their history, distinct organizational modes, and political stances of reform environmentalism versus a more transformist or radical climate justice frame, respectively, their relations have been marked by contention and competition, as will be seen below.[11] Yet that said, the two networks nonetheless remain linked by a shared history, meeting spaces, some members in common, informal information exchange, support for Southern governments' positions, and coordinated action.

CAN is the oldest and largest network participating in the UN climate talks, emerging out of the 1992 Rio Earth Summit. Thus, any impact that civil society actors have had on the treaty process can largely be credited to its members. The network's leaders are among the most established environmental reform groups such as World Wildlife Fund and Greenpeace. But they've recently been joined by influential social justice, aid, and development NGOs like OXFAM and Christian Aid, which reflects the increased salience of the climate issue in the larger Global Justice Movement's ever-shifting agenda. CAN's secretariat in Washington DC coordinates activities, information exchange, and strategy among 12 regional offices worldwide, publicizes its campaigns, raises funds, and collects membership dues. Its stance, while increasingly critical, has largely focused on 'sustainable development'—that is, human and economic development that doesn't compromise either's continued growth or unduly harm the planet. In this regard, it reflects the liberal socio-economic and political discourse of universal, yet differentially assigned, rights and obligations based on each country's level of economic development. CAN's lobbying and campaigning efforts promote government regulation at both the national and international levels through 'fair, ambitious and binding' targets and treaties, sustainable economic growth supported by technology and aid transfers to the South, and individual behavioral change (see Gibson, 2011; Hadden, 2011).

CAN's network structure and aims thus approximate the more hierarchical, reformist, and limited agenda of a so-called 'first generation advocacy model', with its attendant tensions (see Bennett, 2005; Reitan, 2007). These came to a head in the UN climate talks two years prior at the COP13 in Bali. CAN members, including Friends of the Earth International and some of its national affiliates, voiced concerns about lead Northern NGOs promoting their own governments' interests over those of poor and developing countries. They also accused them of blocking the network from adopting more critical and direct action stances against powerful state and economic actors and in defense of the planet and its vast majority of people. These critiques resonated with some Southern-based networks and *embedded partisan NGOs* (Reitan, 2011) who were coming to the climate talks for the first time (Gibson, 2011; Hadden, 2011). The dissidents began meeting and staging actions separate from CAN and, by the COP13's end, 20 groups issued a press release launching a new network, Climate Justice Now! (CJN, 2007).

The latter's name highlights their commitment to struggle for social, ecological, and gender justice simultaneously, as well as their demand for reparations for 'climate debt' to be paid to the South. Since a number of its members can be said to have 'spilled over' from (Hadden, 2011)—or 'coalesced' with (Reitan, this volume)—the anti-neoliberal, Global Justice Movement, CJN's climate justice frame embodies an eco-marxist tendency. It is also telling that CJN's critical and more confrontational stance against the UNFCCC process—charging it as undemocratic and marginalizing of voices from the South most affected by climate change and as proposing false and profit-oriented solutions that fail to address the scale of the crisis—are the very same criticisms its participants leveled against their former CAN comrades upon their exodus.

Going into the COP15, the more established CAN had to compete with the upstart CJN for UN accreditation badges, and many of the former were incensed to find that 40% went to the latter. The two networks were made to share the NGO room in the official Bella Center as well as to coordinate times for press conferences—both of which were conflictual. When NGO access to the center was severely curtailed in the final days of negotiations, CAN members migrated to the Klimaforum space, where CJN had been hosting well-attended and open informational and mobilization meetings all week. Yet as one of us observed, CAN proceeded to string tape and check badges in its cordoned off section of the hall, excluding non-network activists and the public from their 'sensitive' discussions (and then bursting into tears and walking away when questioned about it).

These fractious relations notwithstanding, it's important to note how the first generation CAN and the 'second-generation, direct action social justice'-modeled CJN (Bennett, 2005; Reitan, 2007), nonetheless coordinated around the COP15. Informally, the two networks shared information via their overlapping members such as Christian Aid, the Washington, DC-based Institute for Policy Studies, and some national delegates of Friends of the Earth. Because the two networks' meetings ran back-to-back, it was not uncommon for some CAN members to stay after to liaise or participate with CJN. Further, both networks supported the joint demand of the Africa group, Least Developed Countries (LDCs), Alliance of Small Island States (AOSIS), the Group of 77 Developing Countries (G77), and China to hold industrialized nations to legally binding reduction targets and to a second commitment period under the Kyoto Protocol.[12] Additionally, CAN is credited (if grudgingly) by CJN members for their ability to produce daily policy newsletters, the ECO, which is widely distributed and read by negotiators and civil society observers alike.

Regarding coordinated and joint action, both networks mobilized on 12 December for the permitted march called by CAN members' Global Campaign for Climate Action (GCCA; see Björk, 2010; Hadden, 2011). CJN, however, joined the third and more radical network Climate Justice Action (discussed below), to march that day under the anti-systemic banner of 'System Change not Climate Change'. Some CJN members have credited CAN for their ability to orchestrate mass marches such as that on '12/12', where up to 100,000 turned out, in addition to media-savvy and popular sign-on campaigns such as TckTckTck, which the younger, less well-resourced, and more confrontational CJN has not yet been able to do.

Articulating Leftist Revolutionary and Radical Strands with Post-Autonomist Praxis

A reinvigorated leftist radicalism, increased pragmatism, marxist–anarchist convergence, and growing valorization of indigenous struggles were all embodied in a third network, spearheaded by anti-systemic groups and direct action autonomists at the COP15: Climate Justice Action (CJA). Organizationally and demographically, CJA stands in contrast to both CAN and CJN in that most of its participants were young, urban, European women and men (fairly gender-balanced), whereas the other two networks were comprised of more traditionally organized and professional NGOs and transnational organizations, as well as older and more geographically diverse participants. CJA's most active organizers were from Danish and German direct action, anti-capitalist and autonomist groups and the No Borders and Climate Camp networks, who hatched the idea for the new network shortly before the 2008 WSF in Belém. At that forum, they were joined by a number of CJN's mass-based organizations and more embedded partisan NGOs including GJEP, Via Campesina, Indigenous Environmental Network, and Focus on the Global South.

Even more so than the CJN, this diffuse collectivity strove toward a second-generation, direct action network ideal—with all its attendant difficulties: CJA was launched in 2008 through a series of international mobilization meetings as a horizontal network based on consensus decision-making and the principles of autonomy and trust. Of the three networks it has been the most outspoken critic of capitalism and firmly committed to civil disobedience and direct action to safeguard the environment. CJA was forged by activists coming from both anarchistic and marxist orientations into what one of its lead organizers (Müller, 2010) described as a broadly 'post-autonomous' network, which reflected the rapprochement that marxist theorist David Harvey and others have hailed as the contemporary leftist zeitgeist. The network's statements and actions bordered on outright antagonism toward the UN and interstate system, and instead championed solutions to the climate crisis emanating from grassroots, workers', and popular social movements linked into a global 'movement of movements'.

Consensus decision-making in a new and diverse network whose prominent members were also the most radical meant that CJA's planning meetings and online discussions were volatile from the start. As the COP15 grew nearer, the consensus process came to a standstill and, in the event, broke down. During the summit itself, key decisions were mostly made by a core group of activist-spokespersons—whose phones were being tapped and who, one by one, were arrested—

and then 'consensed to' in giant meetings at the convergence centers. But in spite of internal derision and decision-making breakdown exacerbated by police surveillance and a concerted decapitation strategy, CJA activists—and especially the Copenhagen logistical group Climate Collective—went to great efforts to assure that the hundreds of youth who turned up at the Ragnhildesgade and Teglholmen convergence centers were housed, fed, entertained, informed, and able to forge smaller affinity action groups and to participate to some degree in the larger CJA decision-making.

Notably, CJA activists also worked closely with impacted communities such as the Indigenous Environmental Network and Via Campesina through their support of the Trade to Climate Caravans, which was a one-week tour that brought 60 farmers and frontline community members from the anti-WTO protests in Geneva to the climate negotiations in Copenhagen. Conversely, indigenous representatives attended several CJA action planning meetings to provide input on the aims and tactics of the proposed Reclaim Power action. Of particular concern for these participants was ensuring that vulnerable people had the opportunity to lead the march but also avoid arrest or undue persecution, should police repression ensue. Finally, CJA mobilized thousands to take part in mass, direct, and antagonistic action over several days, the largest being the 16 December Reclaim Power march on the Bella Center of approximately 3,000, which was co-organized by CJN.

CJA can be viewed as an ambitious experiment in increased openness and pragmatism drawing together all activist tendencies present in Copenhagen and thus the broad swath of the transnational environmental movement. This experiment was coupled with a valorization of autonomous indigenous movements, which we detected to varying degrees among all Western tendencies in the climate change struggle (see also Powless, this volume). For while CJA promoted direct action, localized solutions, and horizontality, they also pledged to coordinate closely with other international climate and social justice groups across the political spectrum coming to Copenhagen and to facilitate their taking action while there. This 'post-autonomist' approach was a pragmatic effort by some in CJA to avoid the secrecy and (self-)marginalization commonly associated with anarchists and the radical left subculture (Müller, 2010).

This new openness was not without its critics even further to the left, so to speak. Evidence of intra-anarchist fracturing existed alongside simultaneous coalescence with the larger climate, indigenous, and global justice movements. This fracturing was embodied in Never Trust a Cop (NTAC). Critical of CJA's more open, collaborative approach and its eschewing the 'shut it down' position in favor of 'no deal is better than a bad deal' (Hadden, 2011), the smaller NTAC broke away in the lead-up to COP15 to pursue separate campaigns, such as the Hit the Production action aimed at shutting down the Copenhagen harbor. Yet even this was not a complete break, as NTAC activists were indirectly linked to CJA via the Climate Collective, who coordinated solidarity housing and information-sharing for both, and some NTAC joined the autonomous 'green bloc' (who were mostly preemptively arrested) during CJA's Reclaim Power action.

It was within the CJA where we see the clearest evidence of convergence among post-marxism and post-anarchism into post-autonomy, blending policy-oriented critique and tactics with consensus-based participatory democracy, broad alliance-building, and contentious outside mobilization. CJA utilized many tactics to amplify and bridge their revolutionary and radical roots into an inclusive, collaborative post-autonomist campaign against the UNFCCC. To build a coalition from the ground up, they held open international planning meetings beginning in 2008 and through the COP15. They first established the core of the network, while in later meetings they strategically opened out to other actors. Efforts were spearheaded by the

Danish network, Klimax!, who brought together around 100 people from 25 countries at the first meeting in Copenhagen. A second, at COP14 in Poznan, Poland, drew roughly 80 people from nearly 30 countries, the majority being CJN members. The third was held at the 2008 WSF, a crucial moment to network with the many indigenous activists present in Belém. The remaining 2009 meetings were again held in Copenhagen to focus on the site and meeting logistics. By shifting locales from the Danish capital to the UNFCCC summit to the Brazilian forum and back, coordinators ensured that a broad base of local organizers, impacted indigenous communities and grassroots movements, and sympathetic insider NGOs were engaged in the planning process. To promote transparency, CJA routinely circulated their meeting minutes on the CJA and CJN listservs and posted them on their open access wiki page.

When the COP15 was underway, CJA took several steps to continue constructing their more inclusive, anti-systemic campaign among the hundreds of new activists becoming involved for the first time. To build broadly for their Reclaim Power march, they organized a rally and party in the free community of Christiania where renowned journalist Naomi Klein and scholar-activist Michael Hardt shared the platform with CJA spokesman Tadzio Müller. And for an 'inside strategy', CJA sought out sympathetic CJN allies, liaising with GJEP, Focus on the Global South, Indigenous Environmental Network, and *Smart*Meme. They routinely invited CJN members to attend their nightly coordination meetings in Ragnhildesgade and sat in on several CJN media meetings. Perhaps the strongest example of coordination came when GJEP accredited CJA's Müller and Stine Gry Jonassen to the UNFCCC and gave over one of its coveted CJN press conference slots (which were split between CJN and CAN after some contention) to members of CJA so that they could publicly announce details of their Reclaim Power march from within the official meeting site.[13] Finally, members of CJA and CJN launched multiple 'inside-out communication teams'—one of which was the text messaging between the authors—to coordinate the three-pronged action of Reclaim Power: (1) an NGO walk-out that was to meet the (2) mass march, followed by (3) the People's Assembly for Climate Justice. For the march, CJA organized a speakers' truck, arranged permits, and dispersed into affinity groups clustered into a direct action green bloc, a bike bloc, and a permitted blue bloc to march on the Bella Center and breach the police line and fence to hold the People's Assembly inside the perimeter.

In this confrontational, 'last stand' protest against the UNFCCC, CJN members joined the CJA blue bloc and formed an additional yellow (badge) bloc of NGO delegates—including some CAN members—who were no longer allowed into the Bella Center, under the banner 'No Decisions about us without us—Climate Justice Now!' CJA and CJN also coordinated inside disruptions and a walk-out of some 300 UN observers and participants led by the Indigenous Peoples Caucus. Crucially, this action was also meant to protest the lack of inclusion in the final agreement of the UN Declaration on the Rights of Indigenous Peoples and of Bolivia's demand that the rights of Mother Earth be recognized. Those leaving—including one of us— were halted, pushed, and beaten back by riot police on an icy bridge. Meanwhile, other CJN members, among them the Social and Climate Justice Caravan activists, were invited by CJA to be the main speakers for the Peoples' Assembly which did take place, under heavy police surveillance, outside—not inside—the Bella Center's perimeter fence, for attempts to breach it were repelled with police teargas and billy clubs.

Post-COP15 Reflections

As the COP15 closed to little fanfare with the abrupt 'taking note of' the Copenhagen Accord, the convention was judged by all of the networks to be a failure. Both CJA and CJN issued statements not only condemning the Accord as empty and undemocratic, but also heavily criticizing the UNFCCC and Danish and European police for their unprecedented repression of civil society voices. The CJN (2009) statement struck a despondent, anti-capitalist and eco-marxist tone: 'The UN conference was unable to deliver solutions to the climate crisis, or even minimal progress toward them ... government and corporate elites here in Copenhagen made no attempt to satisfy the expectations of the world. False solutions and corporations completely co-opted the United Nations process.' And while some CAN members, such as the Nature Conservancy, World Wildlife Fund, and National Resources Defense Council at least publicly defended the Copenhagen Accord as a 'crucial step forward', others such as Greenpeace, some Friends of the Earth affiliates, and the Institute for Policy Studies derided the Accord as 'unfair' and a 'non-result'. One close observer of CAN noted: 'The political outcome of COP 15 was a bitter disappointment to groups who had spent years developing careful plans to push delegates towards a more ambitious conclusion' (Hadden, 2011).

Little has changed in the ensuing negotiations to modify this pessimistic assessment. While hope briefly surged around Bolivian President Evo Morales's April 2010 'World Peoples' Conference on Climate Change and the Rights of Mother Earth', which drew some 35,000 participants from over 140 countries, most states have simply ignored the eco-marxist and indigenous Peoples' Accord (PWCCC, 2010) that came out of it. In the face of what is clearly a gross abdication of leadership and denial of responsibility on the part of the world's most powerful governments, we encourage other concerned scholars to experiment with the participatory action methods we've employed here. In doing so, we can gain a better appreciation for the broad diversity of contemporary environmental and other activist praxis as well as for their deep roots in the history of the left—and now branching beyond it. Via PAR, we can also take up roles of movement accompaniment, and in the process help articulate a new 'common sense'. For today's myriad threats emanating not just from potentially cataclysmic climate change but also from the deepening inequalities and perennial injustices that plague all regions of the world, provide scholars with an opportunity—one might even say a duty—to move beyond passive (or 'objective') observers into more active *subjects*[14] and participants in struggle.

We are presented, it seems, with a choice: to simply stand back and interpret the world, or together to seek new ways of changing it. As the PAR pioneer Paulo Freire once said and the Zapatistas have echoed, 'we make the road by walking'. Moving together in this way, we may become conscious, critical, unfettered, and ultimately transcendent of our Western traditions.

Notes

1. We refer to 'marxism' in the lower case to signify that the intellectual and activist lineage inspired by Karl Marx now transcends one man's ideas and texts.
2. It is important to note, however, that some of the earliest proponents of nature conservation in the US and Europe were game hunters, a concern that continues to this day (Rootes, 2007, p. 612). And on historical and contemporary ecological fascism in the West, see Staudenmaier and Biehl (2011).
3. For an elaboration of these three strands in the context of the Alter-Globalization Movement, see Reitan (this volume).
4. This resurgence can be partially explained by climate change being perceived as a zero-sum game, akin to forest preservation and halting nuclear power, which have provoked similarly transgressive praxis. See Rootes (2007, p. 620).
5. On the development of the environmental justice and racism frames, see Agyeman and Evans (2004), Brulle (2000, pp. 207–8), Cole and Foster (2001), Dawson (2010), and Rootes (2007, p. 615).

6 Curran (2007) notes a similar move by deep ecologists toward post-autonomists and post-marxists, by taking up the fight against environmental racism and embracing the view that environmental concerns are as well *social* concerns.
7 For example, there is an ongoing debate between various climate activists over email listservs on the preferred temperature cap. Many reformist NGOs subscribe to the 2°C standard issued by the IPCC and accepted by most Kyoto parties. Since 2008 however, more radical groups and those from the South and impacted communities have begun to challenge this target from both a scientific and justice perspective and have issued a call for a 1.5 or even 1°C cap.
8 A number of scholars, such as Brand et al. (2009), Curran (2007, p. 59), Hadden (2011), Klein (2009), and Reitan (2009), have identified climate change as the newest bellwether issue galvanizing the broader AGM by serving as the most salient mobilizing threat and opportunity following the 2005 and 2007 G8 summits and 2003 US-led attacks on Iraq.
9 *Accompaniment* refers to collaboration based on trust, common understanding and analysis of the problem, and a commitment to solidarity and equality (see Lynd, forthcoming; Whitmore and Wilson, 1999). For a fuller explication of our PAR approach and its strengths and limitations, see Reitan (2007, pp. 32–9). Combining PAR with expressive auto-ethnography and feminist praxis is central to Reitan's current research.
10 In accordance with the University of Miami's Institutional Review Board, all interviews required informed consent and were coded anonymously to protect those who may have been involved in or were planning to participate in events that had the potential to elicit reaction from police or security officials. Interviews are analyzed and presented in Gibson (2011).
11 The membership and structure of, along with contentious relations between, these two networks are explored at length in Gibson (2011) and Hadden (2011).
12 CJN furthermore strongly supported the Bolivarian Alliance for the Americas (ALBA) countries' spokesman Evo Morales in his call for 49% emissions reductions. And the Third World Network, a prominent CJN member, provided expertise to a number of Southern governments, working with their under-staffed delegations long into the night to come up with negotiating positions.
13 Müller was arrested upon his exit by plainclothes police and held on charges of incitement to riot for the summit's duration.
14 We largely accept the post-structuralist position that 'we' (the authors, that is 'I' and 'I') are not modern(ist), autonomous, 'free subjects', but are rather constructed by, and thus subject(ed) to, discourse. That said, we have some capacity—or limited agency—to choose between 'subject positions', and we adopt the critical, marxist notion that the current conjuncture grants an opportunity to choose a more active, engaged, dialogical, and egalitarian relationship with those who the modernist scientific discourse would deem 'objects' of inquiry to be analyzed and explained, not understood or accompanied.

References

Agyeman, J. & Evans, B. (2004) 'Just sustainability': the emerging discourse of environmental justice in Britain? *Geographical Journal*, 170(2), pp. 155–164.
Bennett, W. L. (2005) Social movements beyond borders: organization, communication, and political capacity in two eras of transnational activism, in D. della Porta & S. Tarrow (eds) *Transnational Protest and Global Activism* (Lanham, MD: Rowman & Littlefield), pp. 203–226.
Björk, T. (2010) 12 December initiative—huge success of background for branding?, http://www.aktivism.info/socialforumjourney/
Bookchin, M. (2005) *The Ecology of Freedom: The Emergence and Dissolution of Hierarchy* (Oakland: AK Press).
Bosso, C. J. (2000) Environmental groups and the new political landscape, in N. J. Vig & M. E. Kraft (eds) *Environmental Policy*, 4th ed. (Washington, DC: CQ), pp. 55–76.
Brand, U., Bullard, N., Lander, E. & Mueller, T (eds) (2009) Contours of climate justice: ideas for shaping new climate and energy politics, *Critical Currents*, 6 (Uppsala: Dag Hammarskjold Foundation).
Brulle, R. (2000) *Agency, Democracy and Nature: The U.S. Environmental Movement from a Critical Theory Perspective* (Cambridge, MA: MIT Press).
Carter, N. (2007) *The Politics of the Environment: Ideas, Activism, Policy* (New York: Cambridge University Press).
Chesters, G. & Welsh, I. (2006) *Complexity and Social Movements: Multitudes at the Edge of Chaos* (London: Routledge).

CJN (Climate Justice Now!) (2007) What's missing from the climate talks? Justice!, press release, 14 December, http://www.foei.org/en/media/archive/2007/whats-missing-from-the-climate-talks-justice/

CJN (Climate Justice Now!) (2009) CJN! final statement in Copenhagen, press release, 19 December, http://www.climate-justice-now.org/cjn-final-statement-in-copenhagen/

Cole, L. W. & Foster, S. R. (2001) *From the Ground Up: Environmental Racism the Rise of the Environmental Justice Movement* (New York: New York University Press).

Curran, G. (2007) *21st Century Dissent: Anarchism, Anti-Globalization and Environmentalism* (Basingstoke & New York: Palgrave Macmillan).

Dalton, R. J. (1994) *The Green Rainbow: Environmental Groups in Western Europe* (New Haven, CT: Yale University Press).

Dawson, A. (2010) Climate justice: the emerging movement against green capitalism, *South Atlantic Quarterly*, 109(2), pp. 313–338.

Day, R. J. F. (2005) *Gramsci is Dead: Anarchist Currents in the Newest Social Movements* (London: Pluto Press).

Diani, M. (2003) Introduction: social movements, contentious actions, and social networks: grom metaphor to substance, in M. Diani & D. McAdam (eds) *Social Movements and Networks* (Oxford: Oxford University Press), pp. 1–18.

Doherty, B. (2002) *Ideas and Action in the Green Movement* (London: Routledge).

Dryzek, J. S. (1997) *The Politics of the Earth: Environmental Discourses* (Oxford: Oxford University Press).

Eckersley, R. (1992) *Environmentalism and Political Theory: Towards an Ecocentric Approach* (New York: UCL Press).

Eyerman, R. & Jamison, A. (1991) *Social Movements: A Cognitive Approach* (Oxford: Polity).

Fals Borda, O. & Rahman, M. A. (eds) (1991) *Action and Knowledge: Breaking the Monopoly with Participatory Action-Research* (New York: Apex).

Gazzaniga, M. S. (2011) *Who's in Charge? Free Will and the Science of the Brain* (London: Constable and Robinson).

Gibson, S. (2011) Dynamics of Radicalization: The Rise of Radical Activism against Climate Change, Unpublished Doctoral Dissertation, University of Miami, Coral Gables, FL.

Hadden, J. (2011) When civil society isn't civil: pathways to participation in transnational climate change politics, Paper presented at the International Studies Association annual convention, Montreal, Canada, 17 March.

Haraway, D. (1988) Situated knowledges: the science question in feminism and the privilege of partial perspective, *Feminist Studies*, 14, pp. 575–599.

IPCC (Intergovernmental Panel on Climate Change) (2007) Climate change 2007: the physical science basis. Contribution of working group I, in S. Solomon, D. Qin, M. Manning, Z. Chen, M. Marquis, K. B. Averyt, M. Tignor & H. L. Miller (eds) *Fourth Assessment Report of the Intergovernmental Panel on Climate Change* (Cambridge: Cambridge University Press), pp. 1–21.

Jamison, A. (2001) *The Making of Green Knowledge, Environmental Politics and Cultural Transformation* (Cambridge: Cambridge University Press).

Kemmis, S. & McTaggart, R. (2000) Participatory action research', in N. K. Denzin & Y. S. Lincoln (eds) *Handbook of Qualitative Research* (London: Sage), pp. 567–606.

Klein, N. (2009) The Seattle activists' coming of age in Copenhagen will be very disobedient, *The Guardian*, 12 November, http://www.guardian.co.uk/commentisfree/cifamerica/2009/nov/12/seattle-coming-age-disobedient-copenhagen

Lynd, S. (forthcoming) *Accompanying* (Oakland: PM Press).

Marx, K. (1973 [1845]) 'Theses on Feuerbach', Thesis 11, Vol. 1, in *Karl Marx and Frederick Engels: Selected Works*, 2nd ed. (Moscow: Progress Publishers).

McAdam, D., Tarrow, S. & Tilly, C. (2001) *Dynamics of Contention* (Cambridge: Cambridge University Press).

Melucci, A. (1984) *Altri codici: Aree di movimento nella metropolis* (Bologna: Mulino).

Merchant, C. (1992) *Radical Ecology: The Search for a Livable World* (London: Routledge).

Mertig, A. G., Dunlap, R. E. & Michelson, W. (2002) The environmental movement in the United States, in R. E. Dunlap & W. Michelson (eds) *Handbook of Environmental Sociology* (Westport, CT: Greenwood), pp. 448–481.

Mignolo, W. (2010) The communal and the decolonial, *Turbulence*, 5, pp. 29–31.

Müller, T. (2010) Unpublished email correspondence with the author, 24 October.

Naess, A. (1973) The shallow and the deep, long-range ecology movement: a summary, *Inquiry*, 16, pp. 95–100.

O'Connor, J. (1988) Capitalism, nature and socialism: a theoretical introduction, *Capitalism, Nature, Socialism*, 1, pp. 11–38.

Pepper, D. (1993) *Eco-Socialism: From Deep Ecology to Social Justice* (London: Routledge).

PWCCC (People's World Conference on Climate Change) (2010) People's agreement of Cochabamba, http://pwccc.wordpress.com/2010/04/24/peoples-agreement/

Reitan, R. (2007) *Global Activism* (London: Routledge).

Reitan, R. (2009) The global anti-war movement within and beyond the World Social Forum, *Globalizations*, 6(4), pp. 509–523.

Reitan, R. (2011) Coordinated power in contemporary leftist activism, in T. Olesen (ed.) *Power and Transnational Activism* (London: Routledge), pp. 51–72.

Rootes, C. (2007) Environmental movements, in D. A. Snow, S. A. Soule & H. Kriesi (eds) *The Blackwell Companion to Social Movements* (Malden, MA: Blackwell), pp. 608–640.

Staudenmaier, P. & Biehl, J. (2011) *Ecofascism Revisited: Lessons from the German Experience* (Porsgrunn, Norway: New Compass).

Sylvester, C. (1994) Empathetic cooperation: a feminist method for IR, *Millennium*, 23(2), pp. 315–334.

Tickner, J. A. (1997) You just don't understand: troubled engagements between feminists and IR theorists, *International Studies Quarterly*, 41(4), pp. 611–632.

Touraine, A., Hegedus, Z., Dubet, F. & Wieviorka, M. (1983) *Anti-nuclear Protest: The Opposition to Nuclear Energy in France* (Cambridge: Cambridge University Press).

Vasi, I. B. (2006) The new anti-war protests and miscible mobilizations, *Social Movement Studies*, 5(2), pp. 137–153.

Wapner, P. K. (1996) *Environmental Activism and World Civic Politics* (Albany, NY: State University of New York Press).

Weston, J (ed.) (1986) *Red and Green: The New Politics of the Environment* (London: Pluto Press).

Whitmore, E. & Wilson, M. (1999) Research and popular movements: igniting seeds of fire, *Social Development Issues*, 21(1), pp. 19–28.

Yearley, S. (1994) Social movements and environmental change, in M. Reclift & Ted Benton (eds) *Social Theory and the Global Environment* (London: Routledge), pp. 150–168.

Zibechi, R. (2010) *Dispersing Power: Social Movements as Anti-State Forces* (Oakland: AK Press).

An Indigenous Movement to Confront Climate Change

BEN POWLESS

Indigenous Environmental Network, Canada

ABSTRACT   *Over the last two decades, the Indigenous movement to stop human-induced climate change has grown into a major civil society voice and force, both within the United Nations climate conferences as well as in parallel and autonomous spaces. I first contextualize the movement's roots within the historic rise of an international Indigenous movement framed around human rights. Next I present a characterization of the unique discourses and epistemology held by the International Indigenous Climate Movement in contrast to those of the dominant environmental and governmental institutions and actors. I then outline the agenda, main concerns, and mode of self-organization that this movement has articulated within official negotiations, followed by a discussion of how activists are creating and utilizing alternative, non-official spaces. In both contexts, I briefly touch on the nature of their interactions with non-indigenous social movement actors, and conclude with reflections on the still considerable gaps between Indigenous and non-indigenous actors—both state and civil society.*

In recent years, climate change has evolved from an issue that was understood mostly in technical, scientific terms to one that is now highly charged both politically and emotionally. Human-induced climate change has come to be understood by many as having potentially dramatic impacts on all facets of society, in nearly every state, and indeed threatening the survival of many species on the planet, including our own. As the importance and urgency attached to climate change have increased, so have the varied responses. The issue has been vigorously taken up by international institutions, organizations, governments, and nongovernmental actors alike. All enter the discussions and debates with their own perspectives and agendas, relative power and vulnerabilities.

Indigenous Peoples[1] are among the least powerful and most vulnerable to climate change, and indeed are already being impacted as so-called frontline communities. As a consequence, they have quickly emerged as one of the most engaged non-state actors in the struggle to halt these changes, and, going further, to critique the historical processes and dominant worldview that have wrought these unprecedented threats. This emergent, identity-based climate movement mirrors, and to some extent has grown out of, Indigenous engagement in other international issue areas, especially human rights protections and their governance entities. A parallel exists between the two, indeed, as Indigenous Peoples had been initially absent—and excluded—from both arenas of international treaty negotiations before becoming a formidable voice.

This essay draws on my scholarly research into Indigenous Peoples' rights and struggles and the ways they have been particularly shaped and impacted by environmental changes and conflicts. To the academic literature I have added evidence from my own participation as activist and researcher.[2] As a First Nations youth from Canada, I have spent the last few years doing professional, volunteer, activist, and independent media work with numerous Indigenous Peoples and organizations in different parts of the world, at official international gatherings and civil society forums, and taking part in educational outreach, direct action, and mass mobilizations.[3] In this essay I briefly introduce the broader Global Indigenous Movement, followed by a depiction of what I see to be the unique discourses and epistemology embodied by the Indigenous climate movement, in contrast to the dominant environmental and governmental institutions and actors. Next I overview the main agenda, concerns, and modes of self-organization this movement has developed within official climate negotiations over the years. It is followed by a discussion of how Indigenous climate activists have both created and made use of non-official, parallel, and autonomous spaces, where they also interact with potential allied movements and other actors. Lastly, I make a reflection on where the movement is at the moment, with some brief comments on the considerable gulf that still exists between Indigenous and non-indigenous activists and governments around these issues—noting that there are some hopeful developments and possibilities on this front.

The central argument of this work is that Indigenous Peoples have indeed forged a unique, formidable, and cohesive social movement across borders, working both inside and outside official, governmental spaces and legal processes, in order to contest but also engage the dominant understandings of climate change and their hegemonic and (neo)colonial bases, while, at the same time, creating spaces to assert their own understandings and encounter potential allies. On the one hand, the movement challenges official decision-making processes while demanding inclusion on their own terms. On the other, they are constructing alternative spaces and forms of Indigenous collective power and, to some extent, with allied movements. They are guided by an evolving understanding of the roots of environmental injustice in colonialism and capitalism, as well as by a positive alternative vision of Indigenous knowledge, rights, and lifeways that has resonated beyond Indigenous Peoples and thus can potentially serve as a beacon for the larger climate justice movement going forward. This work makes a contribution to the existing (yet scarce) academic literature on Indigenous social movements in intergovernmental and international processes, as well to the academic literature on social movements in general. It offers both an academic and emic perspective on the Indigenous movement to stop human-induced climate change.

I have been engaged in both study and action around climate change as it impacts Indigenous Peoples for a number of years. I've participated in formal climate negotiations, alternative Indigenous spaces, various types of activism bridging those spaces, and recording and commenting on these struggles as a journalist. Thus many of the reflections below come from direct and first-hand observations of the inner dynamics of the movement. I take full personal responsibility for all portrayals of and inferences from the stated positions of the movement or individual actors.

Any critical comments, however, retain a certain level of generality by not naming individuals, movement actors, or networks explicitly. This is due to an understanding that these relations and groups are themselves complex and not static, an acknowledgement that I cannot speak on behalf of the Indigenous movement, and respect for the evolving nature of intra- and inter-movement relationships and hope for stronger alliances in the future. That said, I will attempt to identify the roots and principles behind some of the conflicts endemic in these relationships. In identifying points of contention or discord between the Indigenous movement and others outside—including potential allies—my goal is ultimately a critical, constructive one (Moose-Mitha, 2005; Reitan, 2007) of fostering greater mutual understanding and finding areas for further research, dialogue, and joint action. A more general aim of this work is to increase knowledge of this movement among the broader academic community in the hopes of encouraging further engaged research and forms of *accompaniment* (see Escárcega, 2009; Lynd and Grubačić, 2008; Reitan, 2007, ch. 2) with both Indigenous an non-indigenous collective actors within the broad and growing movement for climate justice.

Beginnings of the International Indigenous Movement Around Human Rights

The Global Indigenous Movement (GIM) emerged from the long history of Indigenous individuals, professionals, organizations, communities, and networks converging to defend Indigenous rights and ways of life (Álvarez, 1998; Brysk, 2000; Escárcega, 2003, 2010; Escobar, 2008; Henderson, 2008; Lâm, 2000; Niezen, 2003; Wilmer, 1993). Then, as now, movement members have mobilized under a collective identity and ideology, sharing similar goals and objectives. They have done so within formalized, official, (inter-)governmental processes and bodies when possible, but also via 'extraordinary politics' and other resistance efforts when the situation has warranted (Wilmer, 1993, p. 135). Despite their considerable diversity, Indigenous Peoples share a history of oppression and dispossession that constitutes the basis for collective mobilization beyond the confines of traditional political systems or official state borders. Their collective efforts seek to challenge and reshape the political sphere and terms of engagement, rather than simply accepting or becoming part of that sphere on pre-defined terms (Brysk, 2000, p. 33).

Another longstanding feature of Indigenous activism that helps explain today's International Indigenous Climate Movement (IICM) in particular revolves around the recognition of Indigenous Peoples as collective rights-holders, as opposed to simply individual rights-holders who happen to belong to a group. Stemming from this collectivist notion, Indigenous agitation generally displays a high level of international coordination and collaboration, involving deep and broad relationships of trust, mutual identification, and interest across distinct Indigenous movements and peoples, and to a lesser extent, with non-indigenous allies (Brysk, 2000, pp. 33–34, 69; Henderson, 2008; Wilmer, 1993, p. 137).

Further, more than many other movements, the GIM is highly transnational, owing in part to the unresponsive or outright hostile and predatory national governments within whose borders they reside. The fraught nature of Indigenous–state relations accounts for the first shifts to the international and transnational levels of contention by Indigenous Peoples. Their going to the United Nations in search of rights and protections is something akin to the 'boomerang effect' (Keck and Sikkink, 1998), and, once set in motion, has become a 'spiral model' (Risse and Sikkink, 1999). The spectrum of state reactions from unresponsiveness to outright oppression results in distinct levels of internationalization across countries and communities and even issues (Brysk, 2000, p. 26; Escárcega, 2003, p. 77; Niezen, 2003, p. 15). To illustrate, I will present two brief examples of the emergence of domestic and transnational Indigenous movements, from the 'First World' and from Latin America, as precursors to the GIM in general and the IICM in particular.

Indigenous Peoples' first attempt at international leverage and involvement began in the 1920s. Representatives of the Haudenosaunee (Iroquois) Confederacy of North America joined with the Maori of Aotearoa (New Zealand) to lobby the League of Nations and the British Commonwealth members in 1922 and 1923. Their mission ultimately left in failure after being disrupted especially by the British government. Three decades later, national Indigenous movements began to coalesce in Canada, the United States, Australia, and New Zealand in the wake of the civil rights movements in North America. These nascent networks and movement actors served as the first impetuses to inform Indigenous groups in those countries of their shared histories and experiences with others around the world, for up until that point, they knew little of what was happening to each other. Yet many groups would soon come to regard the national scene as unresponsive and ineffective in this period, which precipitated their scale shift (Reitan, 2007) or boomerang to the international level and the UN forums. Throughout those years, alliances were sparse, as progressive, non-indigenous social movements mainly concerned themselves with their own identity struggles or broader economic and social justice demands made to the state, holding little regard for or knowledge about the unique challenges and harms facing Indigenous Peoples (Escárcega, 2003; Jelin, 1998; Lâm, 2000; Niezen, 2003; Smith, 2005).

In Latin America, Indigenous movements emerged out of environments less unresponsive than hostile to public participation, much less mass mobilization (Álvarez et al., 1998, p. 9). Thus, these nascent movement actors were unconditioned to and dissuaded from interacting with the state apparatuses, which meant that they were able to foster political visions and struggles on their own, appropriate to their locality and reflective of their diversity (Varese, 2006, p. 217). In recent years, Indigenous groups have grown increasingly effective at bringing these unique visions and struggles fostered in relative autonomy to the forefront of politics across Latin America, presenting subaltern perspectives that fundamentally challenge the exclusionary and colonialist nation-state, while demanding differentiated citizenship and rights, democratization on their own terms, and an Indigenous vision of a pluri-national polity, or state. As a response to this hostile historical environment and being forced to live within arbitrary and illegitimate borders imposed on and dividing Indigenous groups, the Indigenous movements in Latin America tended to develop in a very transnational way from the beginning, similar to, although with distinct reasons from, their North American counterparts (Postero and Zamosc, 2004, pp. 2–3; Smith, 2005, p. 108; Varese, 2006, p. 228).

Furthermore, Indigenous Peoples in Latin America have been more negatively impacted by neoliberal economic reforms than those in the North, in that these processes have precipitated the gradual erosion of state sovereignty, coupled with political elites who openly intervene in favor of private interests like multinational corporations to the detriment of Indigenous Peoples. With the blessing or blind eye turned by the state, these corporations have aggressively moved into Indigenous territories that were previously unexploited to extract resources, aided by weak or nonexistent laws protecting the environment, human rights, or historic treaties or agreements. So while the state remains important in this calculus as the body responsible for mitigating—or aggravating—the impacts of economic and political policies on Indigenous Peoples, movement actors have chosen increasingly to supravene the state, leading, as in North America, to the transnationalization of their activities and participation especially within the UN forums (Varese, 2006, p. 3; Warren and Jackson, 2003).

Thus, a transnational Indigenous movement can be said to really have emerged during the 1970s largely in response to these closed doors at the national level and seemingly more open ones at the level of the UN.[4] Here, Indigenous Peoples began to appreciate that the UN was uniquely endowed with considerable legal and moral, or *soft* power (Nye, 2005), to set norms, and more importantly, define peoplehood and the rights associated with it (Anaya, 2004; Escárcega, 2003, p. 5; Lâm, 2000). By 1982, the Working Group on Indigenous Populations was created under the UN system, which was the first international venue to be substantially influenced by the movement for Indigenous rights (Brysk, 2000, p. 130; Escárcega, 2003, p. 135; Muehlebach, 2001). The Working Group was to become one of the most highly attended human rights bodies, with special allowances created for the participation of Indigenous Peoples not otherwise recognized by the international system. This forum was also unique in that it allowed Indigenous Peoples to challenge states from 'below' to be more responsive and accountable to their concerns by requiring that Working Group decisions be reached by consensus, which effectively gave a veto to a non-state actor over state decisions. This also marked the beginning of an Indigenous caucus, a trend which would continue into climate negotiations, where delegates meet separately from those of the state in order to deliberate and arrive at consensus positions of their own (Escárcega, 2003; Henderson, 2008; Lâm, 2000).

In 1987, this Working Group was given the historic mandate to produce a draft declaration to promote Indigenous rights. A document was tabled the following year, and worked on for another five, before being transferred to another jurisdiction, where it underwent further laborious revisions and languished for years. A full two decades later, in 2007, the final document was presented to the UN General Assembly. Just four states voted against it—Australia, New Zealand, the US, and Canada, all settler countries with large Indigenous populations. Each would later bow to national and international pressure and express their support—albeit with caveats. Thus was passed the UN Declaration on the Rights of Indigenous Peoples (UNDRIP), creating a new set of rights standards for Indigenous Peoples, and turning these into a central demand and meterstick of the GIM (Henderson, 2008, pp. 51, 67). This arduous process, right through the final vote, however, also put Indigenous Peoples on notice that there were still powerful states opposed to their gaining full rights and recognition under international law. This complex and often adversarial relationship with certain states in particular in the international context carried over to the UN climate change negotiations and the emerging ICM.

Summing up, Indigenous Peoples were effectively able to become a force in the international arena and to use their collective power in challenging the rights, sovereignty, and accountability of states. These efforts can be seen as part of a broader movement to limit state sovereignty that began with the creation of the first human rights instruments after World War II, countering the ultranationalist and statist ideologies that preyed on, discriminated against, or marginalized many groups, including Indigenous Peoples (Brysk, 2000, pp. 132–3; Escárcega, 2003, pp. 34–5; Jelin, 1998, p. 407; Niezen, 2003, p. 16). State representatives, for their part, challenged Indigenous claims of authenticity, the quality of their ideas and arguments, and their audacity to hold the aspirations they did, even going so far as to delegitimize and demonize the movement by applying epithets such as 'communist' and 'terrorist' (Battiste and Henderson, 2000, p. 4). Yet, as members of stateless nations themselves, Indigenous activists saw their *own* struggle as equally one for sovereignty, and as a means to maintain their self-determination and fend off further human rights violations and state and corporate encroachment. This conflict was laid bare within the debates over the UNDRIP, which in the end acknowledged a right of self-determination for Indigenous Peoples yet excluded the right to secession—in order to appease state interests and actors (Escárcega, 2003, p. 74; Lâm, 2000, pp. 64, 172).

Hence, the Indigenous quest for rights and recognition at the highest level bears a few distinct facets: It exemplifies the long postwar effort to constrain the rights and sovereignty of states. At the same time, it challenges this very 'rights' regime and discourse, which was seen as based on a Western liberal and individualist sense of society and rights, and thus anathema to subaltern views of community and responsibility. This more fundamental challenge has involved articulating and asserting an alternative sense of Indigenous sovereignty and self-determination based on positive protections for culture and communal rights as well as political empowerment, contrasted with the statist understanding of sovereignty and self-determination based on exclusive control over territory and citizenship. Inherent in this assertion has been the recognition of Indigenous rights as collective rights. All of this has coalesced into a powerful attack on many of the founding myths of the modern nation-state and the way that states relate to their societies, peoples, other species, and territory. Moreover, this Indigenous stance stands in considerable contrast to the majority of nongovernmental actors engaged in UN forums, who in their petitioning have had the effects of reinforcing state sovereignty, the inter-state system, and its and philosophical and other foundations (Escárcega, 2003, pp. 34–5; Jelin, 1998, p. 407).

The second major facet of the movement for Indigenous rights at the international level was to expose and challenge the supposed normative consensus and moral order based on Eurocentric values inherent in the international system. This could be seen most visibly in the contortions and distortions of language and meaning in the attempts to translate Indigenous voices and understandings into radically different linguistic and social constructions that could then be 'understood' by international actors. Thus, Indigenous Peoples, by force of their participation and practices, are not just demanding inclusion into such global dialogues such as that on human rights and now climate change, but are also challenging and trying to deconstruct dominant meanings. This is done when they draft their own declarations and hold counter-summits and members-only meetings at new and alternative forums. Both facets described above can be clearly seen in the experience of Indigenous Peoples engaged in climate change negotiations, to which we will now turn (Henderson, 2008; Lâm, 2000, p. 211; Postero and Zamosc, 2004, p. 7; Warren and Jackson, 2003, p. 16; Wilmer, 1993).

The Emergent International Indigenous Climate Movement[5]

Participation of Indigenous Peoples in the international climate change conferences only began in 1998, when the first Indigenous participants attended the United Nations Framework Convention on Climate Change (UNFCCC) Conference of Parties (COP), and there issued an Indigenous declaration. In 2001, they were recognized as a constituency within the UNFCCC, under whose auspices climate talks are held. This allowed the ICM the same rights to participate as other constituencies, such as environmental organizations, and granting, for example, the right to make statements to state parties in attendance and the ability to have private meeting rooms. Beyond being granted these basic things, however, Indigenous Peoples have demanded the creation of an ad hoc working group, similar to a body that exists in the UN Convention on Biological Diversity, the sister convention to the UNFCCC. As with the Working Group on Indigenous Populations described earlier, this would allow Indigenous Peoples to have some of the same rights as states, such as sitting in on private meetings and proposing changes to draft documents. This is one of a number of proposals that have been developed and advanced to considerably increase the effectiveness and voice of Indigenous participation (Grossman, 2006, pp. 39, 43; Macchi et al., 2008, pp. 9, 11).

It was only at the twelfth COP meeting (or COP 12) in 2006 that Indigenous Peoples were successful in getting their issues addressed substantially by states. There, two side events were held that dealt with Indigenous Peoples implicitly. Most explicitly, the Nairobi Work Programme was adopted, which encouraged 'local and Indigenous knowledge' to be considered in adaptation methods to climate change. This was one of the first concrete accomplishments of Indigenous Peoples within the UNFCCC system toward having their traditional knowledge recognized and respected.[6] This would be the first of many such recognitions which have followed over the years, which have always been extensively and critically debated, and often opposed, by a number of colonizing states (Macchi et al., 2008, p. 12).

Even within the formal negotiations, Indigenous Peoples are organized distinctly from other constituencies, more closely resembling a social movement in terms of their cohesiveness, unconventional tactics, and appropriation of public space (Álvarez et al., 1998, p. 19). In meeting as a caucus entire, they strive to come to consensus positions, which are used to collectively lobby states and nongovernmental actors, a practice derived out of experience with the UN human rights system. The caucus has come to call itself the International Indigenous Peoples' Forum on Climate Change, which involves and implicates all Indigenous Peoples' groups participating in the negotiations (Abhainn et al., 2007, p. 133). This stands in contrast to many constituencies which function mainly as loose networks of coordination and communication. Additionally, the Indigenous caucus holds meetings prior to the official negotiation to share information and further develop its positions and strategy.

Within the negotiations, the IICM relies on making interventions in the official meetings and especially in plenary sessions. They organize press conferences and side events, which are attempts to reach out to broader audiences. They meet privately with states and host events or functions off-site. Lastly, and more so than perhaps any other constituency except youth, they organize or join others in direct actions or media stunts (Abhainn et al., 2007, pp. 133–4). These can be interpreted as acts of protest and appropriation of what is normally a state-dominated and -defined space, especially when the actions arise spontaneously or when permission is not sought.

The IICM is challenging states in arenas traditionally dominated by those 'colonizing settler states' that happen to also be the biggest polluters, and some of the most resistant to Indigenous rights—including Canada, the US, and Australia (Grossman, 2006, pp. 42, 49–50). The work done by the IICM in these arenas also opens up space for other groups, in terms of both action and discourse. Grossman (2006, p. 50) sees Indigenous groups able to achieve more than other groups at the UN because they can assert similar rights as states in the negotiations, leveraging their rights to sovereignty under international law to further bolster their position. Yet, Indigenous Peoples' insistence on recognizing climate change as a human rights issue (and an Indigenous rights issue in particular), if successful, would also make it easier for other movements to enact similar human rights protections.

Outside of official negotiations, however, Indigenous Peoples have been prominent figures in decidedly different types of activism vis-à-vis climate change. Many IICM members have been heavily involved in gatherings and events hosted by other civil society groups. At the UN climate negotiations, typically alternative forums are organized to provide opportunities for an audience beyond those who are part of the official negotiations to become informed and engaged in numerous issues, as well as a space for informal information-sharing, networking, and alliance-building among progressive movement actors. Additionally, protests and similar demonstrations are often organized outside the UN meeting space, where Indigenous Peoples typically gather together to march or demonstrate united, again in marked difference from other social movement actors who tend to focus on their individual issues.

Beyond the UN climate conferences, the IICM has also sought out or created other venues to make their voices heard. One of the first and best-known events grew out of the Inuit Circumpolar Committee filing a petition in December 2005 against the US in the Inter-American Commission on Human Rights.[7] They claimed the US was violating their human rights, predominantly cultural rights, by not acting to stop climate change, and they relied both on scientific arguments and traditional knowledge in making these claims. Although unsuccessful, the case did allow for additional petitions to be submitted, making it a first in international law's acknowledgement of the human rights implications of climate change and the impacts in particular on Indigenous Peoples. This is also recognized as one of the first attempts to treat climate change under human rights law, which other groups would later use as a strategy (Grossman, 2006, pp. 47–8).

Other similar spaces where Indigenous Peoples have attempted to challenge and change the dominant climate change discourse and institutions include the UN Permanent Forum on Indigenous Issues and the UN High Commissioner for Human Rights. Two additional gatherings stand out, however, for their uniqueness, scale, and importance. The first was held in Alaska in 2009, where hundreds of Indigenous Peoples converged for days of talks about climate change, joined by representatives of the United Nations. The end result was a declaration which was afterwards widely translated, disseminated, and utilized. The process was effective in allowing Indigenous Peoples to set their own agenda and define their understanding of climate change and its potential remedies, while also building intra-movement solidarity. Translation and time was allotted to allow participants to express themselves and deliberate in respectful circumstances, giving voice and space to many who would not otherwise find it at official UN climate negotiations. At the same time, the gathering also highlighted the diversity of opinions of IICM members, with some divisions arising over the need to limit fossil fuel activities, a prominent source of income for some Indigenous communities.

The second such event was hosted by the Government of Bolivia under Indigenous President Evo Morales in 2010. Bolivia issued an invitation to the world—both state and non-state actors alike—after the fifteenth COP in Copenhagen failed to arrive at a consensus agreement. Over 35,000 people showed up, the majority being Indigenous from Bolivia and surrounding countries. Thus the conference was imbued with a definite tone of Indigenous and especially Andean peoples from the outset, with some of the meetings being conducted in Indigenous languages. The final result, the Cochabamba Declaration, showed Indigenous Peoples to be at the forefront of a movement to tackle climate change based on a trenchant critique of Western political institutions and capitalism, modernity, and colonialism (for a similar argument, see Escobar, 2008). The gathering was also important for creating cohesion and solidarity with non-indigenous environmental movement groups and encouraging participation of those who would not normally attend official negotiations—such as Indigenous farmers or pastoralists. The final declaration was submitted to the UNFCCC, allowing for its potential inclusion into any final agreements to emerge from that official process, though with little progress on that front a few years later. However, its widespread adoption by some states and civil society movements more broadly than just the IICM served in many ways as a sign of success and maturity for the International Indigenous Climate Movement (Climate Connections, 2010).

It bears mentioning that the types of understandings, solutions, and knowledge presented in these declarations, as well as the declarations and statements to emerge out of Indigenous Peoples' participation in the UNFCCC process,[8] were markedly different from those produced by dominant institutions and actors. It can be argued that these texts constitute a modern form of Indigenous knowledge, or a 'new commons' created by the oldest surviving nations

(Wilmer, 1993, p. 32).[9] Throughout these texts, a number of elements stand out in stark contrast to the official documents. They include demands for rigorous emissions reductions to be undertaken far above what has been on the table at the official negotiation rounds, partly in recognition that climate impacts greatly threaten many Indigenous communities (Grossman, 2006, p. 39). Second, there is a strong emphasis placed on a spiritual, non-materialist, and non-commercial relationship with the earth. This is tied to a critique of and sharp disagreement with historical and ongoing processes of control and commodification of the planet (Warren and Jackson, 2003, p. 13).

Similarly, the documents deride the capitalist economic system, market mechanisms, 'techno-fixes', industrialization, and modern 'development' strategies as unable to resolve the climate crisis—which they have in fact created. Further, governments and corporations are openly distrusted throughout. A broad sense of concern over so-called false solutions to climate change, owing to past and potential impacts on Indigenous communities and a lack of consultation, is apparent. Such projects include dams, biofuel plantations, tree farms, nuclear power, 'clean' coal, etc., and are associated with the erosion of Indigenous Peoples' sovereignty, a rise in land grabs, displacement of communities, disruption of traditional practices, as well as state or privatized violence towards community members. The texts portray a complex analysis of the root causes of climate change as resulting from colonial processes and the development of a capitalist economic system dependent upon fossil fuels and resource extraction.

In counterpoint, the IICM has proposed that Indigenous knowledge be recognized and respected as a first step toward addressing and stemming climate change and environmental degradation. They also demand the recognition of Indigenous rights, particularly collective rights associated with the use and control of lands, territories and resources, and the right to 'free, prior and informed consent'. Maintaining a holistic sense of environmental and social integrity and justice is reflected in their analyses, as is strongly advocating their own participation as delegates within the climate negotiations on a par with state actors and as a means to provide necessary corrective perspectives and solutions.

This collective vision, voice, and emerging agenda as seen through recent IICM documents is quite obviously radically divergent from those emanating from the COP forums—with the chief exception of some allied social movement actors in the climate justice movement (see Reitan and Gibson, this volume). When we place the stated positions of these allies alongside documents and statements of the UNFCCC itself, the likes of powerful and big polluters like the Canadian and US governments, other impacted states such as the Association of Small Island States (AOSIS) or a few outliers like Bolivia, and the broad range of civil society groups participating, what emerges is a spectrum of opinions, proposals, and visions closer to or farther from the Indigenous position. I will conclude with some very brief reflections on what distinguishes these various actors from each other and from the IICM. The gaps can be seen as spaces for dialogue as well as a measure of the distance that would need to traversed in order for Indigenous Peoples to feel sufficiently regarded and respected so that an alliance of equals may be forged in our common struggle to preserve our earth.

At the most progressive end of this non-indigenous spectrum, an international consortium of environmental NGOs (see e.g. Climate Action Network International, 2001) share some concordance with Indigenous groups (see Reitan and Gibson, this volume), and yet gaps still exist in how climate change is understood in all of its complexity and historicity. Within the UNFCCC itself (see e.g. United Nations, 1992, 1998), there are many important environmental justice principles included, but we find as of yet no recognition of Indigenous Peoples. Within the mainstream Canadian environmental groups (see e.g. Cundiff et al., 2007; Demerse and Bramley, 2008;

Sierra Club of Canada, 2007, 2008), some concern is expressed for Indigenous Peoples along with other environmental justice principles, but their articulated stances do not yet show a deep understanding or concern on par with that developed in the ICM spaces and documents. Lastly, with regard to the Canadian government's position (see e.g. Hull and Environment Canada, 2008; Williams, 2009) in particular, it shows a near complete disregard for Indigenous Peoples and their demands, or even broader considerations of environmental justice. Indeed, my own experience has tended to corroborate allegations of a 'neo-liberal economic consensus' that has dominated climate negotiations (Dorsey, 2007; Stallworthy, 2009, p. 62).

Much more could be said about these tenuous recognitions and relationships between Indigenous groups and other state and non-state parties, but suffice it to say that there are many problematic elements of the relationship that have thus far kept broader and stronger alliances from being forged. Unfortunately, many of the so-called civil society or NGOs form something of a hegemonic consensus or bloc of environmental organizations which are largely at odds with the ICM perspectives and aspirations, and in some ways mirror the hegemonic consensus mentioned above. These groups maintain much of the power within traditional civil society networks and the UN forums on issues of the environment, and it thus becomes another form of power that needs to be and is being challenged by the ICM, alongside that of the state and inter-state system. But while contentiously engaging with these multiple power blocs, Indigenous Peoples are also throwing down another challenge, and this is to civil society groups to not thwart but rather *support* Indigenous rights, self-determination, cultures, and prospects for survival—and that of the planet.

Considerable work remains in garnering resources, respect, and other forms of needed support from most NGOs and governments alike for frontline communities. Indigenous activists are looking for alliances on these terms, that is, for partners to join in challenging the dominant discourses on the causes, unacceptable consequences, and acceptable solutions to looming environmental catastrophes. It is a challenge based in the newest 'commons' of Indigenous perspectives that have been articulated over many years of international action and coordination, and of listening to each other, to their collective wisdom, and to the earth.

Nevertheless, there have been some bright spots and recent developments in the realm of solidarity that give some cause for hope. One can detect a definite thawing, or even warming up, of support for Indigenous Peoples on behalf of some of the most progressive environmental and social justice NGOs over the past few years especially, along with considerable support from constituencies such as youth and feminists. Some governments have also begun to get behind and take up ICM positions, especially with regard to protections of Indigenous rights and cultures. That said, Indigenous Peoples still too often find themselves in a position of having to work on many fronts against NGOs and states in order to protect and defend themselves in international forums. Yet looking outside of official UN spaces, Indigenous Peoples are enjoying a greater degree of influence, support, and solidarity from movements and actors in those autonomous and parallel spaces, and can even be seen as taking leadership positions on a range of issues that other movements then adopt or adapt into their own analyses and stances (see also Escárcega, forthcoming). This is some progress.

Moving forward, more research, classroom, and media attention needs to be given to understanding and disseminating this new transnational commons of Indigenous knowledge, discourses, and position statements, so that they may reach wider academic, scientific, activist, and popular audiences because, in one sense, the battle over climate change is a battle over meanings and who gets to make claims. Those who frame the issues define the terms of the debate and possible solutions (Dorsey, 2007). We must understand that this process is not simple, in that

Indigenous knowledge has been systematically denigrated over centuries, so much so that it is now regarded both commonly and scientifically —if it is regarded at all— as somewhere between quaint and worthless (Battiste and Henderson, 2000; Kinchenloe and Steinberg, 2008, p. 145; Smith, 2005, p. 60). Thus there is a great need to support the regeneration, renewal, revalorization, and dissemination of this knowledge and those voices that still carry it. That is why it is crucial to support those frontline communities facing the effects of climate change today, and to empower their voices and defend their epistemologies as valuable and necessary. Indigenous Peoples have shown themselves willing and able to lead in many areas on these issues today, and require only that other non-state, state, and inter-state actors alike sit down and talk—or simply catch up. If we are to forge closer alliances toward effective collective efforts to halt catastrophic harm to the planet, then we should allow the long-marginalized and denigrated Indigenous voices and cosmovisions to flourish once more and to serve as a source of guidance for the broader movement.

Acknowledgements

I would like to thank Sylvia Escárcega particularly, as well as two anonymous reviewers, for helping to greatly strengthen this piece.

Notes

1. Indigenous Peoples is capitalized following the custom adopted within much of the Indigenous movement, in recognition of their standing as peoples, as well as out of similar respect afforded with more specific terms, like First Nations.
2. For this methodology, see Denzinet al. (2008), Kovach (2005), Moose-Mitha (2005), Reitan (2007; ch. 2), Reitan and Gibson (this volume), and Tuhiwai Smith (2005).
3. For my work as an independent journalist reporting on Indigenous environmental struggles, see http://rabble.ca/blogs/bloggers/ben-powless.
4. For a comparative analysis of the ways in which UN forums have been among the most open to civil society and social movement actors in comparison with other global governance bodies, see Scholte (2011).
5. The following analysis of Indigenous movements' engagement in the UN climate talks draws chiefly on my own participation, as well as the works of Abhainnet al. (2007), Climate Connections (2010), ETC Group (2010), Grossman (2006), Indigenous Environmental Network (2008), International Climate Justice Network (2002), Monga Bay (2008), Nickels et al. (2006), and Tauli-Corpuz et al. (2009).
6. On Indigenous ecological knowledge, see Fourmile (1999) and Kassam (2009).
7. See http://www.ciel.org/Publications/ICC_Petition_7Dec05.pdf.
8. The analysis in this section comes primarily from examining the following documents: 'The Indigenous Peoples' Declaration' of the World Peoples' Conference of Climate Change and the Rights of Mother Earth (2010); Makelo (2007); The Albuquerque Declaration (1998) available at http://www.nativevillage.org/Inspiration-/Albuquerque%20Convention.htm; Declaration of the First International Forum of Indigenous Peoples on Climate Change (2000) available at http://www.wrm.org.uy/actors/CCC/IPLyon.html; The Alaska Declaration (2009) available at http://www.un.org/ga/president/63/letters/globalsummitoncc.pdf
9. For a discussion of the various historical and contemporary forms and arguments around protecting the 'commons', see Cavanagh and Mander (2004, ch. 5).

References

Abhainn, M., Barnard, K. M. & Grey, S. (eds) *Indigenous Peoples and Climate Change: Vulnerabilities, Adaptation, and Responses to the Mechanisms of the Kyoto Protocol—A Collection of Case Studies* (Chiang Mai, Thailand: The International Alliance of Indigenous and Tribal Peoples of the Tropical Forests Technical Secretariat).

Álvarez, S. E. (1998) Latin American feminisms 'go global': trends of the 1990s and challenges for the new millennium, in S. E. Álvarez, E. Dagnino & A. Escobar (eds) *Cultures of Politics, Politics of Cultures: Re-visioning Latin American Social Movements* (Boulder, CO: Westview Press), pp. 293–324.

Alvarez, S. E., Dagnino, E. & Escobar, A. (eds) (1998) *Cultures of Politics, Politics of Cultures: Re-visioning Latin American Social Movements* (Boulder, CO: Westview Press).

Anaya, J. (2004) *Indigenous Peoples in International Law* (Oxford: Oxford University Press).

Battiste, M. & Henderson, J. (Sákéj) Y. (2000) *Protecting Indigenous Knowledge and Heritage: A Global Challenge* (Saskatoon: Purich Publishing)

Brysk, A. (2000) *From Tribal Village to Global Village: Indian Rights and International Relations in Latin America* (Palo Alto, CA: Stanford University Press).

Cavanagh, J. & Mander, J. (eds) (2004) *Alternatives to Economic Globalization: A Better World Is Possible*, A Report of the International Forum on Globalization (San Francisco: Berrett-Koehler Publishers).

Climate Action Network International (2001) Fair, ambitious & binding: essentials for a successful climate deal, http://www.climatenetwork.org/publication/cans-fair-ambitious-binding-essentials-successful-climate-deal

Climate Connections (2010) The proposals of 'peoples agreement' in the texts for United Nations negotiation on climate change, 16 August, http://climatevoices.wordpress.com/2010/08/16/the-proposals-of-%E2%80%9Cpeoples-agreement%E2%80%9D-in-the-texts-for-united-nations-negotiation-on-climate-change/

Cundiff, B., Hazell, S., Bregha, F. & Mitchell, A. (2007) Tomorrow today, http://www.tomorrowtodaycanada.ca/en_full_conclusion.php

Demerse, C. & Bramley, M. (2008) Choosing greenhouse gas emission reduction policies in Canada, The Pembina Institute (October), http://www.pembina.org/pub/1720

Denzin, N. K., Lincoln, Y. S. & Tuhiwai Smith, L. (2008) *Handbook of Critical and Indigenous Methodologies* (Thousand Oaks, CA: Sage Publications).

Dorsey, M. K. (2007) Climate knowledge and power: tales of skeptic tanks, weather gods, and sagas for climate (in)justice, *Capitalism Nature Socialism*, 18(2), pp. 7–21.

Escárcega, S. (2003) Internationalization of the Politics of Indigenousness: A Case Study of Mexican Indigenous Intellectuals and Activists at the United Nations, Ph.D. Dissertation, University of California–Davis.

Escárcega, S. (2009) Trabajar Haciendo: Activist research and interculturalism, *Intercultural Education Journal*, 20(1), pp. 19–30.

Escárcega, S. (2010) Authenticating strategic essentialisms: the politics of indigenousness at the United Nations, *Cultural Dynamics*, 22(1), pp. 3–28.

Escárcega, S. (forthcoming) The global Indigenous movement and 'paradigm wars': international activism, network building and transformative politics', in J. S. Juris & A, Khasnabish (eds) *Insurgent Encounters: Transnational Activism, Ethnography, and the Political* (Durham, NC: Duke University Press).

Escobar, A. (2008) *Territories of Difference: Place, Movements, Life, Redes* (Durham, NC: Duke University Press).

ETC Group (2010) United Nations science body calls for halt on climate-hacking experiments, 18 May, http://www.etcgroup.org/en/node/5140

Fourmile, H. (1999) Indigenous peoples, the conservation of traditional ecological knowledge, and global governance, in N. Low (ed.) *Global Ethics and Environment* (London: Routledge), pp. 215–246.

Grossman, Z. (2006) International Indigenous responses, in Parker, A., Grossman, Z., Whitesell, E., Stephenson, B., Williams, T., Hardison, P., Ballew, L., Burnham, B., Bushnell, J., & Klosterman, R. (eds) (2006) *Climate Change and Pacific Rim Indigenous Nations* (Olympia, WA: Northwest Indian Applied Research Institute, Evergreen State College), pp. 39–51.

Henderson, J. (Sákéj) Y. (2008) *Indigenous Diplomacy and the Rights of Peoples: Achieving UN Recognition* (Saskatoon: Purich Publishing Limited).

Hull, J. & Environment Canada (2008) Turning the corner: taking action to fight climate change, 29 May, http://www.trbav030.org/pdf2008/TRB08my_Hull_Enviro_Canada.pdf

Indigenous Environmental Network (2008) CORE Manipur and federation of Indigenous and tribal peoples in Asia, *REDD: CO2lonialism of Forests*, April/May.

International Climate Justice Network (2002) Bali principles of climate justice, 28 August, http://www.indiaresource.org/issues/energycc/2003/baliprinciples.html

Jelin, E. (1998) Toward a culture of participation and citizenship: challenges for a more equitable world, in S. E. Alvares, E. Dagnino & A. Escobar (eds) *Cultures of Politics, Politics of Cultures: Re-visioning Latin American Social Movements* (Boulder, CO: Westview Press), pp. 405–414.

Kassam, K.-A. S. (2009) *Biocultural Diversity and Indigenous Ways of Knowing: Human Ecology in the Arctic* (Calgary: University of Calgary Press).

Keck, M. E. & Sikkink, K. (1998) *Activists Beyond Borders: Advocacy Networks in International Politics* (Ithaca, NY: Cornell University Press).

Kinchenloe, Joe L. & Steinberg, S. R. (2008) Indigenous knowledges in education: complexities, dangers, and profound benefits, in N. K. Denzin, Y. S. Lincoln & L. Tuhiwai Smith (eds) *Handbook of Critical and Indigenous Methodologies* (Thousand Oaks, CA: Sage Publications), pp. 135–156.

Kovach, M. (2005) Emerging from the margins: Indigenous methodologies, in L. Brown & S. Strega (eds) *Research as Resistance: Critical, Indigenous, and Anti-Oppressive Approaches* (Toronto: Canadian Scholars' Press), pp. 19–36.

Lâm, M. C. (2000) *At the Edge of the State: Indigenous Peoples and Self-Determination* (Ardsley, NY: Transnational Publishers).

Lynd, S. & Grubačić, A. (2008) *Wobblies and Zapatistas: Conversations on Anarchism, Marxism and Radical History* (Oakland, CA: PM Press).

Macchi, M., Oviedo, G., Gotheil, S., Cross, K., Boedhihartono, A., Wolfangel, C. & Howell, M. (2008) Indigenous and traditional peoples and climate change. IUCN, March, http://cmsdata.iucn.org/downloads/indigenous_peoples_climate_change.pdf

Mignolo, W. D. (2005) *The Idea of Latin America* (Malden, MA: Blackwell).

Makelo, S. A. (2007) The DRC case study: The impacts of the carbon sinks of Ibi-Batéké Project on the indigenous pygmies of the Democratic Republic of the Congo, in M. Abhainn, K. M. Barnard, & S. Grey (eds) *Indigenous Peoples and Climate Change: Vulnerabilities, Adaptation, and Responses to the Mechanisms of the Kyoto Protocol – A Collection of Case Studies* (Chiang Mai, Thailand: The International Alliance of Indigenous and Tribal Peoples of the Tropical Forests Technical Secretariat).

Monga Bay (2008) Indigenous people demand greater say in using forests to fight global warming, 8 October, http://news.mongabay.com/2008/1008-indigenous_redd.html

Moose-Mitha, M. (2005) Situating anti-oppressive theories within critical and difference-centred perspectives, in L. Brown & S. Strega (eds) *Research As Resistance: Critical, Indigenous, and Anti-Oppressive Approaches* (Toronto: Canadian Scholars' Press), pp. 37–72.

Muehlebach, A. (2001) 'Making Place' at the United Nations: Indigenous cultural politics at the U.N. working group on Indigenous populations, *Cultural Anthropology*, 16(3), pp. 415–448.

Nickels, S., Furgal, C., Buell, M. & Moquin, H. (2006) Unikkaaqatigiit—Putting the Human Face on Climate Change: Perspectives from Inuit in Canada (Ottawa: Inuit Tapariit Kanatami, Univerisité Laval, NAHO).

Niezen, R. (2003) *The Origins of Indigenism: Human Rights and the Politics of Identity* (Berkeley: University of California Press).

Nye, J. (2005) *Soft Power: The Means to Success in World Politics* (New York: PublicAffairs Publishing).

Postero, N. G. & Zamosc, L. (2004) Indigenous movements and the Indian question in Latin America, in N. G. Postero & L. Zamosc (eds) *The Struggle for Indigenous Rights in Latin America* (Portland: Sussex Academic Press), pp. 1–31.

Reitan, R. (2007) *Global Activism* (London: Routledge).

Risse, T. & Sikkink, K. (1999) The socialization of international human rights norms into domestic practice: introduction, in T. Risse, S. C. Ropp & K. Sikkink (eds) *The Power of Human Rights: International Norms and Domestic Change* (Cambridge: Cambridge University Press), pp. 1–38.

Scholte, J. A. (ed.) (2011) *Building Global Democracy? Civil Society and Accountable Global Governance* (Cambridge: Cambridge University Press).

Sierra Club of Canada (2007) Planetary citizen's guide to the global climate negotiations: toward a Bali breakthrough', November, http://www.sierraclub.ca/national/postings/scc-climate-guide-nov-2007.pdf

Smith, L. T. (2005) *Decolonizing Methodologies: Research and Indigenous Peoples* (New York: Zed Books).

Sierra Club of Canada (2008) Lead, follow or get out of the way: Sierra Club Canada's Kyoto report card 2008, 13 February, http://www.sierraclub.ca/national/kyoto/kyoto-report-card-2008.pdf

Stallworthy, M. (2009) 'Environmental justice imperative for an era of climate change, *Journal of Law and Society*, 36(1), pp. 55–74.

Tauli-Corpuz, V., de Chavez, R., Baldo-Soriano, E., Magata, H., Golocan, C., Bugtong, M. V., Enklwe-Abayao, L. & Cariño, J. (2009) *Guide on Climate Change and Indigenous Peoples* (Baguio City: Philippines: Tebtebba).

Tuhiwai Smith, L. (2005) *Decolonizing Methodologies: Research and Indigenous Peoples* (New York: Zed Books).

United Nations (1992) United Nations Framework Convention on Climate Change, http://unfccc.int/resource/docs/convkp/conveng.pdf

United Nations (1998) Kyoto Protocol to the United Nations Framework Convention on Climate Change, http://unfccc.int/resource/docs/convkp/kpeng.pdf

Varese, S. (2006) *Witness to Sovereignty: Essays on the Indian Movement in Latin America* (Copenhagen: IWGIA).

Warren, K. B. & Jackson, J. E. (2003) Introduction: studying Indigenous activism in Latin America, in K. B. Warren & J. E. Jackson (eds) *Indigenous Movements, Self-Representation, and the State in Latin America* (Austin: University of Texas Press), pp. 1–21.

Williams, T. (2009) The Climate Change Convention and the Kyoto Protocol. Library of Parliament, 30 January, revised, http://www.parl.gc.ca/content/LOP/ResearchPublications/prb0721-e.htm

Wilmer, F. (1993) *The Indigenous Voice in World Politics: Since Time Immemorial* (Thousand Oaks, CA: Sage Publications).

'No One Is Illegal!' Resistance and the Politics of Discomfort

MAURICE STIERL

Department of Politics and International Studies, University of Warwick, UK

ABSTRACT *This work attempts to recast conceptions of global/ised political resistance. Instead of following systematic accounts of actors seeking global social transformation, it is shown how a Foucauldian understanding of power and resistance—here developed into a 'politics of discomfort'—can help illuminate more situated and cautious approaches to expressions of dissent. It is illustrated how undocumented migrants, or* sans-papiers, *with the support of the German activist network No One Is Illegal (NOII) can assume political subjectivity to confront and resist the dominating power of sovereign state agencies that attempt to marginalise and silence acts of contestation. I argue that NOII's practical resistance, although local, nonetheless has important dimensions 'beyond', as it critiques through its creative actions (global) sovereign hypocrisy, violence, and the 'governmentality of documentation'.*

Introduction

From Puerta del Sol/Madrid, to Tahrir Square/Cairo, Zuccotti Park/New York, and St Pauls/London, the occupation of public spaces in 2011 has gained momentum internationally to become the most recent and among the most significant manifestations of 'global/ised resistance'. These follow other iconic and widely theorised moments of contestation including the Zapatista rebellion against the Mexican state and NAFTA, 'the battle of Seattle' against the Third Ministerial of the WTO in 1999, anti-G8 summit protests in Genoa in 2001 and Heiligendamm in 2007, and acts of subversion during the 2009 Copenhagen climate change summit.

While multifaceted in character, these instances of mass political action share a certain commonality: visibility, 'loudness', and academic recognition. This article seeks to illustrate a form of dissent that may escape traditional understandings of global resistance due to its transversal nature. Political activism that relates to, supports, and listens to undocumented migrants, *sans-papiers*, in their everyday struggles raises pertinent questions with regard to the 'global/ised resistance' discourse in terms of site, scale and ends.

My work contributes to the existing literature first by seeking to offer an alternative reading of resistance as a Foucault-inspired 'politics of discomfort' that, while embedded in relational social conditions, begins as a confrontation 'in one's own head, in the solitude before one's own image' (Müller in Bleiker, 2000, p. 187). Second, it will show how creative expressions of dissent of No One Is Illegal (NOII), a German activist network, constitute resistance that starts 'from where it is at' but comments on underlying oppressive social conditions that span from the local to the global.

The argument proceeds in three sections. The first section briefly scrutinises dominant conceptions of global/ised resistance. It shows that tendencies within the 'resistance/social movement literatures' exist that reproduce sovereign assumptions of *what* and *where* power, resistance, and the political are supposed to be. The second section elaborates a Foucauldian understanding of pervasive power-relations which helps in coming to terms with relational dimensions of contestation and allows for a departure from systematic accounts. This analysis is extended to make the case for a 'politics of discomfort' as a resisting strategy based on self-enquiry, anger, and responsibility. In the final section, a situated case study of the critical network NOII is developed within the Foucauldian frame of 'heterotopia' that exposes the marginalising state/nation/citizen constellation vis-à-vis 'undocumented' migrants.

Global/ised Resistance

Global/ised resistance has many names and faces. It is characterised as 'anti-capitalist', 'anti-imperialist', or 'anti-globalisation' forces, in the form of 'social movements', 'global civil society' or even a 'postmodern transnational political party'. Dissent is practised through 'bottom-up globalisation', 'insurgency from below', or 'counter-hegemonic struggle' (Cohen and Rai, 2000; Eschle and Maiguashca, 2005; Falk 1998; Gill, 2000). Acknowledged expressions of active resistance are diverse but often include the already mentioned 'iconic moments' in Seattle, London, Copenhagen, and Johannesburg. Active protestors in these instances are usually associated with NGOs, environmental groups, anti-war and anti-racism networks, women and gay rights campaigns, religious groups, animal rights defenders, political parties, advocates of the 'Third World' *cum* Global South, and so forth.

Especially within the last two decades the academic discourse has addressed these phenomena from diverse angles and within different analytical frameworks, thereby contributing to an understanding of movement culture, resources, and strategies. Among others, Reitan (2007, pp. 1, 230–42) approaches the 'sea-change in the nature of leftist activism' in a nuanced way by showing how networks in opposition to neoliberal globalisation create solidarity transnationally while retaining their heterogeneous identities. Similarly, Della Porta et al. (2006, pp. 232–48, 18) provide a cautious treatment of how the demand for a new (global) politics transformed into a 'movement for globalisation from below', defined as an inclusive and heterogeneous network driven, however, by a 'common interpretation of reality'.

Nonetheless, in dominant 'global social movement' and 'global resistance' literatures, a certain eagerness persists to categorise diverse manifestations of dissent by attributing names and a 'place to be' so that other, context-specific and subtle practices of resistance may fall out of sight—or become erased. Although no detailed assessment can be provided here, I will point to a few problematic assumptions. Dominant analytical studies interrogating the phenomenon of global movements and resistance have displayed an inclination to situate dissenting practices and collectivities in the realm of the 'civil' and 'social', facing 'powerholders', thus mainly the sovereign state, international organisations, or multilateral corporations (Eschle, 2005). This *a priori* relegation, tied to a static understanding of power, naturalises conceptions of 'powerless social movements' and 'powerful state politics' as opposing forces. Movements engaged in resisting practices are thus portrayed as either somehow *below* or *outside* power and always *against* power. Such strong/weak, above/below binaries uphold images of a dualistic separation of power into 'haves' and 'have-nots' and hierarchical ruler–ruled categories which, again, clearly indicate where power is supposed to reside.

In the wake of Seattle and Genoa many of these prevailing assumptions became reproduced on a transnational level where a 'global civil society' was seen as emerging in a world 'constituted as a bounded political community modelled on the state writ large' (Walker, 1994, p. 696). While 'the political' remained conceptualised in its relation to the global state system, 'global social movements' came to be seen as the vanguard of resistance, notably so as a sustained, collective and united challenge to 'powerholders' (as in Tilly, 1999). Both Della Porta and Diani's (2006, p. 20) definition of social movements as actors engaged in collective actions with 'clearly identified opponents' and 'a distinct collective identity', as well as Murray's (2010, p. 477) statement that due to 'the nature of the enemy—capitalism, the state and all forms of domination and hierarchy—action must be taken on a large scale' seem indicative of widely held conceptions. However, alternative accounts of international summits have illustrated the predominance of white, male, middle-class, English-speaking, urban, computer-literate professionals from the North and West along with the under-representation of the poor, women, and 'people of colour' (Scholte, 2000). The sheer heterogeneity of dissenting actions, actors, perceptions, terminologies, and at times conflicting agendas renders unifying vocabularies questionable. As Death (2010) shows, the social movement literature's reliance on clear power-resistance dichotomies has, in effect, created romanticised visions of a collective will and struggle.

While not doubting the merit of the academic discourse, it should be emphasised that if ambiguous concepts such as 'global resistance' or 'global civil society' are too readily unified and glorified, other critical, dissenting, and localised voices and spaces become marginalised. Coleman and Tucker (2011, p. 404) pointedly illustrate how dominant interpretative frameworks establish 'ready-made objects of analysis', thereby making it difficult to raise issues that fall 'outside'—such as forms of resistance and global ordering that are transversal, multidimensional, and situated in complex power relationships.[1] Eschewing a more relational understanding of power has allowed the prevailing social movement discourse to create 'general ordering categories', thereby ignoring the complex interplay of contesting and ordering forces and the possibility that 'practices of contestation might also bolster or be imbued by the power relations or processes of ordering that they seek to oppose' (Ibid., p. 401).

The following two sections attempt not to immunise actors and practices from the 'paradoxes within' but to illustrate the doubts and concerns as well as the creativity, chances, and capacities in resisting practices. In this way space is opened up for closer scrutiny of modalities of dissent that seem to transcend clear global/local categorisations and fall outside the power/resistance dualism.

Power, Resistance, Discipline, and Discomfort

In his attempt to free the idea of power from its juridico-discursive representation as something totalising, derived from a single source or centre—that is, sovereignty, a Leviathan, king, or state—Michel Foucault, in *The Will to Knowledge* (1998 [1978]), understands power as something that 'comes from everywhere' circulating within the social body. Foucault (Ibid., pp. 92–3) says:

> It seems to me that power must be understood in the first instance as the multiplicity of force relations immanent in the sphere in which they operate and which constitute their own organization; as the process which, through ceaseless struggles and confrontations, transforms, strengthens, or reverses them; as the support which these force relations find in one another, thus forming a chain or a system, or on the contrary, the disjunctions and contradictions which isolate them from one another; and lastly, the strategies in which they take effect, whose general design or institutional crystallization is embodied in the state apparatus, in the formulation of the law, in the various social hegemonies.

For Foucault, power cannot be held exclusively. Everyone is both a wielder of and subject to power. Power 'is the name that one attributes to a complex strategical situation in a particular society' (Ibid., p. 93; 2004 [1976], p. 29). He alludes to power's relational character in *The Subject and Power* (1982, p. 789): '[W]hat defines a relationship of power is that it is a mode of action which does not act directly and immediately on others. Instead, it acts upon their actions: an action upon an action, on existing actions or on those which may arise in the present or the future.' Hence, power relationships can always be actively changed and resisted. The reversibility of relations implies the possibility of acts of deliberate resistance being the determining force: '[R]esistance comes first, and resistance remains superior to the forces of the process; power relations are obliged to change with the resistance' (Foucault in Kelly, 2009, p. 107). Although no form or act of resistance will ever lead to a liberation from power, power-relations can be reconfigured by 'individuals and collective subjects who are faced with a field of possibilities in which several ways of behaving, several reactions and diverse comportments, may be realized' (Foucault, 1982, p. 790).

In stating that the operation of power is only possible if exercised over 'free subjects', Foucault's conception of freedom, even if somewhat opaque, comes to the fore. Foucault's freedom, then, is implied in the subject's endowment with subjectivity, in the ability of the individual and collective subject to exert agency even if such subjectivity always remains tied to a sociopolitical context. In this sense, the subject has the ability to 'permanently provoke': 'For, if it is true that at the heart of power relations and as a permanent condition of their existence there is an insubordination and a certain essential obstinacy on the part of the principles of freedom, then there is no relationship of power without the means of escape or possible flight' (Ibid., p. 794). Therefore, power is not inherently dominating, homogeneous, or something that can be captured and kept exclusively or be released to confront some enemy figure; power is not assigned to a certain stable space or place; it is not unitary; it does not have a singular history; power can never be overcome. At the same time, resistance is not a uniform reaction to some subduing oppressor and not power's stable other; it has no inherent inclination towards emancipation, however defined; resistance can never be eliminated.

A Foucauldian approach to power and resistance renders coherent oppressor–oppressed, dominance–impotence oppositions unsustainable; it does, however, allow for creative human capacity and a multiplicity of subverting projects to resist dominating constitutions of power-relations. Even if we are 'entangled' in 'countless processes of domination and resistance which are always implicated in, and mutually constitutive of, one another' (Sharp et al., 2000, p. 1), we can nonetheless oppose 'dominating power' and seek strategies 'how not to be governed *like that*, by that, in the name of those principles, with such and such an objective in mind and by means of such procedures, not like that, not for that, not by them' (Foucault, 2007, p. 28; emphasis in original).

One such resisting strategy elaborated herein is the subject's active practising of discomfort as a means to render existing configurations of power-relations 'strange', to indeed refuse to be governed, silenced, or disciplined *like that*. It is a refusal essentially personal and practical since it 'refuses what we are' and aspires to what we can become (Foucault, 1982, p. 785). This refusal is situated in the acceptance of a loss of foundation, ideology, and faith, as suggested by Ashley and Walker (1990). The deprivation of pure identity may be lamented, seen as dangerous, and be counteracted by turning fear into a desire to establish new totalities. It may, however, also be greeted with a 'celebratory attitude' that embraces the closing of gates, disallowing the retreat into a 'securely bounded domicile of self-evident being' (Ibid., p. 380). In a 'posture of joyous affirmation' the latter attitude celebrates difference and ambiguity without the desire to impose new truths (Ibid.). Similarly, for Foucault (2002, p. 373), the 'void left by man's disappearance' must not be filled as it is 'the unfolding of a space in which it is once more possible to think'.

Here, I would like to stress the troubling aspect of an emerging sense of crisis that not only translates into an acceptance of 'the end of a substantive idea of the good life' but that struggles to come to terms with this all-embracing uncertainty (Mouffe, 2000, p. 19). Indeed, discomfort, something that disturbs or deprives of ease, has become a troubling but permanent condition. It has become permanent because there are no abstractions and hideouts, no centres of authority and ideology to which one can flee, and no 'endgame' in which a revolutionary upheaval establishes a radically different future that overturns the present. However, it is both this sense of (personal) crisis and the realisation that oppressive power-relations are 'human-made' that can inform a politics confronting the self and the other. In a burdensome process of questioning one's own identity, one struggles for 'self-creation' as '. . . all these present struggles revolve around the question: Who are we? They are a refusal of these abstractions, of economic and ideological state violence, which ignore who we are individually, and also a refusal of a scientific or administrative inquisition which determines who one is' (Foucault, 1982, p. 781).

In discomfort and doubt a consciousness can grow that is not understood as some form of revealed wisdom but as something steered by oneself, through social interaction and within 'matrixes of power'. These networks of power imply that any process of self-enquiry can never be external or prior to society but must be embedded in relational conditions. Abandoning liberal or rationalist ideas about individual agency as autonomous to society does not mean abandoning agency as such. A Foucauldian critique, following Amoore (2008, p. 274), 'is not that which seeks out resolution, reconciliation or the smoothing out of difficulty, but rather that which discomforts and unsettles one's sense of certainty'. A politics of discomfort as a resisting strategy can be grounded in both constant self-enquiry and anger towards those constructions of the present that have become naturalised in its racist, gendered, and exploitative configurations. To be an act of contestation of disciplined meaning, the struggling for social transformation must be practical politics. Bhabha (2000, p. 6; emphasis in original) says:

> The 'human' is identified not with a *given* essence, be it natural or supranatural, but with a *practice*, a task. The property of the human being is the collective or the transindividual construction of her or his individual autonomy; and the value of human agency arises from the fact that no one can be liberated by others, although no one can liberate herself or himself without others.

In furthering this argument a sense of human responsibility emerges. If we accept that networks of power are constitutive of the social and if the 'dream of total mastery' (Mouffe, 2000, p. 77) is dismissed, then an active struggling towards different power-relations can become constructive resistance. Such perspective maintains that due to the complexity of contemporary life there is no eventual resolution of conflict in harmony, no structure, system, or institution that bridges diversity and antagonism, and never a homogeneous collective will. Those who seek to eventually displace discomfort and controversy marginalise and silence those who disagree and in effect exclude the political.

> [T]here is no single locus of great Refusal, no soul of revolt, source of all rebellions, or pure law of the revolutionary. Instead there is a plurality of resistances, each of them a special case ... (Foucault, 1998 [1978], p. 96)

It may be argued that a politics grounded in an idea of unease must face a dual problematic: apathy and co-optation. Apathy and co-optation are related and can be mutually constitutive, fearing the 'danger' of co-optation may lead one to 'surrender'; a growing 'lethargy' may lead more easily to one being 'co-opted' and so on. However, dominating power as a power that 'attempts to control or coerce others, impose its will upon others, or manipulate the consent of others' always-already co-opts (Sharp et al., 2000, p. 2). And hence, indeed, apathy may result. Nonetheless, as the discussion of No One Is Illegal demonstrates, a contestation based on anger, responsibility, and discomfort struggling against a dominating power that seems at times *overwhelming* is shown to have not only the capacity for alternative politics but the already-existing ability as transversal dissent to connect with other individuals and movements on a wider scale.

Resistance in Heterotopia

Before turning to NOII's activism, this work situates its resisting practices in certain matrixes of power or rather, following Foucault (1986, p. 25), in 'heterotopias of deviation', spaces 'in which individuals whose behavior is deviant in relation to the required mean or norm are placed'. In (mis)using the idea of heterotopia to come to terms with the ambivalent 'zone' in which people without documents are pushed into, voluntarily exist and live in, and/or transcend and move out of, it is shown how both discipline *and* resistance exist in these spaces 'of opening and closing that both isolates them and makes them penetrable' (Ibid., p. 26). This study adds to the fascinating examples by Salter (2007) and Budz (2009) of the airport and the refugee ship as heterotopic spaces 'where governmentality is problematized, negotiated, and possibly reconfigured' (Foucault, 1986, p. 20). Here, a different space is examined which, although 'real', may be difficult to conceive. This 'other place within' as a designated realm for all those who do not belong to the citizen body due to the lack of citizen-making documents is inherently contingent without being in any sense 'less real': subjects can choose to remain, can challenge their status, escape and enter the realm of the citizen, but can also move back into irregularity as even citizens now 'may have to struggle for the right to have rights' (Nyers, 2011, p. 185).

Seeing the zone of 'undocumentedness' as a heterotopia gives us certain insights. First, the dominating power invested in sovereign agencies, manifest in the 'state/citizen' discourse, and the 'governmentality of documentation' with all its laws, norms, and guardians shapes this space of undocumentedness while fighting it at the same time. Second, sans-papiers living and creating this space permanently provoke the sovereign system and can actively challenge dominating power. NOII's struggle for and with the undocumented is here discussed as a politics of discomfort. Third, in allowing to connect one space to other spaces, a heterotopic analysis helps illustrate the transversal connections between the zone of the undocumented as being 'in relation with all other sites' (Foucault, 1986, p. 24). It is then argued that NOII's resistance, even though issue-specific, is indeed connected to phenomena beyond.

Governmentality of Documentation

Foucault (2009 [1977–1978], p. 108) defines governmentality as 'the ensemble formed by institutions, procedures, analyses and reflections, calculations, and tactics that allow the exercise of this very specific, albeit very complex, power that has the population as its target, political economy as its major form of knowledge, and apparatuses of security as its essential technical instrument'. It is within this understanding that dominating power operates. Forms of authority and sovereignty become pluralised but remain interrelated. Through 'biopower', contemporary populations are governed. Decentralised apparatuses, or executives for government, exert this power as *dispositifs*, 'made up of various economic components, political unities, discursive elements, and bits of sociocultural information that come together for strategic reasons' (Debrix, 2009, p. 407).

The 'heterotopia of undocumentedness' is a realm in opposition but intimately connected to the regulation of populations and the visibility of mobility. Indeed, this realm is a peculiar side-product of the 'governmentality of documentation' as undocumentedness is in fact produced and the logical outcome of the struggle to regulate and surveille a population. The inherent tension between regularisation and irregularisation, however, does not necessarily lead to the conclusion that as a flawed system it is at 'war with itself'. Rather, it is a system that reinforces these tensions: although 'absolute regulation' can never be achieved, it remains the underlying rationale for pursuing the elimination of undocumentedness, a pursuit, however, that needs undocumentedness and irregularity as its source. The following will briefly depict the sovereign discourse in which the state's dominating power is situated before showing how the German state strategises against the '(foreign) enemy within'.

A state-centric understanding of the world desires order and social coherence which seems guaranteed by a stable state/nation/citizen nexus. In this nexus, citizens, the 'proper subjects' of political life, accord 'powers' to the state and receive protections internally (laws, police) and from external aggression (military, border police) (Nyers, 2003). The community of citizens, the nation, is represented by the state within a clearly demarcated sovereign territory defined by physical borders. When sovereignty is perceived as 'the fulfillment of a historical destiny', dominating power is performed by the construction of 'the other' (Paasi, 1998, p. 69). The 'undocumented' is commonly seen as someone lacking citizen status and therefore the right to claim state representation and protection. The sans-papiers' ascribed identity is defined as an 'aberration of the prior norm' (Soguk, 1999, p. 14) where community, stability, and political subjects stand opposed to isolation, displacement, and 'agents of pollution' (Haddad, 2007, p. 127). Such representation essentially denies the sans-papiers the ability to speak and to exert agency apart from an 'unsavoury' or 'dangerous' kind, as criminals, scroungers, or terrorists (Nyers, 2003, p. 1070). This sovereign discourse shapes and is shaped by strategies of dominating power, illustrated here as the 'governmentality of documentation' within the German context.

In Germany, the constitutional right to asylum, first established when memories of war horrors and forced expulsions were still vivid, was severely curtailed in 1993 as a response to high numbers of people seeking asylum, a situation described by Chancellor Helmut Kohl as a potential 'national emergency' (*Staatsnotstand*) if not counteracted. In the so-called 'asylum compromise' (*Asylkompromiss*) the right to asylum was amended: the 'safe third country' concept was implemented, isolating Germany due to its geographical position; the 'safe country of origin' concept was reworked, allowing more countries to be considered 'safe enough'; the 'airport-regulation' (*Flughafenregelung*) meant that refugees could be kept in the transit zone of the airport and sent back immediately (Meier-Braun, 2002).

Although only briefly mentioned here, these developments must be understood in the European context of gradually creating a common internal and external EU border control regime, common databases (Schengen Information System(s), Visa Information System), a border agency (FRONTEX), as well as the European Neighbourhood Policy, Mobility Partnerships, bilateral agreements, and so forth (Vaughan-Williams, 2008). In this vein, territorial and deterritorialised forms of control became conflated and institutions such as police, immigration services, border controls, military, and intelligence services fused on national, transnational, and supranational levels (Bigo et al., 2007). Due to German and EU strategies, asylum claims diminished in Germany whereas 'illegal immigration' increased significantly.[2]

It is in the context of German and EU legislation, discourse, and norms that the 'governmentality of documentation' as well as the heterotopia of the 'undocumented' need to be understood. Moreover, as Castañeda (2010) shows, undocumented subjects living in Germany face particular hardship due to both the 'norm' to carry personal identification and Articles 87 and 96 of the Residence Act (*Aufenthaltsgesetz*). Article 87, also known as the 'denunciation act', requires undocumented persons residing in Germany to 'be reported to the appropriate authorities if they seek services at public facilities', whereas Article 96, the 'trafficking law', criminalises the act of assisting such persons, 'punishable with a fine or imprisonment, for up to five years' (Ibid., p. 251).

Žižek (in Nyers, 2003, p. 1087) rightly states that the dominant order 'is never simply a positive order: to function at all, it has to cheat, to misname, and so on'. Sovereign (counter-) strategies include: (collective) deportations at night or in chartered aircrafts; outsourcing/privatisation of deportation tasks to (foreign) security personnel; sedating/shackling of deportees; 'everyday' identification checks based on racial stereotypes; extrajudicial manoeuvres; workplace raids; the fostering of alliances with citizens; the criminalisation of undocumented subjects (using regular prisons as detention centres) and of those citizens offering help; evoking images of the undocumented as security threats or 'scroungers'; and delinking immigration officials from locally elected politicians (Castañeda, 2010, p. 252). Thus, the seemingly incompatible 'other space' might indeed be a source for moments of 'sovereign (re)founding', the reaffirmation of the sovereign ideal of a state-centric world order where every undocumented person can be allocated a designated territory 'where she belongs' (Nyers, 2003, p. 1088).

The dominating power, the German state here, has established a complex socio-politico-legal regime in which dispersed 'agencies for government'—from border, police, immigration, health, and employment agencies down to the citizen as watchdog—manage and monitor mobility and the population, thereby (re)establishing dominant notions of sovereignty, citizenship, and identity. Yet, heterotopias are not spaces of singularity; Foucault claims '[the] heterotopia is capable of juxtaposing in a single real place several spaces, several sites that are in themselves incompatible' (1986, p. 25).

Although sovereign governmentality seems at times all-encompassing, there remains room for revolt. Often present in Foucault-informed accounts of 'total institutions', Salter argues, 'is a tendency to assume the smooth functioning of knowledge/power networks in a way that reproduces relations of dominance and obedience with little room for resistance' (2007, p. 63). Indeed, these petty sovereigns with their eagerness to register and regulate are never 'absolute' and do not stand opposed to 'bare life', but face self-determining humans with the capacity to refuse. Undocumented mobility may in some sense reaffirm sovereign principles. But it also ceaselessly creates anxiety in this regime embodying an excess mobility and capable, following Deleuze (in Nyers, 2003, p. 1069), 'to produce the real, to create life, to find a weapon'.

Resistance in the 'Other Space': No One is Illegal and its Politics of Discomfort

The heterotopia is not 'freely accessible like a public place. Either the entry is compulsory . . . or else the individual has to submit to rites and purifications. To get in one must have a certain permission and make certain gestures' (Foucault, 1986, p. 26). The heterotopia of undocumentedness, the space among citizens but not as citizen, is both forced upon and chosen. The regime of asylum can often be more daunting than that of irregularity; 'do not appear if you do not want to disappear' (Foucault, 1998 [1978], p. 84). This 'hidden other space' is a site of assumption, as understandings, figures, and assessments vary significantly depending on 'who speaks'. What we do know is that it is a zone of contestation, not of romanticisation, where multiple actors struggle for narrativity.

NOII is one such actor. Founded in 1997 at the 'Dokumenta X' art exhibition in Kassel, this German-based political network comprises anti-racist and no-border groups, trade unions, religious asylum initiatives, as well as individuals with diverse backgrounds. The initiative represents and supports non-resident migrants living in Germany who are at risk of deportation and other threats to their well-being (NOII, 2011). Although the motives, patterns of behaviour, and living conditions of the undocumented vary significantly, common to most is the constant fear of denunciation and blackmail, since discovery would translate into punishment or deportation (Schönwälder et al., 2006, p. 64). Without legal protection, seeking medical care, work, accommodation, or education for themselves or their children become hazardous endeavours. As a result sans-papiers are frequently exposed to exploitation, blackmail, sexual assault, and violence without means to legally or publicly defend themselves.

NOII demands equal enjoyment of all rights and protection *irrespective* of citizenship and required documents. The network calls for access to health care for sans-papiers and sees education as a human right that cannot be withheld. Tasks are manifold, ranging from informing the public about grievances experienced by sans-papiers to directly supporting the persons concerned in their struggle to flee, hide from, or resist pending deportation, or to obtain legal status. Forms of public protests and commemorations of those deported or killed entail sit-ins, 'caravans', art exhibitions, and performances. NOII seeks at times to make their resistance visible and tangible, while at others operating through clandestine channels.

The network is situated in the space in between citizenship and produced irregularisation, and practises contestation that requires permanent self-assessment. Nyers queries: 'Should advocates relate to non-status immigrants as clients or as allies? . . . [W]hat place is there for abject migrants in the politics of their own liberation' (2003, p. 1081)? With these questions in mind NOII's activism can be analysed as a politics of discomfort, situated in the complex, 'heterotopic' context in which both dominating and resisting powers act and sometimes collide. NOII's contestation can be understood to take three main forms that below I elaborate as 'taking initiative', 'breaking the silence', and 'listening'.

First, NOII activism is motivated both by anger that the treatment of human beings *like that* is possible or just in 'our', or any, society and by a sense of responsibility that if dominant sovereign agencies oppress, criminalise, and deport, resistance must be a practical (counter)task. This is not to say that the response always needs to be directly confrontational and visible. NOII exercises dissent while remaining silent so that 'targets'—state authorities in this case—do not recognise dissenting behaviour, at least for the time being. In 'taking initiative' by providing sans-papiers with medical care, shelter, and access to lawyers, the network subverts the logic of sovereignty in disputing the modern state's ability to determine who to include or exclude and directly intervenes through these 'semi-legal' actions in the 'politics of protection' (Ibid., p. 1071). Such dissent is not merely 'negative resistance'—against state policies, policing, racism, and deportation—but also for freedom of movement, hospitality, and solidarity.

Second, in 'breaking silences', NOII openly problematises the state/nation/citizen nexus by bringing protest to spatial expressions of dominating power, such as the airport or detention centre. Deportations of foreigners as moments of 'sovereign (re)founding' not only express who belongs and who does not but represent 'the compulsory allocation of subjects to their proper sovereigns, or, in many instances of statelessness, to other surrogate sovereigns' (Walters, 2010, p. 90). In opposing deportations NOII illustrates the inherent violence in these 'sovereign moments' and practises discomfort by making oppression visible. When deportee Aamir Ageeb died in 1999 at the hands of the German Federal Police while being forcibly deported on board of a Lufthansa aircraft, NOII launched the 'Deportation Class' campaign targeting airlines taking part in the rendition of sans-papiers (No Borders, 2011).[3] In nationwide campaigns and with ties to other European networks, NOII activists protested at airports and Lufthansa's annual shareholders' meeting, through online demonstrations and art exhibitions.

NOII practises discomfort by unsettling 'common-sense' assumptions that the state's 'prerogative' to decide upon matters of inclusion and exclusion is legitimate or inevitable. In directly turning to passengers and asking for their participation, activists speak out for the sans-papiers who is silenced, sedated, or shackled and confront others with the violence and inhumanity inherent in this state act. Not only a transit zone for those on business or holiday, anti-deportation activism recasts the airport as a political and *dis*-comfortable site and demands passengers' individual and collective responsibility. Since its launch, the 'Deportation Class' campaign has repeatedly prevented aircrafts from taking off with deportees on board, forced Lufthansa to publicly explain itself, and succeeded in influencing the German pilot association to re-evaluate its policies. However, these affronts to dominating power can be counteracted. In the case of deportee Ageeb, police officers placed shackles around arms and legs and a helmet on his head and notified crew members of the necessity of such preventive measures since Ageeb had committed rape and three acts of murder—accusations that were later found to be outright lies. Ageeb died by suffocation. In 2004, all police officers charged in his death were released on parole.

As a response to combined public pressure, frequently halted aircrafts, and the visibility of deportees on commercial flights, home secretaries of the 'G5' (France, Germany, Italy, Spain, and England) agreed on a collective deportation strategy. Accordingly, charter flights collect deportees in different European countries before transporting them to their country of origin (No Racism, 2011). Nonetheless, these counter-strategies respond to the creativity of resistance in that subversion obliges dominating power to react, and thus, according to De Genova (2010, p. 59), resistance is always superior:

> The deportation, then, reveals itself to be a feckless and frenetic machinery, its rigid and convulsive movements doomed to always present but a tawdry caricature of the human freedom that always precedes it and ever surpasses it.

The third form of resistance emphasised here, 'listening', revolves around the questions 'who can be political and what place is there for the undocumented to practise resistance themselves'? The concept of citizenship produces an 'authentic identity' in opposition to the 'non-identity' of the sans-papiers who are seen as lacking meaningful agency. In this account sans-papiers need to *become* citizens first to acquire the right to speak and be heard. Until they enter the sovereign realm as foundational subjects, one needs to speak and act *for* them. Thinking about the 'amorphous being' as political agent is *dis*comfortable and questions conventional state–alien or helper–victim dichotomies. NOII activists attempt to resist 'by listening' and by 'enabling themselves to listen.'

For example, Deportation Class (2010) campaigners published a newsletter highlighting the best means for sans-papiers to prevent deportation themselves. NOII advises deportees to remain cooperative until the airplane is boarded due to the likelihood of physical and psychological mistreatment by police forces. Then, when police agents lose jurisdiction, the sans-papiers are encouraged to resist through insisting to speak to the captain, by threatening to bring up charges against crew members, or by gaining passengers' solidarity. In accepting the undocumented as political agents and not passive victims, NOII opens spaces for the sans-papiers to articulate their resistance and for others to listen. Through such 'impossible activism', the sovereign account of where the political must be is called into question (Nyers, 2003, p. 1080). Balibar (in Nyers, 2006, p. 123) notes:

> The sans-papiers, the excluded among the excluded . . . have ceased to simply play the victims in order to become the actors of democratic politics. Through their resistance and their imagination, they powerfully help us give [politics] new life.

Sovereignty's oppressive hierarchy of the superior state/nation/citizen above the faceless sans-papiers becomes exposed and, with it, the violence and conflict *within* the sovereign system. The presence of the undocumented migrant as an agent in her own right disrupts 'administrative routine' that expects unproblematic expulsions of docile non-citizens, highlights sovereign domination, and invites solidarity: 'To say that no human is illegal is to call into question the entire architecture of sovereignty, all its borders, locks and doors, internal hierarchies' (Nyers, 2003, p. 1089).

In practising the slogan 'No One Is Illegal', political activists struggle with others, for others and oneself. Returning, then, to the important questions raised by Nyers, it seems that no clear or unambiguous answers can be found. NOII and its allies follow diverse strategies, consider the sans-papiers as in turns clients, comrades, or friends, speak with and on behalf of them, and most importantly open spaces and possibilities for them to speak. At the same time, questions relating to the broadening and strengthening of the network as well as its self-understanding remain contentious. Repeatedly debated issues include: how can we widen the network so that local communities engage; in what way does 'privilege' allow predominantly white middle-class Europeans to be engaged in such struggle, and at what costs; relatedly, how can we overcome the network's West-European and North-American dominance and biases; and what is the best approach that allows us to listen to migrant struggles without recreating helper-victim power dichotomies?

Heterotopia and Beyond

For Foucault (1986, p. 24), heterotopias have the 'curious property of being in relation with all the other sites, but in such a way as to suspect, neutralize, or invert the set of relations that they happen to designate, mirror or reflect'. The sphere of undocumentedness embodies such a curious property. It has already been shown how this space becomes (ab)used as an ever-present and needed object for moments of sovereign recreation and antagonism. But instead of purely mirroring the space of the citizen-subject, the 'other space' distorts the former, renders 'strange' the common-sense categories of inside and outside, and exposes the grimace of sovereignty and its complex violence and hypocrisy. Resistance questions the portrayal of the state as protector and our socialisation into the logic of sovereignty, stability, and safety. In this sense NOII's resistance is practising discomfort as it localises the source of *dis*-ease in these contradictory manifestations of dominating power and instead of retreating, challenges the 'state-centered ontological resolution' (Rajaram and Grundy-Warr, 2007, p. xii).

While the struggle of the sans-papiers is issue-specific, undocumentedness is connected to a myriad of sites. Hannah Arendt's (in Habermas, 2008, p. 301) prescient prediction that 'stateless persons, refugees, and those deprived of rights' would symbolise our times means that flight, migration, and refuge connect and are a response to complex processes of global ordering. For De Genova (2010, p. 2), the 'deportation regime' and the illegalisation of human mobility represent a global response and 'part of the larger strategy of these states and the incipient planetary regime constituted by their concerted effort to regulate the freedom of movement'. Walters (2010, p. 272) points to the practice of deportation 'as a form of the international police of population', while Mezzadra (2004, p. 272) regards migratory movements as illuminating 'an unspoken genealogy of contemporary processes of globalisation'.

In this sense, the heterotopia of undocumentedness can be seen as situated and local as well as international and global. The resistance discussed here critiques these transversal characteristics of the contemporary global order while not necessarily constituting 'global resistance' as understood in mainstream literatures. NOII's struggle, its network-character, and the diversity of its members render the eagerness to 'give names' inadequate. National and international allies of NOII in the No-Border, anti-racism, or anti-deportation movements, include individuals ranging from anarchists to churchwomen, from doctors to bloggers, each with their own reasons to struggle for and with the sans-papiers.

Attributing commonalities and a coherent worldview, or placing movements into the straitjackets of 'civil society' or 'social movement' is to needlessly restrict the scope of possible action. The struggle of undocumented migrants and their supporters does not necessarily have to find a place in the 'global literatures' or ask for 'a visa from some common regime to establish its validity' (Foucault, 2004 [1976], p. 6). Instead, such contestation always-already constitutes transversal resistance. By introducing a sense of crisis that opens 'spaces within the existing order as a continuous disturbance of 'the political'' (Rossdale, 2010, p. 489), it is a form of subversion that disrupts the sovereign common sense, the normality of oppressive deportations, struggles for new narratives, and gradual transformations in societal values. Such dissent 'starts from where it is at' but cannot be located purely in the domestic, the transnational, or global.

Conclusion

NOII activism as a practical expression of a politics of discomfort enables rearticulations of dominant ontologies of agency towards 'individual responsibility with others for others and oneself.' Instead of creating new totalising accounts, the political is seen as existing in transversal spheres, not merely in citizenship as defined by the state. This is not to say that such a network is to become *the* model for future forms of resistance or is free of (internal) frictions; rather, NOII has been able 'in some places, at some times, in some struggles' (Walker, 1988, p. 146) to demonstrate capacity for creative and alternative politics. Lately, some NOII branches in Germany have become weaker, and others have disappeared altogether.

At the same time, however, NoBorder movements gather momentum and we witness the 'internationalisation' of and greater collaboration between anti-deportation, sanctuary, occupation, NOII, and migrant solidarity movements. Via Internet forums, workshops, no-border camps, and solidarity protests these diverse groups exchange information and practise the slogan 'neither here nor elsewhere'. NOII's tactics of resisting deportations at airports or deportation centres have become widely employed in many other countries. And indeed, undocumented migrants, former detainees, refugees, or denizens form an integral part therein, share their experience, and thereby crucially shape resisting strategies.

Resistance, here, has been shown to exist in 'spaces of potentiality'. In these spaces, state apparatuses as the dominant power attempt to discipline and silence, though never succeed in muting dissent completely. Groups like NOII challenge the state's monopoly to decide who to include and exclude, and who warrants protection, human rights, and dignity. The production of undocumentedness may be seen as 'modern civil death', as the expulsion from state rights and state protection. However, its very creation creates resistances. Non-citizen dissent is not to be romanticised, for it reflects a permanent state of hardship and precarity. And yet, such resistance constitutes an 'excess of life' and of movement, and thereby a continuously creative, troubling, symbolic, and practical confrontation.

Notes

1. Transversal, here, is understood as proposed by Bleiker (2000, p. 7) as the acceptance that contemporary struggles and political dynamics transgress local, national, and international spheres.
2. The term 'illegal im/migration' describes the unlawful crossing of the state border and/or an unauthorised stay in a country. This work proposes the term 'undocumented' or 'sans-papiers' both because the term 'illegality' criminalises and because 'immigration' relates to a one-sided perception of migration. Also, although Squire et al. (2011, p. 4) cautiously employ the notion of 'irregular migration', irregularity is only used here when discussing the state discourse and its production of 'spaces of irregularity'. Other than that, 'undocumented' is preferred as it points to the mere lack of certain documents rather than value-laden images of irregular, thus abnormal, and suspicious beings.
3. Following the 1963 Tokyo Convention, an international treaty regulating offences against penal law while 'in-flight', airline companies are directly responsible for the mistreatment of deportees by either state police forces or the airline's security personnel (UN, 1963).

References

Amoore, L. (2008) Foucault against the grain, *International Political Sociology*, 3(2), pp. 274–276.
Ashley, R. K. & Walker, R. B. J. (1990) Conclusion: reading dissidence/writing the discipline: crisis and the question of sovereignty in international studies, *International Studies Quarterly*, 34(3), pp. 367–416.
Bhabha, H. K. (2000) On minorities: cultural rights, *Radical Philosophy*, 100, pp. 3–6.
Bigo, D., Carrera, S., Guild, E. & Walker, R. B. J. (2007) The changing landscape of European liberty and security, CHALLENGE Project, Research Paper no. 4, February.
Bleiker, R. (2000) *Popular Dissent, Human Agency and Global Politics* (Cambridge: Cambridge University Press).
Budz, M. (2009) A heterotopian analysis of maritime refugee incidents, *International Political Sociology*, 3(1), pp. 18–35.
Castañeda, H. (2010) Deportation deferred: 'illegality', visibility, and recognition in contemporary Germany, in N. De Genova (ed.) *The Deportation Regime* (London: Duke University Press), pp. 245–261.
Cohen, R. & Rai, S. M. (eds) (2000) *Global Social Movements* (London: The Athlone Press).
Coleman, L. M. & Tucker, K. (2011) Between discipline and dissent: situated resistance and global order, *Globalizations*, 8(4), pp. 397–410.
Death, C. (2010) Counter-conducts: a Foucauldian analytics of protest, *Social Movement Studies*, 9(3), pp. 235–251.
Debrix, F. (2009) Nothing to fear but fear: governmentality and the biopolitical production of terror, *International Political Sociology*, 3(4), pp. 398–413.
De Genova, N. (ed.) (2010) *The Deportation Regime* (London: Duke University Press).
Eschle, C. (2005) Constructing 'the anti-globalisation movement', in C. Eschle, & B. Maiguashca (eds) *Critical Theories, International Relations and the Anti-Globalisation Movement* (London: Routledge), pp. 17–35.
Della Porta, D. & Diani, M. (2006) *Social Movements* (Oxford: Blackwell Publishing).
Eschle, C. Constructing 'the anti-globalisation movement', in C. Eschle, & B. Maiguashca (eds) *Critical Theories, International Relations and 'the Anti-Globalisation Movement* (London: Routledge), pp. 17–35.
Falk, R. (1998) Global civil society: perspectives, initiatives, movements, *Oxford Development Studies*, 26(1), pp. 99–110.
Foucault, M. (1982) The subject and power, *Critical Inquiry*, 8(4), pp. 777–795.
Foucault, M. (1986) Of other spaces, *Diacritics*, 16(1), pp. 22–27.

Foucault, M. (1998 [1978]) *The History of Sexuality, An Introduction, Volume I, The Will to Knowledge* (London: Penguin Books).
Foucault, M. (2002) *The Order of Things* (London: Routledge).
Foucault, M. (2004 [1976]) *Society Must be Defended: Lectures at the Collège de France 1975–6* (London: Penguin).
Foucault, M. (2007) *The Politics of Truth* (New York: Semiotext(e)).
Foucault, M. (2009 [1977–1978]) *Security, Territory, Population* (New York: Palgrave Macmillan).
Gill, S. (2000) Toward a postmodern prince? The battle in Seattle as a moment in the new politics of globalisation, *Millennium*, 29(1), pp. 131–140.
Habermas, J. (2008) Citizenship and national identity: some reflections on the future of Europe, in T. Pogge & D. Moellendorf (eds) *Global Justice—Seminal Essays* (St. Paul: Paragon House), pp. 285–310.
Haddad, E. (2007) Danger happens at the border, in P. K. Rajaram & C. Grundy-Warr (eds) *Borderscapes, Hidden Geographies and Politics at Territory's Edge* (Minneapolis: University of Minnesota Press), pp. 119–136.
Kelly, M. G. E. (2009) *The Political Philosophy of Michel Foucault* (London: Routledge).
Meier-Braun, K. H. (2002) *Deutschland, Einwanderungsland* (Berlin: Suhrkamp Verlag).
Mezzadra, S. (2004) The Right to Escape, *Ephemera*, 4(3), pp. 267–275.
Mouffe, C. (2000) *The Democratic Paradox* (London: Verso).
Murray, D. (2010) Democratic insurrection: constructing the common in global resistance, *Millennium*, 39(2), pp. 461–482.
No Borders (2011) http://www.noborder.org/archive/www.deportation-class.com/
No One Is Illegal (2011) http://www.kmii-koeln.de
No Racism (2011) 'Asylum Airways': EU-Sammeldeportationen mit Chartermaschinen, http://www.no-racism.net/article/1320
Nyers, P. (2006) *Rethinking Refugees* (London: Routledge).
Nyers, P. (2003) Abject cosmopolitanism: the politics of protection in the anti-deportation movement, *Third World Quarterly*, 24(6), pp. 1069–1093.
Nyers, P. (2011) Forms of irregular citizenship, in V. Squire (ed) *The Contested Politics of Mobility* (London: Routledge), pp. 184–198.
Paasi, A. (1998) Boundaries as social processes: territoriality in the world of flows, *Geopolitics*, 3(1), pp. 69–88.
Rajaram, P. K. & Grundy-Warr, C. (eds) (2007) *Borderscapes, Hidden Geographies and Politics at Territory's Edge* (Minneapolis: University of Minnesota Press).
Reitan, R. (2007) *Global Activism* (London: Routledge).
Rossdale, C. (2010) Anarchy is what anarchists make of it: reclaiming the concept of agency in IR and security studies, *Millennium*, 39(2), pp. 483–501.
Salter, M. B. (2007) Governmentalities of an airport: heterotopia and confession, *International Political Sociology*, 1(1), pp. 49–66.
Scholte, J. A. (2000) Cautionary reflections on Seattle, *Millennium*, 29(1), pp. 115–121.
Schönwälder, K., Vogel, D. & Sciortino, G. (2006) *Migration and Illegality in Germany* (Berlin: AKI Research Review 1).
Sharp, J. P., Routledge, P., Philo, C. & Paddison, R. (2000) *Entanglements of Power* (London: Routledge).
Soguk, N. (1999) *States and Strangers* (Minneapolis: University of Minnesota Press).
Squire, V. (ed) (2011) *The Contested Politics of Mobility* (New York: Routledge).
Tilly, C. (1999) From interactions to outcomes in social movements, in M. Giugni, D. McAdam & C. Tilly (eds) *How Social Movements Matter* (Minneapolis: University of Minnesota Press), pp. 253–270.
United Nations (1963) Convention on offences and certain other acts committed on board aircraft, Tokyo, http://www.un.org/en/
Vaughan-Williams, N. (2008) Borderwork beyond inside/outside? Frontex, the citizen—detective and the war on terror, *Space and Polity*, 12(1), pp. 63–79.
Walker, R. B. J. (1988) *One World, Many Worlds* (London: Zed Books).
Walker, R. B. J. (1994) Social movements/world politics, *Millennium*, 23(3), pp. 669–700.
Walters, W. (2010) Deportation, expulsion, and the international police of aliens, in N. De Genova (ed.) *The Deportation Regime* (London: Duke University Press), pp. 69–100.

Balkanization of Politics, Politics of Balkanization

ANDREJ GRUBAČIĆ

California Institute of Integral Studies, USA

ABSTRACT *There are two sides of Balkanization: 'Balkanization from above' is a historical project of breaking inter-ethnic solidarity and regional sociocultural identity, violent incorporation into the nation-state system and capitalist world-economy, and more recently, imposing neoliberal colonialism. 'Balkanization from below', on the other hand, stresses social and cultural affinities, customs in common resulting from mutual aid and solidarity and fostering inter-ethnic self-activity—which was largely severed by Euro-colonial intervention. This pluri-cultural reality finds expression in anti-authoritarian politics of local self-government, communal land use, and federative movements. Activists and scholars would do well to recuperate this precious, historical vision of a trans-ethnic, anti-authoritarian society that a Balkan federation would make possible. We must examine the implications of 'Balkanizing' theory and 'Balkanizing' politics if this vision of 'federalism from below', sustained by networks of autonomous and culturally-diverse communities, is to be built—a prospect with significance far beyond the Balkans.*

Introduction

I grew up in Belgrade—or, more precisely, between Belgrade and Sarajevo—but I always considered myself Yugoslav. I do not see any reason to stop doing so now. Yugoslavia might not exist anymore, but Yugoslavia for me, and for people like me, was never just a country—it was an idea. Like the Balkans itself, it was a project of inter-ethnic coexistence, a trans-ethnic and pluri-cultural space of many diverse worlds. The Balkans I know is the Balkans from below: a space of bogoumils—those medieval heretics who fought against Crusades and churches—and a place of anti-Ottoman resistance; a home to haidouks and klephts, pirates and rebels; a refuge of feminists and socialists, of antifascists and partisans; a place of dreamers of all sorts struggling both against provincial 'peninsularity' as well as against occupations, foreign interventions and that process which is now, in a strange inversion of history, often described with that fashionable phrase, 'Balkanization'.

My family was a microcosm of this deeper Balkan reality. My grandparents were socialists, partisans, and antifascists—dreamers who believed in self-management and the Yugoslav 'path to socialism'. This idea—and especially the Yugoslav and Balkan dream of an inter-ethnic, pluri-cultural space—was dramatically dismantled in the 1990s. That was the beginning of my struggle to understand my own identity and the problem of Yugoslav socialism. I went on to look for another path toward what my grandparents understood as communism. It seemed to me that the Marxist-Leninist way of getting 'from here to there'—the project of seizing the power of the state, and functioning through a 'democratically' centralized party-organization—had produced not a free association of free human beings, but a bureaucratized expression of what was still called, by the official ideology of a socialist state, Marxism. Given my distrust of bureaucratic Marxism, I became an anarchist very early on. Anarchism, in my mind, meant taking democracy seriously and organizing prefiguratively—that is, in a way that anticipates the society we are about to create. Instead of taking the power of the state, anarchism is concerned with socializing power—with creating new political and social structures not after the revolution, but in the immediate present, in the shell of the existing order. The basic goal, however, remains the same. Like my grandparents, I too believe in and dream of a region where many worlds fit, and where everything is for everyone.

I survived the violence of the Yugoslav wars and NATO interventions, but in the end it was my political work in Belgrade—in the country that I still refuse to call by any other name but Yugoslavia—that made it difficult for me to stay there. With the kind help of many generous friends, I found refuge in the United States. Although I moved to the United States in 2005, I was already a foreigner well before that moment. I became a foreigner in the early 1990s, when the political ideas of inter-ethnic cooperation and mutual aid as we had known them in Yugoslavia were destroyed by the combined madness of ethno-nationalist hysteria and humanitarian imperialism. Being here, on the other side of the world, away from home and reading news from Yugoslavia—or whatever other name local elites and foreign embassies now use to describe it—was then and remains now equally disconcerting. The new, former state-socialist republics were neoliberalized, privatized, or colonized and caught in an uneasy tension between sclero-nationalism and neoliberalism. A foreigner with papers to prove it, I remain an outsider trying to make sense of what has happened to the idea of the Balkans and to the country I came from. At the same time, I have and continue to find myself to be a Yugoslav, a man without a country but also, as an anarchist, a man without a state.

I feel absolutely no loyalty to Serbian, Croatian, or Bosnian national causes. I have no other emotion but utter contempt for the people who helped destroy Yugoslavia, and I feel the same about the people who are now selling what is left of it. I stand equally distant from the traditionalists and from so-called transitionalists. I believe that the obligations and responsibilities that stand before us (all of us who believe in this deeper conception of the Balkans) are to restore and to revive the idea of Balkan federalism; to infuse it with a new, contemporary meaning; and to fight against the interconnected impositions of Euro-American imperialism and provincial ethno-nationalism. In other words, we must simultaneously and passionately struggle for another, Balkanized Europe and a different, Balkanized world. The future of Europe, should there be one, is in the Balkans, not the other way around.

In this essay I would like to introduce a distinction between two kinds of 'Balkanization'. First one is what I call 'Balkanization from above'. I use this expression to describe a project, remarkably consistent in history, of breaking Balkan inter-ethnic solidarity and regional sociocultural identity; a process of violently incorporating the region into the system of nation-states and capitalist world-economy; and contemporary imposition of neoliberal colonialism.

These imperial and colonial attitudes still define the terms 'civilized world', 'international community', and 'civil society'. Balkan people were never too impressed by civilization. As early as 1871, the founder of the Balkan socialist movement, Svetozar Marković, ridiculed the entire 'civilized world', from the *London Times* to the obedient Serbian press. The civilized world, he wrote, 'was composed of rich Englishmen, Brussels ministers and their deputies (the representatives of the capitalists), the European rulers and their marshals, generals, and other magnates, Viennese bankers and Belgrade journalists' (Marković, 1987, p. 146). Marković was an anti-authoritarian socialist who believed, as do I, in a pluri-cultural Balkan federation organized as a decentralized, directly democratic society based on local agricultural and industrial associations. This is the kind of antinomian imagination that needs to be rediscovered: a horizontalist tradition of the barbarians who never accepted the civilized world that is now collapsing.

The second kind of Balkanization is 'Balkanization from below'. We might describe it as a tradition and narrative that affirms social and cultural affinities, as well as on customs in common resulting from inter-ethnic mutual aid and solidarity, and resulting in what can be termed an inter-ethnic self-activity, one that was severed through Euro-colonial intervention. I maintain that in the Balkans this pluri-cultural reality finds its political expression in the anti-authoritarian politics of local self-government, communal use of land, and various movements for Balkan federation. The latter project included, in its most expansive and most inspiring proposal, all countries of former Yugoslavia, Albania, Bulgaria, Romania, Greece, and Turkey. It is necessary, today more than ever, to stage a lively debate between utopian proposals that dream of the (left) libertarian organization of society, always in thoughtful dialogue with local institutions and traditions.

Balkanization from Above

A decade or so ago, during the European humanitarian adventure in the Balkans, Michael Nicholson (1994, p. 16), an eminent British journalist, wrote in his *Natasha's Story*:

> The ferocity of the Balkan peoples has at times been so primitive that anthropologists have likened them to the Amazon's Yanamamo, one of the world's most savage and primitive tribes. Up until the turn of the present century there were still reports from the Balkans of decapitated enemy heads presented as trophies on silver plates at victory dinners. Nor was it unknown for the winners to eat the loser's heart and liver ...

I was born in a good communist Balkan family where we have never enjoyed such delicacies. Perhaps naively, I suspect that most of my fellow tribesmen have never tasted them either. So, the question emerges: how is it possible that this distinguished British gentleman is able to produce such an appallingly disturbing description?

No less disturbing is, for want of a better term, a sociological analysis offered by another eminent man of letters, Simon Winchester (1999, p. 26), in his *The Fracture Zone: A Return to the Balkans*, where he 'observes':

> Just as the peninsula—these strange and feral Balkans—is outlandish and unlike the rest of Europe, for its inhabitants, the wild peoples of the Balkans, who evolved into something that varies substantially from whatever is the human norm.

Somewhat more recently, on the other side of the ocean, Michael Ignatieff, self-taught political theorist, announces, with quite remarkable honesty, a prospect of 'Nation-building in Bosnia,

Kosovo, and Afghanistan because they are laboratories in which a new imperium is taking shape, in which American military power, European money and humanitarian motive have combined to produce a form of imperial rule for a post-imperial age' (Ignatieff, 2003, p. 32) That is, in these ungovernable barbarian frontier zones of failed states and ethnic conflict, A 'temporary imperialism', in the form of limited occupation, is necessary. 'Bosnia after Dayton offered laboratory conditions in which to experiment with nation-building', he continues, as 'the reconstruction of the Balkans has not been an exercise in humanitarian social work, it has always been an imperial project . . . [because] nation-building is the kind of imperialism you get in a human rights era'. (Ibid.)

I believe that the only way to understand these remarkable attitudes is to situate them in the tradition of Balkanization from above. How do we account for statements like these? This form of Balkanization is, one might say, an invention of European colonial modernity and its Balkanologists. One could even make a little joke and suggest that Euro-American politics in the Balkans was, historically, guided by three B's: Balkanization, barbarity, and bombs. People in the Balkans are barbarians, or so this Euro-imperial line goes, they tend to Balkanize, and the only way to prevent that is to bomb them (or sell them bombs so they can do it themselves).

If we take a historical view, I think that we could identify a phenomenon or, rather, a whole complex of elite reactions, which I propose calling 'political Balkano-phobia': an elite fear of autonomous spaces. Balkanization from above came into existence as an elite response to autonomous processes from below. European colonial modernity arose, in no small part, as a result of successful fights for the formation and territorial unification of a regional identity. The state-architects of Europe of that time were, in fact, obsessed with the demon of the Balkans, Balkanization being taken here in the sense of a 'Balkanization from below', an alternative process of territorial organization, decentralization, territorial autonomy, and federalism. Balkanization from below, a process of constant fission and fusion, was a remarkably threatening alternative for the emerging large, centralized, coercive systems. With the modern invention of Balkanity, Balkanization (from above!) became a name, and an excuse, for a process of eliminating the threat of autonomous political spaces that lack any specialized and permanently constituted, coercive authority separated from society, as well as of eliminating the region's memory of its anti-modern and anti-statist struggles.

I believe that the invention of 'Balkanity' as a political and geo-cultural concept should be located within the historical landscape organized by the 1878 Congress in Berlin. It is my argument that the modern history of the Balkans properly begins in the Berlin Congress—home to 'carve-up of the Balkans', 'the Great Game' in Central Asia, and the 'Scramble for Africa'—after which, as Maria Todorova (1997) suggests, the adjective 'Balkan' ceased to be a vague geographical concept and was transformed into one of the most consistently pejorative epithets in Western political discourse.

It is interesting to note that this is the same period in which Bram Stoker writes his famous Gothic novel, *Dracula*. Here, as Vesna Goldsworthy (1998, p. 12) shrewdly observes, we are introduced to a new and strange world:

> Dracula's world represents everything that is anathema to the Victorians—passion, sex, unrestrained violence. . . . Dracula must not simply be killed but completely destroyed by the united representatives of the West—an Englishman, a Dutchman and an American . . . Their mission to restore order in the Balkans represents a fictional expression of the attempts in the late 19th and 20th centuries by the Western powers to impose peace on the peninsula.

The colonial imagination of Stoker lived on with the queen of mystery novels. In *The Secret of Chimneys*, Agatha Christie depicted a 'Herzoslovakian' peasant, Boris Anchoukoff, with 'high

Slavonic cheekbones, and dreamy fanatic eyes'. He is, we learn, 'a human bloodhound from a race of brigands' (Glenny, 1999, p.13).

The next steps in defining Balkanization from above emerged during The First and Second Balkan Wars of 1912 and 1913, widely believed to offer definitive proof of 'medieval' behavior on the part of Balkan warriors. Reading contemporary documents it is easy to see how the supposed violent nature of the Balkans was used as an alibi for the future interventions of always-benevolent European powers.

However, the crucial moment of development of Balkanization from above was a courageous action by Gavrilo Princip and his comrades in 1914. Misha Glenny (1999, p. 13) quotes John Gunther's popular book *Inside Europe* (1940) which:

> summarized feelings on this side of the Atlantic: 'It is an intolerable affront to human and political nature that these wretched and unhappy little countries in the Balkan peninsula can, and do, have quarrels that cause world wars. Some hundred and fifty thousand young Americans died because of an event in 1914 in a mud-caked primitive village, Sarajevo. Loathsome and almost obscene snarls in Balkan politics, hardly intelligible to a Western reader, are still vital to the peace of Europe, and perhaps the world'.

My contention is that the destruction of state-socialist Yugoslavia was a project of the same century-long process of Balkanization from above. In contrast, Socialist Yugoslavia was a result of a long tradition of movements for Balkan unity, a manifestation of Balkanization from below. After the defeat of real existing socialism, the Yugoslav state, with its indigenous socialism, and its Global South, nonaligned orientation, could no longer be tolerated. Through the historically well-established pattern of imperialist intervention and local collaboration, this typically Balkan experiment has been destroyed in a series of bloody ethnic wars. Europeans and Americans have successfully blocked every peace initiative during the conflict. Balkanophobic racism in 'the civilized world' has diverged into 'paternalistic Balkanism', reserved for the helpless and childlike Bosnians and Kosovars, and 'raw Balkanism', meaning the evil Serbs.

Former Yugoslav republics were immediately transformed into veritable laboratories of 'state-building', 'multiculturalism', 'truth and reconciliation', 'democracy-promotion', and 'economic privatization'. Political choices became restricted to local chauvinist and pro-European options. Alternatives were declared non-patriotic or anti-European. The so-called nongovernmental organizations and other organs of civil society, that monstrous creation of American democracy-promotion, joined hands with nationalists and outright fascist extremists against the pro-Balkan left. The International Tribunal in The Hague was established in order to promulgate and further refine the official (European and American) truth of humanitarian ideology. Intervention on behalf of this ideology ('humanitarian intervention') was wildly popular among Euro-American elites, and has been used as a justification in every imperialist adventure since, from Iraq to Afghanistan to Libya.

It is interesting to note that the term 'Balkans', with its 'race of brigands', was barely used during the Communist period. Four of the countries were subsumed into the phrase 'Eastern Europe' while Greece and Turkey were 'Nato's southern flank'. It is no accident that when Yugoslavia collapsed in 1991, the term Balkans came back. At the same time as the 'savage Balkans' was reintroduced, the propaganda myth of the artificiality of the now former Yugoslavia, and its 'dark Balkan origins', emerged from the woodwork of metropolitan academia.

Today, in this new era of integration, the Balkans, former Yugoslavia, and Balkanization are presented and projected to the world opinion as nothing but the historical residue of 'primitive nationalisms', which once again pose a threat to delirious European bureaucratization—just like in the era of the Berlin Congress—at its core. The EU is unsettled by the prospect of a politically rebellious region, inside of, and against, imperial agglomeration.

It would be possible to make an argument that both the late nineteenth century Europe and the neoliberal bureaucratic Europe were built against and in opposition to the Balkans. There is a historical continuity between Berlin and Lisbon. The road to both leads through the Balkans and, most crucially, through the former Yugoslavia and its mud-caked village of Sarajevo, today once again under occupation of the ever watchful 'international community'.

Balkanization from Below

I have already described Balkanization from below as a narrative that insists on social and cultural affinities, as well as on customs in common resulting from inter-ethnic mutual aid and solidarity, and resulting in what can be termed an inter-ethnic self-activity, one that was severed through Euro-colonial intervention. In the Balkans, this many-headed hydra has its own political program and vision. The name for this vision is Balkan federation. There are two principal manifestations of this program, one that I will call federalism from above, based on the idea of federated socialist states, and another that rests on a horizontalist principle that I will call federalism from below.

One of the first expressions of Balkan federalism is the Democratic Eastern Federation. Founded in 1865, it is a syncretic mix of democratic, socialist, and national ideas. From that moment onward, the history of Balkan federalism diverges. One line of development will lead to the established political and cultural elites of the Balkan states who were always receptive to the ideas of federalism. Conservative and liberal politicians, even kings (like Otto of Greece and Milan Obrenović of Serbia), briefly and randomly presented themselves as supporters of some kind of federalism. Likewise, federalism from above is expressed in the politics of communist parties. Almost all communist parties before the war had a Balkan federation (a federation of socialist states) as a part of, or even a centerpiece of, their respective programs. In this vein, the most important federalist efforts can be found in the Balkan Conferences of the interwar period, and in Tito's federalist plans right after World War II.

There is another, far more interesting line to follow in the development of Balkan federalism. It is also well known that many anarchists took part in the revolts of Bosnia-Herzegovina and of Bulgaria (1875–78). Malatesta was not successful in his attempt to enter Bosnia, but his comrade Stepniak was and he left us an important testimony about the struggle against the Ottomans. Moreover, socialists participated in the movement for Macedonian autonomy (Boatmen, Revolutionary Macedonian Organization), as well as in the anti-Ottoman revolts in Crete, even the interstate Greco-Turkish war in 1897. Some of the anti-authoritarian socialists, like Svetozar Marković or Botev, supported a Balkan federation built from below, a stateless federation that would establish itself as the result of social revolution and not interstate arrangements and would be based on the confederationist organizing of traditional Southern Slavic agrarian communities.

It is crucial today to return to the ideas of Svetozar Marković, our Balkan Mariátegui. According to Marković, local conditions will determine the nature of new society that the working class will establish in each country. The problem of bread, he wrote, is a problem of direct democracy. It is hard not to see the similarity between Marković's eclectic, ethical socialism—which he defined not as a new economic system, but a new way of life—and proposals arriving from contemporary peasant movements gathered around Via Campesina. In a dialogue with anarchism and Marxism, he sought a *Balkanized socialism* based upon communal institutions and instincts rather than inexorable historical laws. He argued for socialist movements that are not only anti-colonial with respect to the West and the East, but also revolutionary with respect to the Balkan past. His Balkanized socialism was ethical and visionary, eclectic and humane, and on all accounts unacceptable to his state-socialist critics who dismissed him as 'utopian socialist'. His aim, he wrote in 1874, was internal social reorganization on the basis of sovereignty and communal self-government, and federation in the Balkan Peninsula. Herein, in his federalist plans, lies what is perhaps his greatest contribution: his feverish attempt to subdue the separate nationalisms of the Balkan peoples in favor of an all-inclusive, directly democratic federalism. This anti-authoritarian eclecticism is itself a most precious feature of Balkan societies and their revolutionary tradition. The ability to connect local and global, subaltern and modern, is what I advocate under the name of Balkanization of politics.

Svetozar Marković died at the age of 28. His death was a result of years spent in exile and prisons of the Serbian state. One of his last acts before his death was to help found the first school for women in Serbia. He was buried on 16 March 1875, in the presence of thousands of peasants, some of who shouted at the police sent to maintain order to remove their hats in the presence of the saint. Many decades after the death of Svetozar Marković, on 15 July 1924, a new publication, *La Federation Balkanique*, appeared. This was a fortnightly periodical published in Vienna in all the Balkan languages as well as in German and French. In a spirited editorial the program of this publication was defined as follows:

> The principal task of our publication as its title has already shown, is to propagate the idea of liberation and the right of self-determination of the Balkan people as well as that of federalization . . . We wish that they may cease to be the common prey of European imperialism and Balkan chauvinism: that they may cease to be the arena where the latter settle their disastrous internal quarrels . . . The working masses will finally be eager to unite its forces into a single Balkan front directed against chauvinism and conquering Imperialism from whatever quarter they may come. We want liberty and peace for our countries and our peoples! We know also that this liberty and this peace are not graciously granted but must be conquered by a desperate struggle! And we are beginning this struggle! (Stavrianos, 1964, p. 132)

This is the struggle and the principle that a new generation of Balkan revolutionaries must begin anew, with the same passion, but in a contemporary context, with new organizational forms, new political sensibility, and new language. After the horrors of bureaucratic socialism, after many episodes of ethno-nationalist violence, in the ruins of Eurocentered neoliberalism, I believe it is crucial that we revive horizontal federalism in the form of a Balkan federation: with no state, and beyond all nations. We stand in a long and magnificent tradition.

Before I am accused of painting too rosy of a picture, let me just say a few words about another painful dichotomy inscribed in the history of the peninsula, the one between nationalism and regional inter-ethnic self-activity. The history of the Balkans is obviously not only a history of inter-ethnic cooperation. It is also a bloody history of nationalist atrocities that we are responsible for, that are self-inflicted. Not more then anywhere else in Europe, perhaps, and not without encouragement from outside, but nevertheless very real. The authoritarian left in the Balkans, with its stubborn insistence on 'national sovereignty' and support for the nation-state form as a necessary stage in social liberation, played a negative role in defining a position on nationalism. I would not like to be misunderstood here. When I say that I advocate regionalism and pluri-culturalism, or that I criticize a Jacobin model of a mono-cultural state, I do not mean to say that we can evade the violent aspects of our brutal nationalist past. We have to confront in the same breath the terror visited upon us by Euro-colonial violence and our own self-inflicted brutalities. For the past to become a principle of action in the present we have to stop living in the past and instead integrate it into the present in an emancipatory way. In order to build a pluri-cultural Balkans the present has to be liberated from the past.

It should be clear that I am not advocating an erasure of the past, but a work of remembrance as part of the work of freedom. This cannot be done by embracing any form of particularism, ethnic or regional. Following Achile Mbembe (2001), I would like to borrow a term for this always incomplete project, riddled with tensions and contradictions, which both embraces and transcends the question of specificity, and call it *Balkanopolitanism*—a way of being from the Balkans articulated through an openness to difference and a transcendence of nationalism. Balkanopolitanism, as a regional project actively seeking out new experiences and rejecting 'the confines of bounded communities and their own cultural backgrounds' (Ibid.), would transcend Balkan nationalisms through curiosity for the foreign and an openness to hybridity. If Arturo Escobar (2008) is right when he suggests that being place-based is not the same as being place-bound, then Balkanopolitanism would be a precious gift to the project of global universalism, where, in the words of Léopold Sédar Senghor, the world becomes a meeting place of giving and receiving (*rendez-vous du donner et du recevoir*).

But how can a national issue be dealt with in a more programmatic sense? I believe that nationalism can only be answered within a regional framework, and I believe that the Balkans can provide a model for another Europe, a Balkanized Europe of regions, as an alternative to both a transnational European super-state and nation-states. A Balkanization of Europe would be premised on the politics of autonomous regions and a plurality of cultures. I see the region—an entity once eroded by the centralized nation-state and capitalism—as the basis for the regeneration and reconstruction of the social and political life of Europe.

I think that new Balkan revolutionaries should embrace and defend the project of a contemporary Balkan federation as one of radical decolonization, pluri-culturality, social change from the bottom-up, analogous to, and in active communication with such contemporary projects as the pluri-nationalist politics of the indigenous people of the Andean Federation, Anarchists against the Wall in the Middle East, or grassroots movements from Africa who chant that 'we are the poors'.

This Balkans, neither capitalist nor bureaucratic-socialistic, would be a trans-ethnic society with a Balkanopolitan, pluri-culturalist outlook. An outlook which previously existed but was lost in its incorporation into nation-state frameworks; an outlook that recognizes multiple and overlapping identities and affiliations characterized by proliferation and multiplicity; an outlook that recognizes the unity produced out of difference. This would be a Balkans based on voluntary cooperation and mutual aid, direct democracy of neighborhood assemblies and city federations, free associations that extend themselves and cover every branch of human activity, with a self-managed economy with participatory planning, structured within the regional frame of a state-dissolving federation.

To build such a world we would need a new type of politics from below. It should be clear that by politics I mean an organic, dialogical, shared, and participatory activity of the self-governing public, and not a statecraft, a set of operations that are premised on the seizing of state power and which are realized through a political party, nor any political movement that replicates the state in its organization. I am talking about an anti-authoritarian politics that is utopian, in the sense that it celebrates political imagination and attempts to bring into being other possibilities for human existence, one that conquers a point of view beyond the given, and refuses the rationalization of the real, the rationalization of the imposed colonial and state-national alternatives. I am talking about a new, restored politics of mutual aid, mutual solidarity, pluri-cultural identity, and freedom.

Moving from the Balkans of nationalism and exploitation to the (federated) Balkans of solidarity and struggle is possible only in the context of inter-ethnic accompaniment and concrete struggles that prefigure a 'no-state solution' of regional federalism. The Freedom Fight movement in Serbia, anti-authoritarian movements and migrant groups like Clandestina in Greece, and Bulgarian anarchist federations are some important cases in point. But we need many more.

We, 'the revolutionaries of the future', need to go back to, and build upon, what is the most precious part of our history, and that is a pluri-cultural vision of multi-ethnic, indeed trans-ethnic, anti-authoritarian society. We need to understand the scandal borne by the word 'Balkans' and rediscover the trenchancy of its idea. The kind of society we are talking about is possible only within the framework of a Balkan federation, with no state, and beyond nation: a world where many worlds fit. If this is not our reality today, it follows that our duty, our only duty, is to fight to make it our reality tomorrow.

Balkanizing Theory

What are the implications of Balkanization from below for theoretical work? What I termed 'invention of Balkanity' lies at the very heart of European universalism. The modern/capitalist European universalist project included, as its 'other side', the invention of the Balkans. This Balkans was discovered as a symbol of everything mysterious and threatening in European culture. The Balkans became a 'wild Europe', an entangling, intricate labyrinth inhabited by creatures of sin and insolent nations, incapable of governing themselves: a place in the heart of European darkness. A place outside, if on the doorstep, where people need to be evangelized in the name of civilizing missions, human rights, and civil society. This is the Balkans as a black hole in world history, an endless reservoir of violence and negativity, a chaotic gap in world time. This cultural element cannot be overstated.

In recent years, a group of progressive and radical Balkanologists initiated a serious theoretical attempt to correct the epistemological centrism of European scholarship. Milica Bakić-Hayden (1995), drawing from Edward Said's conceptual world of Orientalism and situating the Balkans in this category of historical explanation, introduced a new heuristic of 'nesting orientalism' as a variation on the Orientalist theme. Further, Maria Todorova (1997) has recognized different traits in the constructed identity of the Balkans, not 'merely as a subspecies of orientalism', but as a 'specific rhetorical paradigm'. There is an independent trajectory in defining the hegemonic representation of the peninsula, which she terms 'Balkanism'. Even more perceptively, Tamara Vukov, in a still unpublished paper, adds to this debate with her useful analysis of 'neo-Balkanism', in which she locates the Balkans within the historical reality of global capitalism.

While welcoming this epistemic change of perspective, and acknowledging the value of the aforementioned research, my inclination is to relate the particular historical time/space of the Balkans to the processes of global capitalist coloniality that Anibal Quijano (2001) describes as 'coloniality of power'. Coloniality of power, according to Quijano, presupposes a new model of global power, an inauguration of the first modern/colonial/capitalist world-system, which was structured around a notion of race. While it might be possible to understand the history of European interpretative violence inflicted upon 'European Turkey' as one of 'nesting orientalisms', it seems to me impossible to understand the history of the Balkans, after its invention in the wake of the Berlin Congress, outside of the new global hegemonic model and technology of power. In place since the Conquest of the Americas, the model articulates race and labor, space, and peoples, according to the needs of capital and for the benefit of European peoples.

It is important, in my view, to take into more serious consideration Enrique Dussel's (1995, p. 111) distinction between 'two modernities': one that is 'Eurocentric, provincial, and regional', and the other that is world-oriented and includes the 'other side', that which was dominated, exploited, and concealed. Dussel insists that we need to deny the innocence of modernity, because it is only then possible to 'discover' the hidden 'other side' of modernity: the peripheral colonial world, the indigenous peoples, the enslaved black, the oppressed woman, the other Balkans: the victims of modernity, all of them subjected to an irrational act that contradicts modernity's ideal of rationality. Dussel calls this 'transmodernity', understood as a world-wide ethical liberation project in which alterity, which was part and parcel of modernity, would be able to fulfill itself (1995, p.124) The alterity and 'exteriority' of the Balkans, and its 'white but not quite' inhabitants, should not be thought about as a pure outside, untouched by the modern. It refers to an outside that is precisely constituted as difference by hegemonic processes.

I hope that all these approaches can help introduce a fresh conceptual framework for the understanding of recent and not so recent historical intertwining of 'Balkanist' and nationalist discourses. In order to change the Balkans, we need to start thinking otherwise about and from the Balkans. Here I would like to suggest that such an understanding requires its own collective and emancipatory research project, a project of thinking otherwise from the interior exteriority of the border, and that might be called 'Balkanology from below'. This emancipatory research program would contribute to developing, from this side of 'the other side of modernity', the very possibility of talking about 'worlds and knowledges otherwise'.

Radical Balkanologists, organized in such a community of argumentation, could benefit greatly from the intellectual work of the so-called modernity/coloniality group, represented by Quijano, Escobar, Dussel, Mignolo, and other activist scholars. It would be an unfortunate mistake to see the impressive work of this group as solely a paradigm for Latin America, rather than as an other way of thinking that runs counter to the great modernist narratives, or as an 'other paradigm' useful for situating the (hidden) Balkans. At the same time, in unlocking the radical potential for thinking from difference and towards the constitution of alternative local and regional worlds, and taking seriously the epistemic force of local histories and thinking theory through from the political praxis of subaltern groups, radical Balkanologists would do well to follow in the steps of Peter Linebaugh and Marcus Rediker (2000) and other historians from below who have been adventuring for traces of the 'many-headed hydra' of rebels and revolutionaries, and hidden stories of popular struggles across the proletarian Atlantic. The beautiful, dazzling history of anti-authoritarian Balkans is replete with exciting struggles and utopian political perspectives. This project, of Balkanology from below, could be imagined as a uni-disciplinary (Wallerstein, 1996) or un-disciplinary (Escobar, 2008) program, with members coming from many different fields, un-disciplining the disciplines, and establishing a single field of study. This might help us learn how to free our past and our future from 'the Eurocentric mirror where our image is always, necessarily, distorted' (Quijano, 2001, p. 580).

References

Bakić-Hayden, M. (1995) Nesting orientalisms: the case of former Yugoslavia, *Slavic Review*, 54(4), pp. 917–931.
Dussel, E. (1995) *The Invention of the Americas* (New York: Continuum).
Glenny, M. (1999) Only in the Balkans, *London Review of Books*, 21(9), pp. 12–14.
Goldsworthy, V. (1998) *Inventing Ruritania: The Imperialism of the Imagination* (New Haven, CT: Yale University Press).
Ignatieff, M. (2003) *Empire Lite: Nation Building in Bosnia, Kosovo, Afghanistan* (London: Vintage).

Linebaugh, P. & Rediker, M. (2000) *The Many-Headed Hydra: Sailors, Slaves, Commoners, and the Hidden History of the Revolutionary Atlantic* (Boston: Beacon Press).
Marković, S. (1987) *Celokupna Dela* (Beograd: Narodna Knjiga).
Mbembe, A. (2001) *On the Postcolony* (Berkeley: University of California Press).
Nicholson, M. (1994) *Natasha's Story* (London: Pan).
Quijano, A. (2000) Coloniality of power, ethnocentrism, and Latin America, *Nepantla*, 1(3), pp. 533–580.
Stavrianos, S. L. (1964) *Balkan Federation: A History of the Movement Toward Balkan Unity in Modern Times* (Hamden, CT: Archon Books).
Todorova, M. (1997) *Imagining the Balkans* (Oxford: Oxford University Press).
Wallerstein, I. (ed.) (1996) *Open the Social Sciences* (Palo Alto, CA: Stanford University Press).
Winchester, S. (1999) *The Fracture Zone: A Return to the Balkans* (London: Viking).

The Living and Being of the Streets: Fanon and the Arab Uprisings

ANNA M. AGATHANGELOU

York University, Toronto, Canada

ABSTRACT *The North Africa and Middle East (MENA) insurrections point to the transformative potential of the convergence between massive numbers of unemployed young people and modern communication networks in response to the 2008 global financial crisis and the failed 'War on Terror'. Yet theorists have wondered about the timing and significance of these revolutions, along with their relationship with social rebellions in other times and places. This work stages a conversation with Frantz Fanon about the spacing of temporality of revolutions, focusing on his understanding of the anti-colonial revolution and the significance of the least sovereign (and potentially most revolutionary) subjects in the decolonization and anti-slavery struggles. I then engage with the MENA revolts and uprisings arguing that they are revolutionary advances toward a socialism that is able to check the snatching of land and slaughtering of others for development.*

Since the beginning of the Middle East and North African (MENA) insurrections—combining the latent force of massive numbers of unemployed young people with the dynamism of modern communication networks following the 2008 global financial crisis and the failed 'War on Terror'—theorists have wondered about the meaning of these revolutions. Are they revolutions, uprisings, or revolts (Coombs, 2011)?[1] The outcomes of these debates help us understand the current crises of power and shifts in world politics. While the MENA revolts depend on new technologies and express decentralized forms of organization, echoing the *worldwide anti-globalization movements*, their form and scale in the context of normative and terror acts is unprecedented. Multiple groups in the MENA region took to the streets, using contemporary social, technological, and social forms (i.e. new social media technologies, songs, poetry) and their own bodies to spark leaderless rebellions against the global empire of capital. Through such actions, the young revolutionaries constituted the 'street' as a new global space of contestation, reaching beyond their geographical and issue-based boundaries to link with others questioning spatialities of power and neoliberal logics of segregation, and confronting key postcolonial predicaments.

But what are the key lessons from these insurrections in the region and worldwide? Can the 'spontaneous' and diverse crowds organize themselves into a broader revolutionary movement that can dirempt the dominant structures of neoliberalism? Can this diverse mass open a new the question of anti-colonization and freedom and engage in decolonization to disrupt the neocolonial segregations of imperial 'reformers' without permitting the Orientalist fantasies and racial fetishisms of the region to violently reassert themselves?

To answer these questions I engage the MENA uprisings directly. I argue that these movements emerged by responding to and contesting neoliberalism and its devastating impact on MENA societies, economies and polities. For the past two decades, neoliberal logics have compounded the system of power imbalance in colonial/slave ways in which foreign interests are served through a small native elite that also benefits at the expense of the majority. These uprisings can also be read as the anti-colonization struggles continue (with national liberation struggles having remained 'incomplete', where global power reasserted itself at the expense of the majority). These *acts of* decolonization and anti-slavery not only question the familiar institutions of neoliberal markets and sovereign states and their leadership, their arrival also points to a disruption of the familiar political. These acts also draw on multiple methods to challenge those leaders who have despotically ruled them.

I therefore stage a conversation with Frantz Fanon who provides us with clues on how to read neoliberalism and its spaces through his extensive engagement of how the colonial dominant strategy was the zoning and segregating of the world in order to govern it. For Fanon the colonized spaces were 'storm zones' of repeated revolts pregnant with revolutionary advances toward a socialism that does not depend on snatching of land and slaughtering of the black and the colonized for development. Second, engaging with Fanon allows us to understand the key postcolonial predicaments such as the leadership of revolution as well as the national bourgeoisie including the presence of class structures today. For Fanon, the *national bourgeoisie* was problematic from the beginning and hence, his privileging instead of the *national liberation movement* with its focus on the coming into being of the *wretched*. This unseating of the bourgeois and national in favor of the wretched and liberation puts into crisis all the inherited diremptions of civil society, the socio-pathological colonial/authoritarian state, and perhaps, even dislocates the idea of freedom. For Fanon the wretched precipitates a foundational crisis in the colony due to their incommensurability with the field of onto-political thought.

This conversation with Fanon foregrounds the second section of the essay about the contribution of the MENA revolts: namely, their insights into the history of revolutionary movements and the methods they employ to reach beyond their geographical and issue-based boundaries to link with others in struggle. I argue that these revolts broaden the idea of revolution and social movements by not only striving to achieve certain social, political, and economic goals, but also by coinciding with the commencement of new modalities of intervening in global processes of *spatiality*, *segregation* and *corporeality*. I conclude with critical praxical insights, noting that these revolutionary moments have multiple trajectories intertwined with multiple structural organizations[3] that may converge and diverge from other movements. These insights highlight the idea that alter forms of life that open new ethical and political questions about freedom exist and point to their endurance including the existence of ontologies of revolt/revolution as process. In this they also produce and articulate new 'modes of existence' and new subjectivities that reach beyond the region.

Revolutionary Movements in the Twenty-first Century: In Conversation with Fanon

In *The Wretched of the Earth* Fanon gives clues to understanding revolution and the tensions within colonial spaces. He shifts the conversation from the colonizer to the colonized by challenging three main premises. First, for any act to be considered radical and revolutionary, it must accept Western progress as its originating source and invest it with an ontological primacy. Second, the possibility of successful revolutions requires a national bourgeoisie with close ties to neocolonial and imperial dominant powers. Third, colonial practice and ideas provide Western states and their constituencies with the authority to determine the extent of successful revolutions and thus to define the form of intervention required. Instead of accepting these premises, Fanon pushes us to recognize that revolution and its related practices are simultaneously ontological, epistemological, and ethical and must be fought on all three registers.

As Fanon's work was forged in the fire of North African revolution and decolonization, now is an opportune time to engage it anew. He provides clues on how to read neoliberalism, space, and bodies, and theorizes extensively revolution. For example, his focus on segregation/zoning of rich and poor, black and white, men and women allows us to link the concept of spatiality to the current segregation and zoning of the world (rural and urban, rich and poor, black and white, etc.). In addition, his idea that a *solidarity* that permanently disrupts the social pathologies of the neocolonial/authoritarian state can be achieved through *combat* constitutes the colonial subject as a revolutionary of daily practice and way of being. His critique also reorients our vision to the consideration of corporeality as the locus of revolutionary politics and subjectivity. Finally, Fanon's critique of the national bourgeoisie as opposed to the national liberation movement pushes us to think anew the central role of and the arrival of the colonial subject. Was sovereignty and its contingent sovereign subject ever an efficacious response to a world saturated with imperial power and constituted through violence?[4]

Attuned to the vast, decolonizing movements around him, Fanon expressed his understanding of the need to disrupt imperial and colonial expropriation. His direct involvement in and reflections on the African revolution and Pan-African movements, along with his membership in the Algerian delegation to and speeches at the 1958 All-African People's Congress in Accra, make him a paramount theorist of a revolution that decolonizes and de-slaves spaces and bodies simultaneously.

Fanon writes that decolonization begins with recognizing the spatiality of three registers simultaneously, psyche, body, and the earth; the colonial power works through all three through *segregation*. This does not mean that the three cannot analytically be understood separately; rather, their relationship is porous and, hence, productive of power. Decolonization and anti-slavery struggles have to begin with this understanding. In *The Wretched of the Earth*, Fanon (1967 [1961], p. 3) claims the colonized world can be most clearly understood by 'penetrating its geographical configuration'. Fanon complicates this by arguing that the colonization of the land results in the colonization of the psyche and the body (Ibid., p. 44): 'the arrival of the white man in Madagascar shattered not only [the colonized] horizons but its psychological mechanisms' (Ibid., p. 67). For Fanon, the snatching of bodies out of their land (and enslaving them) entails an existential slaughtering (see Agathangelou, 2011; Mbembe, 2001). While Fanon recognizes that the colonized's geographical, psychic, and physical space has been colonized through theft and segregation, he argues that decolonization requires a 'revolution' which itself 'is about territory: political, economic, geographic, ideological, and cultural' (Fanon, 1967 [1961], p. 104). This anti-colonial revolution brings into being the wretched and the earth anew. Fanon speaks of the logic of 'tabula rasa which characterizes at the outset all decolonization' (Ibid., pp. 124–5). For him, this logic makes possible a new understanding about the fatefulness of colonial law and sovereignty which becomes challenged by the mere existence of the wretched, embodying a generalized impropriety.

For Fanon, merely making social, political, and institutional changes cannot solve colonization and slavery, as they constitute and are constituted by the psychic and bodily schema of the subject, which are in a dynamic relation with the environment and its constitution. While he recognizes that slavery and colonization destroy the corporeal schema of the colonized and the material schema of the earth, what we understand and what earth is, through such techniques as zoning and segregation, he argues that decolonization begins by creating places within which the *black* and *colonial* man can articulate his vision and act accordingly. To challenge colonialism is to usurp its 'coercive structuring of space as the defining reality of social domination, indeed of social being' (Sekyi-Out, 1996, p. 76).

Colonization divides the world into two, the colonized zones and the European zones: 'what divides this world is first and foremost what species, what race one belongs to' (Fanon, 1967 [1961], p. 5). Fanon reminds us that racism is not merely a superstructural effect of a determinant economic base; it is also an organizing principle of society. But for Fanon, class, sexuality, and race are co-constituted as opposed to being causally related: none predetermines or is a consequence of the others. He argues this in both *Black Skin, White Masks* (1967 [1952]) and *The Wretched of the Earth* (1967 [1961]). Any international order, he tells us, is simultaneously a racial and an economic order. The borders within colonized regions, argues Fanon, segregate the wealthy from the poor and produce clearly demarcated racial formations. The colonized sector is a world of 'white folks', a world whose 'belly is permanently full of good things' (Fanon, 1967 [1961], p. 4). On the other side of this zone is a 'sector of niggers, a sector of towelheads' that is 'hungry for bread, meat, shoes, coal, and light' (Ibid., pp. 4–5). Thus, racial asymmetry is realized corporeally, territorially (i.e. the environment), and economically, not just conceptualized as a variable of the economy (Fanon, 1967 [1952]).

This world spatially orders first, beings based on flesh, and, in turn, this spatial order becomes constitutive of colonized subjects. The subject turned flesh 'is a man tucked away' (Fanon, 1967 [1952], p. 15), trapped in the cramped 'native quarters' (p. 4). He finds himself dreaming of 'jumping, swimming, running, and climbing' (p. 15) outside this colonial zone. Fanon's analysis engages with the physicality and spatiality of colonial power relations; for him, land is a *living relation with other living and non-living material entities*, not just an abstract value of equality or freedom. The colonial subject knows that the 'most essential value' is access to land as it may 'provide bread,' life, and the dignity of life, that is, of not being 'arrested, beaten, and starved' (p. 9). But space is never neutral; movement across zones is either controlled or facilitated depending upon the power relations that trigger it.[5]

Fanon disrupts dominant understandings in psychoanalysis and phenomenology (i.e. Freud, Lacan, Merleau-Ponty, Sartre) of space and bodies.[6] He foregrounds an intertwined relation among earth, bodies, and space and argues against space as a container within which bodies or other objects circulate. For Fanon, earth, bodies, and place become constituted in relation to each other. Such recognition requires a focus on how we understand the constitution of space and racial bodies and how those material entities become the raw material of racial fetishisms and toward the constitution of the slave as flesh and the colonized as a kind of a subject. Fanon explains: 'A slow composition of myself as a body in the middle of a spatial and temporal world—such seems to be the [bodily] schema. It does not impose itself upon me; it is, rather, [a] definitive structuring of the self and of the world—definitive because it creates a real dialectic between my body and the world' (Fanon, 1967 [1952], p. 112). This 'dialectic' composes the socially situated, corporeal self that makes Fanon.

These elements and the movements that constitute the earth and the bodily schemas, for Fanon, are grounded in a colonial and white geo-power whose interest is to 'rewrite the geographies of national stratified space with new bioregional economic maps knitted into global ecologies—complete with ... zones of 'dying forests', 'regional desertification', ... 'depleted farmland' (Luke, 1999, p. 140). For Fanon, the situation in which he finds himself (as our situation today) is racist and requires a complex understanding of the formation of the world and bodily schema:

> Below the corporeal schema I had sketched a historico-racial schema. The elements that I used had been provided for me not by 'residual sensations and perceptions primarily of a tactile vestibular, kinesthetic, and visual character,' but by the other, the white man, who had woven me out of a thousand details, anecdotes, and stories. I thought that I what I had in hand was to construct a physiological self, to balance space, to localize sensations, and here I was called on for more. (Fanon, 1967 [1952], p. 111)

Fanon's conceptualization of co-constitutional dimensions provides a useful starting point for theorists to take seriously the widening disparities between and within geographical zones, nation-states, and subjects (i.e. as bodies and as flesh).[7] In the contemporary moment, the systems of power that produced colonial formations have reformulated; hiding behind the promises of neoliberalism, they are producing anew an uneven and unequal world. Globalization theories, however, have failed to consider these processes with what I call a *geo-colonial-racial locus of political focus*. Paying attention to the geo-slavery-racialization of economic formations creates space for *anti-geo-slave-colonial* struggles. Equality based on a monolithic dimension of power produces ineffective social change, for economic inequality will continue to manifest itself through geo-slave, colonial, and racial inequality. In short, while theorizing the relation of race, flesh, bodies, land, and space is necessary for theorizing world movements today, it is not enough to incorporate them. Rather, we must think them through anew.

The task of the colonist is to replace indigenous histories and cultures with newly constructed spatial-geo-slave, colonial, and racial ideologies. In *Black Skin, White Masks* (1967) [1961], Fanon explains how this task is realized. The racial domination of the colonies is legitimated through propaganda (p. 69) and religious institutions that equate darkness with evil and inhumanity (pp. 6–7), thereby instilling 'a mood of submission' in subjugated peoples. Gradually, these mechanisms of domination become embedded in a variety of institutions operating to mediate the polarized geo-slave, colonial, and racialized economic systems of colonial worlds. Most importantly, racial significations are internalized in the psyches, the structures of society, and its land through language.[8] For Fanon, this movement to the white world constitutes a transformation of being, a new ontology. He argues that movement across the land and traversing the borders of its multiple life-worlds has the effect of uprooting one from one's former physical space and leads to psychic changes, an 'absolute mutation' (p. 19) and a 'new way of being' (p. 25). A black man becomes whiter if he moves to 'white' land (i.e. France), using the language of the white man and inhabits this other world (p. 38).[9]

Hence, for Fanon any revolutionary project has to account for this simultaneous violence and reconstitution, as well as the spatiality of situation. As the positionality of different people (i.e. white, black, Algerian)[10] is seen differently by various historico-racial schemas, the effect on their corporeal schemas also differs. Instead of having a lived body, black and other non-white persons are snatched out of their land and their communities and become aware of their bodies as objects. But 'it is no longer a question of being aware of [one's] body' (Fanon, 1967 [1952], p. 112). Rather, the black and colonized man functions to grant perspective to the white man as he transforms the body into will and reason, into Western epistemology and Western ontology: 'The White man had the anguished feeling that I was escaping from him and that I was taking something with me . . . [I]t was obvious that I had a secret' (Ibid., p. 128). Fanon highlights place and movement simultaneously; the segregation and snatching of bodies from their land (through slavery and colonization) requires the prioritization of the temporal over the spatial. Fanon exposes this logic and pushes us to engage with the 'catch-up' required by the insertion of a model that locates whites in modernity and consigns some to the *primitive* and others to the undeveloped. Place becomes significant beyond an understanding of a geographical point with regards to organizing and engaging in revolutionary work. Fanon's insistence on the relationship of space, subject formation, and the corporeal points to how colonialism works: it snatches, it segregates, it displaces and it slaughters.

Fanon's writings analyze the Algerian situation in both the national and international realm. *The Wretched of the Earth* situates the events in Algeria within an extensive discussion of liberation movements across the world. In this work, Fanon disrupts dominant understandings of the global, political sociality, and the sovereign agent of world revolutions by complicating the condition of the 'colonized'. Although the colonized live in the same physical space, he says, they are divided on many fronts and have 'little reason to think of themselves as sharing a political identity or as belonging to one nation with a potentially sovereign will' (Gordon, 2011, p. 41). The first instruction given to those under colonial rule is to stay where they are and not to cross the boundaries. No wonder aggressive feelings develop, or that these aggressions seek an outlet.

Arguing with and against Marx, Fanon (1961, p. 61) notes that the proletariat in the colonial countries is not the suppressed mass of poor industrial workers, but poor peasants. If one sets Fanon's arguments in the context of the current revolutions, his ideas resonate, pushing toward a nuanced understanding of violence and how necessary it is in the unfolding of the relationship among land, sovereignty, imperialism, and the revolutionary subject. His analysis problematizes the idea that the source of worldwide authority is the sovereignty of the liberal subject. He argues that any nationalist bourgeoisie, including the colonial one, is not an inventive, productive, and entrepreneurial class as Marx discusses in the *Communist Manifesto*, but a 'vampiric' bourgeoisie profiting from the colonial economy. They cannot promote the revolution. Instead, he looks to the peasants, the intellectuals, the outcasts, and the unemployed (Ibid., pp. 126–39).

For Fanon, the revolutionary struggle depends on the dispossessed peasantry with nothing to lose. Their spontaneous rebelliousness comes from the expropriation of their land, and the slaughtering of their bodies; they forge a revolutionary movement with those intellectuals who oppose the bourgeoisie. For Fanon this is an act of disrupting slavery, decolonization, and geo-slavery-colonial-politico-ontological vision. It is also the only method of disrupting what I call the *slaughtering foundations of governance* (see Agathangelou, 2011; Bamyeh, 2007) in which the colonizers actively work to shape the balance between the peasants and the intellectuals (Fanon, 1961, pp. 148–205).

Thinking along with Fanon, the multiple divisions that exist amidst the different classes in a given space and era pushes us to consider the presence of many ethical systems and their competing enunciations. For instance, if we read Fanon's careful distinction between the *national bourgeoisie* and the *national liberation movement*, we recognize that these actors' approaches to land and to slave and colonization relations are subtended by different worldviews. The national bourgeoisie, Fanon tells us, seek to rectify the political context of the oppression and degradation of social life by taking over the colonial institutions while continuing to support those interests. The national liberation movement's capability to forge through collective struggle the Algerian nation would depend squarely on the ratification of communal life:

> 'In stirring up these men and women, colonialism has regrouped them beneath a single sign. Equally victims of the same tyranny, simultaneously identifying a single enemy, this physically dispersed people is realizing its unity and founding in suffering a spiritual community which constitutes the most solid bastion of the Algerian Revolution'. (Fanon, 1965, p. 120)

It is such a ratification of communal life that seeks to create systems that are not a threat to any form of life (Fanon, 1970 [1959], p. 101).

Fanon's intervention disrupts the dominant idea that the West and the national bourgeoisie are the only ones that can rectify the degradation of multiple forms of social life. In fact, Fanon notes that such an ethical positing necessarily depends on violence which and is itself and the possibility of any sovereign subject inextricable with it. If the ontological foundations of Western governance are erected on the slaughtering of slaves, land, capital, and alter-worldviews, then its contingent economic, social, and political systems are the purveyors of death. Fanon notes that in Algeria the colonizers' ideological approaches do not capture the spectrum of ethical injunctions associated with subjectivity. Rather, the national liberation movement requires that 'the will to break colonialism' not be linked 'with another quite different will: that of coming to a friendly agreement with it' (Fanon, 1961, p. 124). Fanon pushes here for a project that broadens Marx's idea of property relations by recognizing originary accumulation or Marx's primitive accumulation as the major presupposed resource for the erection of the sovereign and the secret of capitalist accumulation. For Fanon, it is not enough to focus on the erection of the sovereign in the form of state, capital, and subject structure as such a focus evades how terror is necessary and how it marks the emergence of all relations in the colony. He states: 'history teaches us clearly that the battle against colonialism does not run straight away along the lines of nationalism . . . the native devotes his energies to ending certain definite abuses: forced labor, corporal punishment . . . it so happens that the unpreparedness of the educated classes, the lack of practical links between them and the mass of the people, . . . and, let it be said, their cowardice at the decisive moment of the struggle will give rise to tragic mishaps' (Fanon 1967 [1961], p. 148).

The current revolutions embody some of these tensions. On the one hand, not all who have struggled escape domination; indeed, many seem eager to embrace the new globalism, even if the 'colonial legacy has not completely transformed itself into the comparative advantage of linguistic competence plus low wages and a 12-hour temporal head start' (Philip, 2010). On the other hand, thousands are engaged in decolonizing acts to shape their world. Fanon's 'masses' are no longer willing to wait for multiple formations of neoliberal projects to 'save' them.

The MENA Revolutions

Many explain the revolutionary movements in the MENA region as either 'novel' events or the result of public authoritarianism under neoliberal regimes—rising food prices, high unemployment, and government corruption; but as El-Ghobashy (2011) says, such narratives do not do justice to the revolutions. They erase the nuanced unfolding of the 'contingency of the event[s]' (Ibid., p. 1) and focus on their exceptionality and a linear understanding of temporality without accounting for the intertwinements of spatiality and temporality of neoliberalism with other formations.

An exception is Timothy Mitchell (2010) who exposes the ways neoliberalism is itself a spatial project promising 'prospects without limits'. All these prospects demand more expansion and snatching of land in a Fanonian sense, segregation of zones, and snatching and displacement of bodies in spaces that make them flexible ontologically and for exploitation. The same sociopolitical and economic processes create new concentrations of wealth and resources on the one hand, and of economic vulnerability and poverty on the other, along with new urban spaces catering to and harboring these groups, thus producing a new social architecture.

Similarly, Safaa Marafi (2011) argues that the neoliberal dream is based on the segregation of spaces, using Cairo to make her point. She contrasts Al-Rehab City, where visitors and residents enjoy new markets and commercial activities, with the larger city of Cairo which now houses those who are economically vulnerable, socially and spatially stigmatized, and rendered politically weak. In the latter, the local government is an increasingly dominant actor, intervening in and regulating their daily practices. Al-Rehab is a qualitatively different but parallel form of urban captivity, containing groups who are commanding ever-larger economic resources, and who have increasingly tenuous ties to the rest of the society, including the local government whose role has diminished significantly. The spatial segregation feeds into and reproduces the social distances between groups: some are increasingly socially and spatially isolated as they live the dream of neoliberalism; others are left 'out' with no structures of support.

These spatial segregations constituting the neoliberal dream have consistently brought to the fore projects of endurance (Povinelli, 2011, p. 123) generated possibilities for revolution. For Fanon, 'in an initial phase, it is the action, the plans of the occupier that determine the centres of resistance around which a people's will to survive becomes organized' (Fanon, 1970 [1959], p. 32).

Following Bamyeh (2011), these revolutions generate the possibility of a new patriotism, that is, a new political space wherein a subject willing to be in solidarity with others worldwide is constituted, as s/he struggles to transform spaces, corporeal schemas and, indeed, the ontological conditions of existence. I argue that the current revolutions point to a *practical solidarity*, to the emergence of the wretched, as a major ethical principle that can be used to review the question of transformation from the standpoint of all political networks about sovereign and other claims. In Povinelli's words: what carnal forms, and in what configurations, have the right to exist, survive, be killed? What can be exhausted because this exhaustion is necessary for the endurance of something else? (p. 23). There are a number of basic expressions associated with these specific revolutionary moments, including the power and convergence of different forces, revolting to radically change the conditions that generate daily violence, civic fighting against violence that is inextricable from the very possibility of different racial, gender, and other identities, and political participation.

Praxical Solidarity in the Neoliberal Segregated Zonings

The *context* of the uprisings is not unknown. First, neoliberalism has had a devastating effect on the region whose major constitutive element is 'rent' (from oil, gas, minerals, and tourism) with a clan-based ruling class, and a political entourage and technocrats in the middle. This rentier economy employs a small labor force and recruits neocolonial mercenary contractors to secure fenced communities and control the unemployed and underemployed young workers, in societies where 50–65% of the population is under 25 years of age. To paraphrase Petras (2011), this is *neocolonization by invitation*.

Second, neoliberal shifts in the name of 'reforms' such as deregulation, laissez faire access to domestic markets, reduction of food subsidies to the poor, and elimination of state employment have exacerbated the existing system's power asymmetries, generating anew colonial and slave conditions in which class-clan regimes and foreign interests are served by a small native elite running the show. Historical predicaments of colonialism and imperialism, as well as contemporary tensions between those who hold the reins of the economy (real estate developers, financial speculators, importers), clan rulers who control the wealth, and marginal street labor, have shifted the terms of the contestations of power. Recognizing the false promises of neoliberal 'reformers,' the constraints imposed by US and EU immigration regimes, and the inability of the class-clan regimes to draw on their segregation strategies, the *de classé* masses (the *Arab Street*) confronted the clientelistic oligarchies (Petras, 2011), turning the street into a social and economic *locus of contestation of geo-slave-and-colonial-world power*.

In Tunisia, a revolt triggered by Mohamed Bouazizi who set himself on fire caused President Zane-el-Abidine Ben Ali to flee to Saudi Arabia on 14 January 2011. That same month, protests erupted in Algeria (5 January) and Jordan (7 January) following in Tunisia's lead. Seeing the many revolts in the rest of the region, Saad al-Hariri's government in Lebanon collapsed (12 January) as well, while protests occurred in Saudi Arabia (28 January) and Sudan (30 January). On 25 January, hundreds of thousands assembled in Tahrir Square in Cairo and in other cities throughout Egypt to demanded radical reforms. On 11 February 2011, Hosni Mubarak finally resigned after the killing of 800 protesters. In Libya, in the middle of February 2011, the revolutionary movement escalated into a NATO intervention in March leaving thousands dead. Yemenis organized against the ruling regime in the third week of January; loyalists and the security forces of President Ali Abdullah Saleh, in office since 1978, shot hundreds of demonstrators. The 14 February marches in Bahrain led to the mid-March 2011 military intervention of the Gulf Cooperation Council (GCC) and Saudi Arabia. From 18 February on, protests took place in Oman and Iraq—the latter being violently squashed by US-trained anti-riot police (Mohammed, 2011); on 25 March, protests began in Syria, turning into a full-fledged civil war by year's end.

In short, MENA region revolutionaries reoriented the praxical tradition and ruptured the image of Arabs as obedient; 'with a rock in one hand, and a cellphone in the other', they demonstrated claiming that the world they had struggled so hard to create was not open to them (Ryan, 2011). They disrupted multiple mythologies and dominant Orientalist ideas. For example, the Egyptians took matters into their own hands, showing that authoritarian leadership is not the only one that 'can do the job for [them]' (Shatz, 2011). For many years, the Arab rulers' motto that they were 'authoritarian' but 'moderate' and 'responsible' leaders dominated the political and economic landscape of Egypt. Mubarak's negotiations with multinationals and with the US for military aid (in return for passage through the Suez Canal) secured his power. He also provided security for the US and Israel services such as 'interrogating radical Islamists kidnapped by the CIA as part of the extraordinary rendition programme, maintaining the peace with Israel, tightening the siege of Gaza, [and] opposing the "resistance" front led by Iran' (Ibid.). Such actions made it possible for American military aid to 'continue to flow, at a rate of $1.3 billion a year' (Ibid.). While Mubarak argued this would benefit the majority, millions were left scrambling for jobs and food.

As a result, the Egyptians took to the streets, unplugging terrorized and gendered subjectivities from sovereign apparatuses and neoliberal regimes. The transformation from obedient into the wretched of the earth, in practical solidarity with one another in the streets, transformed how people think about revolutionary leadership, their relationship to their land, and their own subjectivity. In Fanon's articulation, it has dislodged the common assumption that change and transformation are the result of 'little vanguards' (Fanon, 1970 [1959], 1).

In Tunisia, Ben Ali, like other African leaders, took over the violent practices of the colonialists. Instead of working toward a national anti-colonial liberation movement, the emerging ruling party developed authoritarian principles and sold itself as a base for Western capitalism:

> The more the society ingratiated itself with the West, the more the ruling sections of the political class felt a sense of impunity, believing that Western support could shield them from popular opposition. (Campbell, 2011)

Here too, the recognition that African leadership was invested in the imperial and neocolonial–neoliberal erections of market and political regimes pushed people into the streets to shatter the object of autocratic state power (Mitchell, 2010; Petras, 2011). The popular songs of Ben Amr in Tunisia told the president that his people were dying; the people chanted these songs, unleashing an energy that was 'bound to this profound human reality and to its socialist future, and not to the apparent omnipotence of great systems' (Fanon, 1970 [1959], p. 1).

In Tunisia, in Sidi Bouzid, the economic terror of capitalism which was extensively supported by the US and France came to the fore with Bouazizi's self-immolation. People took to the streets, at once denouncing and revealing the extent of the corruption of the dictator who had been in power since 1987. As Fanon tells us, there needs to be clarity about the formation of the classes and their interests. In Tunisia, the national capitalist class dominated the ruling party, which cooperated with foreign multinationals to establish free trade zones where workers could not organize. The youth were a pool of cheap reserve labor regulated by religious and political leaders. Yet like Bouazizi, many 'were not waiting for a dictator to declare the year for them; they were bent on taking the year and making the break for a new decade' (Campbell, 2011).

The multiple protests in the MENA region are continuing to unfold a year later. These uprisings disrupt the dominant problematic characterization that Arabs either obediently follow the *rule of law* under authoritarian regimes, or else violently take to the streets without rational thought. Rather, this authoritarian and 'legal fetishism' sets their lived concrete experiences within contexts not fully domesticated by Europe (Farley, 1997, p. 457). These myriad forms of organizing and political solidarities seen in these recent uprisings disrupt the idea that revolutionary violence is itself law-making and functional of political institutions and rather point to a second ethical principle, namely that political solidarity 'spreads' to the next generation and puts into crisis civil society and the state as the purveyors of justice and substantive democracy (Tahrir Documents, 2011).

The protests in the streets challenge imperial and neoliberal governance that depends on geo-colonial, sovereign, and necropolitical power[11] and dominant methods of snatching, slaughtering, and segregating of multiple forms of life in zones positing claims; under 'the mantle of grand political programs . . . the economic principles of the post-revolutionary regime (fairness, equal opportunity, and absence of corruption)' (Bamyeh, 2011, p. 6) and gender justice are addressed. The movement to the streets expresses an ethic that trespasses dominant understandings of the 'sense of the world' (Nancy, 2011), the community, and the revolutionary subject (Motha, 2011). The Tunisian, Egyptian, and Yemeni revolutions highlight that different communities live and work together, including the Muslims and Copts in Egypt who formed joint groups for food, sleeping, defense, and prayer. These practical solidarities are the 'becomings' of the systems that kept them in place and the contours/barriers of a new subject formation.

Diremptions of Civil Society and Colonial/Authoritarian States: The Coming Into Being of the Wretched

Bamyeh's (2011) analysis complicates, as does Fanon's (1967 [1952], p. 226), the formation and spaces of the revolution, its agents, and its leadership, along with the practice of the revolution as it unfolds in the contemporary moment. Fanon speaks of feeling solidarity with the revolt in Santo Domingo: 'Every time a man has said no to an attempt to subjugate his fellows, [he] has felt solidarity with this act. . . . I will not make myself the man of any past. I do not want to exalt [a Negro civilization of] the past at the expense of my present and my future' (Ibid., p. 226). For Fanon it is not enough to fetishize revolutionary acts and lands as such racialized fetishistic attachments to a racial other act as a stand in for the fear of a supposedly sovereign subject's disintegration. Ultimately, this racial fetishization may politically hold us hostage to fantasies of the other while also freeing us from the possibility of being mutually exposed to ourselves and others (i.e. mutual exposure of our existential struggles ($υπαρξιακή\ αγωνία$)). One must engage in daily revolutions, even though such revolutions 'can throw everything into confusion in a new way, fundamentally upsetting colonised society and "upsetting its limits"' (Gibson, 2011, citing

2004, p. 15). Fanon also cautions about 'the brutal violence and counter-violence' of revolutions and 'the 'sclerosis' that knee-jerk anti-imperialism brings' (Ibid., p. 113).

Fanon (2004, p. 195, cited in Fanon-Mendès-France, 2011) warns us of militant revolutionaries whose goal to organize the society quickly leads them to bypass those 'liturgical acts' which 'are privileged occasions given to a human being to listen and to speak . . . and put forward new ideas'. These liturgical daily acts are 'seemingly banal, but in the local engagements time becomes 'space for human development,' as Marx puts it, 'no longer . . . of the moment or the next harvest but rather of the rest of the world'' (Ibid., p. 135). Fanon continues:

> Man's liberation is a universal fight based on the defense of private and public freedoms, the primacy of the general interest, the reduction in inequality, accountability of the elected, and the sovereignty of right. (Ibid.)

Fanon's nuanced understanding of the revolution and the possibility that the struggle may be snatched by corporate and geo-colonial powers is important today. For instance, in the Tunisian revolution like the 1988 riots in Algeria the 'political crowds' objected to the failure of the state to 'honor its socialist-oriented identity [and yet] this leaning was sacrificed when the protest movement fused politically with the market-oriented economy of the Islamist movement' (Khalil, 2011, p. 9).

Referring to the 1988 Algerian protests, Roberts (2002, p. 6, cited in Khalil, 2011, p. 9) asks: 'What has this bourgeois Islamic Puritanism, with its essentially positive acceptance of laissez-faire capitalist political economy . . . got to do with the character and behavior of social movements in Algeria and, in the first instance, with the outlook of the Algerian crowd?' Turning to Tunisia, Khalil thematizes the Arab and Islamic lived experience, as a question of time rather than identity, like Fanon but within the contemporary context by considering the insights revolutionaries around the world have gained from multiple movements in the region and elsewhere, specifically where Islam plays a significant role in the spatiality of social relations:

> Is there an intrinsic relationship between unideological, non-sectarian popular revolts and the emergence of politically repressed Islamist opposition groups?. . . . The question can be posed in the context of a desire to rewrite history. In Tunisia, the return, legalization and support enjoyed by the main Islamist party . . . gives rise to the question of new definitions of political authority, of the people. . . . The political crowds of the Tunisian revolution denaturalized the language used by the State, de-naturalized poverty, and de-naturalized an absolute character of secular, European, and republican models devoid of all real republican values. (Khalil, 2011, p. 9)

They have also denaturalized the imperial–neoliberal idea of land as a space for golf, tourism, and real estate developments. Such uprisings disrupt dominant understandings and highlight Islam's own history of revolt, along with its 'moral economy' that produces the expectation that states will act according to political and economic ethical principles.

The uprisings and revolts in the MENA region open space for the reinsertion of popular struggles of society into worldwide struggles by refusing to accept a notion of history that is transhistorical and universal. Previous Islamic and anti-globalization uprisings have been significant in shaping a spatially malleable vision of socialism that does not depend on the theft of people's existential relations and exploitation of the majority. The spontaneous revolutionary acts of practical solidarity and decolonization have posited a system that does not depend on the recovery of sovereign masculinity (the ultimate value of Western-liberal and juridical discourses) from their deposed neoliberal and authoritarian regimes. Rather, the new system looks to constituting anew the contours of social systems and subjects by renewing multiple forms of life.

The spontaneous acts of decolonization that brought together men and women of the middle and working classes, homeless peoples, and the youth disrupted the gendered order of 'imperialism and patriarchal/Islamic occupation' that claims that women's contribution to social development is rather represented in economies of passivity and sacrifice (Mikdashi, 2012). The presence of women, children, men, and transgendered peoples from diverse classes and backgrounds highlights that their interventions are have been central to and revolutionary practices. They put themselves on the line to constitute their bodies and the world order's value anew, and their practices disrupt the dominant codes in the economies underpinning the foundations of global governance.

The major constituent elements of this new sense of the world and the new revolutionary subject disrupt the sectarian, sexual, and sovereign segregations that have consistently claimed class, gender, secularism, and sovereignty as able to 'save' or somehow suture the de-ranged spatio-experiences and lives of those who are barred from the privileged groups and spaces. Revolutions as acts of anti-colonization and anti-slavery push asunder the boundaries of the struggle.[12] The central ethical element of revolution is not the struggle for bread or the struggle against authoritarian regimes; it is the movement of the 'different' subjects asymmetrically positioned in stratified systems of governance to eliminate all forms of oppression, theft, and above all, dismantle a structure and global order whose foundations depend on the slaughter of the slave and the colonized. Indeed, these revolutionary expressions are evidence of a human dignity preparing humanity for the renewal of the wretched of the earth and for remaking the earth itself anew (Fanon, 1970 [1959], p. 1; see also Bamyeh, 2011).

The Acted Revolutionary Truth: Corporeal Disruptions

After Bouazizi's immolation, the Tunisians, Egyptians, Bahrainis, Libyans, Syrians, and Yemenis literally put their bodies on the line to constitute themselves as the masses able to govern. This young fruit and vegetable vendor, also a university graduate, reached the breaking point after being slapped twice across the face by a female police officer and having his goods confiscated when he was unable to pay the bribe she demanded. The intimate and yet public sexualized working-class humiliation which accompanied the slap led to Bouazizi's setting himself ablaze, dying two weeks later. Within a context where grievances and violence are intertwined and sexed relations are striated, a state uniformed woman slapping a working-class man highlighted sexual and corporeal brutality, economic grievances, and state violence and intergenerational 'spreadings' (Irigaray, 1985, p. 288).

Meanwhile, in Egypt in June 2010, Alexandria (male) police killed Khaled Saeed, a young man who worked on computers, for posting a video that showed police discussing how to share out the seized property from a drug bust. He was in an Internet café uploading the video when (male) police dragged him away and beat him to death. Briefly stated, Saeed's death mobilized protests against a regime that took its power for granted. Bouazizi's self-immolation and Khaled Saeed's beating ruptured the world order's dominant strategies of geo-colonial power formation and revealed the simmering desire for transformation.

Unlike much of their leadership, the MENA protesters do not assume the West as the normative referent of transformation. They took to the streets when they realized that their regimes' gratuitous violence converged with the West's liberal wars.[13] They used all technologies available to them to disrupt the terms of the geo-colonial and corporeal order and to disrupt the dominant practice of state-corporate collusive control of such tools. Using their own bodies as technologies of power disrupted the idea that they or their lands were or ever could be subjected completely corporations and the political regime to the rules and dominant practices of violence such as the snatching of land for profits.

The desire for transformation came through clearly in the slogans and chants of workers and poor farmers who converged on Tunis after Ben Ali's fall to demand the removal of the ruling party and the interim leader: 'We have come to bring down the rest of the dictatorship'. Traveling through the night in a caravan of cars, trucks, and motorcycles from towns across the rocky region far from Tunisia's luxurious tourist beaches, and in defiance of a curfew and 'state of emergency', they turned their bodies and voices toward collective strife against the order that had systematically stolen their lands and lives. In Egypt, people protested on blogs and designed banners and posters displaying Khaled Saaed's corpse (ElBaradei, 2011). They also formed a community around opposition to police brutality and other government abuses.

The protesters have reoriented the praxical tradition of a Western modernity to a revolution that posits the possibility of configuring anew the effects of the geo-slave-and-colonial state and corporeal powers. They have done so by foregrounding corporeality, space, and state and civil society violences and the objects of violence. More so, the emergence of these revolutionaries into the streets showed them as the central loci of contestation for the simple reason that they precipitate a crisis to the neocolonial–neoliberal structures and their corporate and elite agents (ranging from businessmen to real estate agents to political leadership). In their chants, songs, and slogans, the MENA protesters employ the grammar of revolution, while disrupting the juridico-grammatical injunction that violence and terror are opposed by the state or the civil society. The resonant music flowing across the land and through bodies feeds off of and into the creative responses to violence and oppression. Their regime's use of gratuitous violence is no longer contained. The corporeal street protests and the music mock the ordinary violence of the everyday, the violence against multiple forms of life including people's spaces. They remind people that hierarchical ordering of desires and needs is a strategy that emerges from privilege: its ethical value is containment and suffocation, not the recognition and affirmation of the ethics that emerge from solidarity practices against geo-slave-and-corporeal orders.

Drawing on the land and the body as the fundamental sites of contestation of the dominant global order requires one (a la Fanon) to recognize certain distinctions: one is either *for* an order that is willing to slaughter its people in the name of national or other kinds of development and promises; *or* one seeks to transform its economic, social, political systems by 'get [ting] as close as possible to the Revolution, to get ahead of the Revolution if possible, in short to be in on it' (Fanon, 1970 [1959], p. 81). As if responding to the class made by revolutionaries including Fanon, women, children, the working class, and rural peoples took to the streets. The youth (*shabab*) transformed their spaces and bodies and regrouped their forces: nothing and no one could make them retreat (Abourahme and Jayyusi, 2011). Many younger people and women participating in the social revolts emerging as the wretched realized that systematic programs are required to articulate a different vision and practice of horizontal and participatory leadership, generating spaces and institutions that had marginalized them through policies or social practices (Abou-Habib, 2011, 2012).

In the streets of Tunis and Cairo, bodies became the sites that contested those objects and technologies that systematically worked to segregate, discipline, contain, kill them, or let them die. The acted truths constituted a grammar of revolution which inoculated them against the 'terrorist' epithets beginning to circulate in newspapers of Europe and North America:

> 'We are not thugs,' said Samer Abdul Razek, 29, who lost a friend Jan. 28 when he was shot in the head by a sniper. Razek, a student of literature, was bleeding from a stomach wound he suffered when hit by a rock thrown by security forces. 'I want this government and military rule to end'. (Fadel and Mansour, 2011)

The politics, of 'protection' and the problematic criminalization of the working class and protesters' bodies are disrupted in a world profoundly shaped by the convergence of originary relations and globality, with its accompanying political, economic and sovereign relations (see Agathangelou, 1997; Amin, 1997; Fanon, 1970 [1959], p. 12; Grovogui, 2010, 2011; Muppidi, 2004; Said, 1978).

MENA Revolts and Uprisings and New Modes of Existence Beyond the Region

Even with so many attempts to erase them, the recently unfolding revolutionary becomings ask us to *see* the concrete conditions and the places from which they emerge. These disruptions of colonization require deconstructing 'the absoluteness of power' or 'the particular mechanisms of tyrannical power' which 'converge on the [spaces of the] black body' which itself is understood as not-yet, a problem that challenges dominant understandings of ontology as Fanon reminds us in *Black Skins and White Masks*. By bringing the organic contingencies of lived relations into intimate collision with the violent practices of state and capital, the very idea of revolution is being revolutionized. The 2011 uprisings continue the nationalist struggles to rid colonized spaces of foreign powers, reconstituting anew the difficult questions/practices that began with national liberation movements. They are also directed towards 'Arab problems' (Khalidi, 2011), including ridding their societies of military regimes.

A revolutionary moment is not equivalent to revolution as an ongoing process. They are *temporally different*; this distinction is analytically crucial as it allows us to recognize what Fanon says in *Wretched of the E*arth about the importance of desires and the objective moment or of the real and the imaginative. In fact, the MENA revolutions highlight that the question of freedom may subtend the questions of space and time.

MENA citizens are challenging entrenched regimes whose policies, transnational interests, and daily practices rob them of their dignity. They are disrupting the daily slaughter of peoples and communities and positing a vision that takes seriously the conjunction of existential conditions and labor relations. If there is a 'universal yearning' for dignity and non-violence, it is not based on Western values but on the 'unresolved' question of what freedom is and how one makes it real.

While it is important to acknowledge spontaneity and novelty, it is equally important to remember that the space being opened up for genuine politics can quickly be routinized and recaptured by the 'old'. It can once again be filled by the framing of the revolts as part of imperial and neoliberal agendas from the 'liberal' to the most 'radical' circles. Indeed, much of the 'sense' (of law, decision, judgment, value) of these revolutions/revolts/uprisings is already global, as interests that want to consolidate their powers with no real change have appropriated them. Ultimately, the recurring nature of the violence which constitutes social reproduction and replenishes capital shapes our economies beyond property relations and our spaces beyond segregated nationalist expressions or autocratic terror regimes. As Fanon would put it, we are all already in on it.

Acknowledgements

Special thanks to Ruth Reitan, the two reviewers, Elizabeth Thompson, and Kostantin Kilibarda for the careful read and excellent suggestions. Special thanks also go to Kole for helping me shorten the title and to Lissa Chiu, Tamara Spira, and Heather Turcotte, Kyle D. Killian, Mikael Lawrence Killian, and Aleksi Christos Killian for the many conversations on the question of revolution.

Notes

1 Coombs defines revolution as the 'announcement of affirmation of the systematic overhaul of existing socio-economic conditions, within which the popular mobilization plays an essential role even while it remains insufficient to represent the overhaul itself' (2011: 139).

2. I want to thank the anonymous reviewers; their organizing suggestions have sharpened the argument.
3. This idea emerges out of conversations with Heather Turcotte on abolitionist histories/struggles.
4. For the erosion of the modern liberal state, see Jean Luc-Nancy (2005). Some have argued that the EU is engaging in 'constitutional steering'; see Skoutaris (2012).
5. In *Black Skin, White Masks* he shows that one's experience of the body is entangled in one's reality and live experience of timing of space.
6. See Agathangelou (2011) for the ways Fanon understands the earth, bodies, and space.
7. See Anna M. Agathangelou (2011) who argues that the slave and ancestors (i.e. constituted as flesh) do not figure in terms of globality which has serious implications on the ways we theorize and understand revolution.
8. Fanon tells us about his experience of being called names: 'Dirty nigger!' or simply, 'Look, a Negro . . . I came into the world imbued with the will to find a meaning in things, my spirit filled with the desire to attain to the source of the world, and then I found that I was an object in the midst of other objects' (Fanon, 1967 [1952], p. 109).
9. In Fanon's words: 'Negroes who return . . . convey the impression that they have completed a cycle . . . They return literally full of themselves' (Fanon 1967 [1952], p. 19).
10. Fanon sustains the distinctions between the racial positionality of Algerians and the blacks of Martinique. I do the same here as such a material and analytical distinction has implications in the way we read the constitution and emergence of the wretched and toward revolutionary relations and practices.
11. For a definition of necropolitical power, see Mbembe (2003). He states: 'Politics is therefore death that lives a human life' (p. 15) and the figure of sovereignty is 'the generalized instrumentalization of human existence and the material destruction of human bodies and populations' (p. 14).
12. See Kostantin Kilibarda (2012) for a brilliant analysis of the interventions made by the aboriginal communities in Canada in the occupy movements.
13. This realization was assisted by the Wikileaks publishing cables, supposedly given to them by the US soldier and intelligence officer Bradley Manning, who now faces life imprisonment, in this: see Al jazeera (2011).

References

Abou-Habib, L. (2011) Women, social movements, and revolution: winds of change in the MENA region, *Women's Learning Partnership*, http://www.learningpartnership.org/blog/2011/02/winds-of-change-mena/

Abou-Habib, L. (2012) No spring for Arab women: a sober report from CSW and a wake up call, *Women's Learning Partnership*, http://www.learningpartnership.org/blog/2012/03/wlp-at-the-56th-csw-in-new-york-sharing-different-ideas-confronting-global-challenges-to-women%e2%80%99s-rights-and-equality/

Abourahme, N. & Jayyusi, M. (2011) The will to revolt and the spectre of the Real, *City*, 15(6), pp. 625–630.

Agathangelou, A. (1997) The Cypriot 'Ethic Conflict' in the production of global power, Ph.D. Dissertation, Syracuse University.

Agathangelou, A. M. (2011a) Bodies to the slaughter: global racial reconstructions, Fanon's combat breath, and wrestling for life, *Somatechnics Journal*, 1(1), pp. 209–248.

Agathangelou, A. M. (2011b) Making anew an Arab regional order? On poetry, sex, and revolution, *Globalizations*, 8(5), pp. 581–594.

Al jazeera (2011) Breaking through information monopoly, http://www.aljazeera.com/indepth/features/2011/10/2011104115312389414.html

Amin, S. (1997) *Capitalism in the Age of Globalization* (Zed Books).

Amin, S. (2011) Audacity, more audacity, *The Bullet, Socialist Project*, no. 577, http://www.socialistproject.ca/bullet/577.php

Bamyeh, M. A. (2007) *Of Death and Dominion: The Existential Foundations of Governance* (Evanston, IL: Northwestern University Press).

Bamyeh, M. A. (2011) Arab revolutions and the making of a new patriotism, *Orient—German Journal for Politics, Economics and Culture of the Middle East*, 52(3), pp. 6–10.

Campbell, H. (2011) Tunisia's revolution: Self-organisation for self-emancipation, *Pambazuka News: Pan-African Voices for Freedom and Justice*, 514, http://www.pambazuka.org/en/category/features/70472

Campbell, H. (2012) African worldview on revolutionary ruptures and pace of change in 2012, *Pambazuka News: African Voices for Freedom and Justice*, http://www.pambazuka.org/en/category/features/79610

Coombs, N. (2011) Political semantics of the Arab revolts/uprisings/riots/insurrections/revolutions, *Journal of Critical Globalisation*, Studies, 4, http://www.criticalglobalisation.com/issue4.html

Fadel, L. & Mansour, M. (2011) Protesters, police clash in Cairo, *Washington Post*, http://www.washingtonpost.com/world/protesters-police-clash-in-cairo/2011/06/28/AGhKGzpH_story.html

Fanon, F. (1967 [1961]) *The Wretched of the Earth*, C. Farrington (trans.) (New York: Grove Press).
Fanon, F. (1967 [1952]) *Black Skin, White Masks* (New York: Grove Press).
Fanon, F. (1970 [1959]) *A Dying Colonialism*, H. Chevalier (trans.) (New York: Pelican).
Fanon-Mendès-France, M. (2011) Frantz Fanon and the current multiple crises, *Pambazuka News: Pan African Voices for Freedom and Justice*, 561, http://pambazuka.org/en/category/features/78515
Farley, A. (1997) The black body as fetish object, *Oregon Law Review*, 76(3), pp. 457–535.
El-Ghobashy, M. (2011) Politics by other means, *Boston Review*, November/December, pp. 1–3.
Gordon, J. A. (2011) Revolutionary in counter-revolutionary times: elaborating Fanonian national consciousness into the twenty-first century, *Journal of French and Francophone Philosophy*, 19(1), pp. 37–47.
Grovogui, S. (2010) The Global South: A Metaphor, Not an Etymology, *Global Studies Review*, 6(3).
Grovogui, S. (2011) To the Orphaned, Dispossessed, and Illegitimate Children: Human Rights Beyond Republican and Liberal Traditions, *Indiana Journal of Global Legal Studies*, 41, pp. 41–63.
Irigaray, L. (1985) *This Sex Which is not One* (New York: Cornell University Press).
Khalil, A. (2011) The political crowd: theorizing popular revolt in North Africa, *Contemporary Islam: Dynamics of Muslim Life* (December), pp. 1–21.
Kilibarda, K. (forthcoming) Lessons from #Occupy in Canada: Contesting Space, settler Consciousness and Erasures within the 99%, *Journal of Critical Globalization Studies*.
Marafi, S. (2011) The neoliberal dream of segregation, http://dar.aucegypt.edu/handle/10526/2262
Mbembe, A. (2001) *On the Postcolony* (Berkeley, CA: University of California Press).
Mbembe, A. (2003) Necropolitics, *Public Culture*, 15(1), pp. 11–40.
Mikdashi, M. (2012) The uprisings will be gendered, *Jadaliyya*, 28 February 28, http://www.jadaliyya.com/pages/index/4506/the-uprisings-will-be-gendered
Mitchell, T. (2010) Dreamland: the neoliberalism of your desires, http://www.merip.org/mer/mer210/dreamland-neoliberalism-your-desires
Motha, S. (2011) The end of sovereignty in North Africa, *Critical Legal Thinking: Law and the Political*, http://www.criticallegalthinking.com/2011/04/19/the-end-of-sovereignty-in-north-africa-in-the-world/
Mohammed, Y. (2011) Iraqi women's activist rebuffs U.S. claims of a freer Iraq: this is not a democratic country, *DemocracyNow!*, 16 December, http://www.democracynow.org/2011/12/16/iraqi_womens_activist_rebuffs_us_claims
Muppidi, H. (2004) *The Politics of the Global* (University of Minnesota Press).
Nancy, J. L. (2005) On finitude and sovereignty, Lecture at Birkbeck Institute for Humanities, Adieu Derrida Series, May 2005.
Nancy, J. L. (2011) What the Arab peoples signify to us, *Critical Legal Thinking, Law and the Political*, http://www.criticallegalthinking.com/2011/03/31/what-the-arab-peoples-signify-to-us/
Petras, J. (2011) Roots of the Arab revolts and premature celebrations, *Intifada*, 4 March, http://www.intifada-palestine.com/2011/03/james-petras-roots-of-the-arab-revolts-and-premature-celebrations/
Philip, K. (2010) Postcolonial technopolitics: reflections on the Indian experience, *Johannesburg Workshop in Theory and Criticism*, http://www.jwtc.org.za/volume_3/kavita_philip.htm
Povinelli, E. (2011) *Economies of Abandonment: Social Belonging and Endurance in Late Liberalism* (Duke University Press).
Roberts, H. (2002) *Moral Economy or Moral Polity? The Political Anthropology of Algeria Riots. Crisis States Programme Working Papers* (London: London School of Economics).
Ryan, Y. (2011) How Tunisia's revolution began, *AlJazeera.com*, http://www.aljazeera.com/indepth/features/2011/01/2011126121815985483.html
Said, E. (1978) *Orientalism* (London: Penguin).
Sekyi-Out, A. (1996) *Fanon's Dialectic of Experience* (Cambridge, MA: Harvard University Press).
Shatz, A. (2011) After Mubarak, *London Review of Books*, 17 February, pp.
Skoutaris, N. (2012) On sovereign debt crisis and sovereignty: A constitutional law perspective, Presentation at York University, Toronto, 8 March.
Tahrir Documents (2011) How to revolt, http://www.tahrirdocuments.org/2011/03/how-to-revolt/

Index

Note: references to figures are in **Bold**

acted revolutionary truth 140–2
Adbusters 26
AFL-CIO 49
AFSC 19
Agathangelou, Anna M 10
Al-Rehab City 135
Alvarez, Sonia 59
anarchism 118
anti-globalization 1
ANSWER 23
Anti-/Alter-Globalization Movement (AGM) 1;antinomies 31; bellwether issues 16,17; composition 2, 15–16;'global left' 1; theorizing 2–3; transnational coalescence 16; transnational presence 16
Arab Spring 25
Arab uprisings 129–44
ARENA 22
Articulacion Feminista Marcosur 61–3
Asian Floor Wage campaign 53
Asian Peace Alliance (APA) 19,22
Association of Small Island States 97
autonomists 4
AWID 61

Bakic-Hayden, Milica 125
Bakunin, Mikhail 4–5
Balkanity, invention of 120
Balkanization 117–27; anti-authoritarian politics, and 124; below, from 122–5; civilization, and 119; contemporaray federation, proposal for 124; from above 119–22; invention of 120; nationalist atrocities, and 123
Balkanizing theory 125–6
Balkanopolitanism 124
Battle in Seattle 2
Bella Center 79–80
Bello, Walden 23
Ben Ali 137
Ben Amir 137
Berlin congress 120
Berlin Social Forum 34

Bernstein, Eduard 5
Bieler, Andreas 9
Black Skin, White Masks 133
Blair, Tony 21
Bolivia 96
Bouazizi, Mohamed 136,140
bridge builders 16
Building Solidarities: Feminist Dialogues 62

Cairo 135
Cairo Anti-War Conferences 22,23–4
Campaign Against Fundamentalisms 61
capitalism:crisis, and 45; inner logic 45; structural setting 44
casualisation 46
Chile 25
Christie, Agatha 120–1
class: conceptualization 32
Climate Action Network 80–2
climate activism; miscible movements 78
climate change 73–88; mounting concern over 76
Climate Collective 83
Climate Justice Action 82
climate justice movement 77–8
Climate Justice Now! 80–2
coalescence 18
coalescence of global peace and justice movements 15–28
coalition building 59–60
coalition of the willing 25
Cochabamba Declaration 96
Code Pink 20
Cold War : emancipatory efforts 33; trade unions, and 43
collective deportation strategy 112
colonial and white geo-power 132
colonist, task of 133
colonization, disruptions of 142; effect 132
color-coded blocs 5
Confederation of German Trade Unions 36
contemporary activism: nature of 3
contemporary rhizomatic logic 38

INDEX

contributing authors 9
Conway, Janet 10, 34
COP 12 95
COP15 75, 78–80; meeting spaces 79; mobilization 79; observation field notes 80; participatory action research 78–80
COSATU 49
critical globalization scholarship 8–10

decent work, decent life initiative 47–50; alleged Northern bias 49; Third World, and 48; tripartite allegations, and 48
decolonization 131
Deleuze, Gilles 30–1
democratic deficit 25
Democratic Eastern Federation 122
Deportation Class 113
Desai, M 68
DGB 49
Diani, Mario 77
diremptions of civil society and colonial/authoritarian states 138–40
discomfort 106–7
Dussel, Enrique 126

ecologism 75
El-Ghobashy 135
EMCALI 53
environmental activism 73–88; historical tension 75; ideological strands 74; leftist praxis 74–8; post-COP15 reflections 84–5; transnational movement 73
environmental justice 77
EPSU 54
ETUC 47
Euro-colonial violence 123–4
European colonial modernity 120
European Commission 48–9
European Metalworkers' Federation 53
European Social Forum (ESF) 24–5, 30
European Union 48–9

Fanon, Frantz 129–44; decolonization, on 131; neoliberalism, and 130
feminism 57–71; coalition, and 59–60; solidarity 57
Feminist Dialogues 62
feminist strategies 65–7; alliance-building 65–7; coalition, and 59–60;cross-movement solidarity 65–7
FGS 21–2
first World Social Forum 33–4
Foucault, Michel 105–6
frayed braid 2–8; leftist strands 3
freedom, concept of 106
French revolution 4
Funke, Peter Nikolaus 9

future strategies for labour 52–4

Gandhi, Nandita 63
German state 110
Germany constitutional right to asylum 109
Gibson, Shannon 10
Glenny, Misha 121
Global Anti-War Movement (GAWM) 18–22; emergence of 19
Global Assembly 24
global civil society 105
global commodity chains 46
Global Indigenous Movement 91
global justice actors: US domestic level 20–1
Global Justice Ecology Project 79
global justice scale down in Asia 21–2
global justice scale down in UK 21
global left 1
Global Peace and Justice Movement 22–5
global political economy: transformations of 32
global social forum process 30
Global Social Forum Rhizome 29–42; accomplishments 38–9; developing framework 34–9; heterogeneity 36–7; horizontalist ethos of forums 31; limitations 38–9; multiplicity 37–8; resistance relay, as 31
globalisation 43–56; exploitation, and 47; production, and 46; structural change, and 46
Globalise Resistance 19
globalised resistance 104–5; academic discourse 104–5
Goldsworthy, Vesna 120
governmentality of documentation 109–10
green movement: radical wing 75–6
Grubacic, Andrej 10
Guattari, Felix 30–1

Hardt, Michael 84
Harvey, David 45
Hersel, Philip 36
heterarchy 38–9, 40
heterotopia 108–14
heterotopia and beyond 113–14
Holloway, John 7
horizontalist political ethic 7
humanitarian ideology 121

Ignatieff, Michael 119–20
IICM 91; actions of 95
IMF 20
indigenous activists 3
Indigenous Environmental Network 83
indigenous movement to confront climate change 89–102; NGOs, and 97–8

indigenous peoples 89–102; erosion of sovereignty 97; Eurocentric values, and 94; Latin America 92; social movements 90; UN, and 93
Intergovernmental Panel on Climate Change 76
Inuit Circumpolar Committee 96
Iraq; attack on 19
ITUC 47–8

Jakarta Peace Concensus 22,23

key global justice movement bridge-builders **19**
Klein, Naomi 84
Kohl, Helmut 109
Kyoto Protocol 77

La Federation Balkanique 123
Labour and Globalisation Network 50–1, 50–2
Latin Americ: indigenous movements 92
League of Nations 92
left-right dichotomy 4
Leninist critiques 7
Lidl 37
Linebaugh, Peter 126
liturgical daily acts 139
local forum: nature of 36
Luxemburg, Rosa 5

Marafi, Safaa 135
Markovic, Svetozar 122–3
Marx, Karl 4
Marxism 118
Masuku, Bongni 49
Mbembe, Achile 124
MENA insurrections 129–44; grammar of revolution 141; image of arabs as obedient, and 137; Islam, and 139; multiple protests 138; neoliberal shifts 136; new modes of existence beyond region, and 142; novelty 142; practical solidarity 136; spontaneity 142; worldwide struggles, and 139–40; youth, role of 141
Merk, Jeroen 53
militant particularism 39
Mitchell, Timothy 135
Mobilization for Global Justice 20
moderate strands 4
Mohanty, Chandra Talpade 59
Morales, Evo 85, 96
movement coalescence 25–6
movement crossovers 17
movement of movement 38
Muller, Tadzio 7–8, 84

national bourgeoisie 134–5
national liberation movement 130, 134–5
neocolonization by invitation 136
neoliberal globalisation agency of labour in 47–52
neoliberalism capitalism 32–3
Neumann, Achim 37
Never Trust a Cop 83
New Left 39
NGO advocacy networks 6
Nicholson, Michael 119
No Border movements 114
No one is illegal 103–16; activism 111–12; demands 111; practising discomfort 112
Norway: Campaign for the Welfare State 53

Occupy movement 3, 25–6 Asia 26; Britain 26
Occupy Wall Street 25
Old Left 39; tendencies 4
open-space, politics of 35
organised labour: challenge for 52
other possible communism 7
outsourcing 46

Participatory Action Research (PAR) 9
participatory research methods 8–10
patriarchy 67
politics of discomfort 103–16
post-anarchism 7
post-autonomism 7–8
post-autonomist praxis 82–4
post-Marxism 7–8
power 105–8; relationship 106
Powless, Ben 10
praxical solidarity in neoliberal segregated zonings 136–8
praxis of transversality 68
Princip, Gavrilo 121
production structures: nuanced approach 44
public sector workers: cooperation 53
Pulignano, Valeria 53

Quijano, Anibal 125

racial domination of colonies 133
radical Balkanologists 126
Ramonet, Ignacio 37
Reclaim Power 83–4
red-green debate 76
Rediker, Marcus 126
Rees, John 23
Reitan, Ruth 9, 10
RENGO 49
resistance 103–16
resistance in heterotopia 108–14
resistance in the other space 111–13

INDEX

resistance relay 38
revolutionaries of the future 125
revoluntary movement 142
revolutionary movements in the 21st century 131–5
Rhizomatic Left 39
rhizome: image of 29; meaning 35; multi-connectivity 35–6; multiplicity 37–8
rooted cosmopolitan 17–18

Saeed, Khaled 140
Sandoval, C 60
Santo Domingo 138
scale shifts 17
Seattle protests 33
Shah, Nandita 63
social democratic reformers 6
social forum literature 30
Solidaires 50–1
solidarity: struggle for 60
state-centric understanding of world 109
state socialist projects: failure of 32
Stierl, Maurice 10
Stoker, Bram: *Dracula* 120
storm zones 130
StreetNet International 50–1
STW-UK 19, 21
SWP 19, 21

techno fixes 77
theorizations of solidarity 58–60
theory 30
The Wretched of the Earth 130, 131, 134
Todorova, Maria 125
total institutions 110
trade unions: social democratic labour parties, and 48; new social movements, and 52
traditional social movement issues 9
transnational civil society 6
transnational coalescense 16–18
transnational feminisms 57–71; alliances at WSF 60–5; patriarchy, and 67
transnational social movement coalescence **17**
transnational solidarity 43–56
transversal politics 60
transversality: commitment to 69
Trotsky, Leon 45

TUC 49
Tunisia 136, 137–8, 140–41

UNCED 75
UNDRIP 93
UNFCC 94
UN High Commissioner for Human Rights 96
UN Permanent Forum on Indigenous Issues 96
United for Peace and Justice (UFPJ) 19, 20
United Nations 58–9
upward scale shift 18
US-led wars: opposition to 25
US Third World feminism 59

Via Campesina 65, 83
virtual ethnography 30

welfare state 49
Western unitary state ideals: challenge to 8
WICEJ 61
Winchester, Simon 119
worker: definition 50
Workers of the world unite 43–56
Working Group on Indigenous Populations 93
World and European Social Forums 22
World March of Women 63–5; alliance-building 65; coalition-building approach 66; feminist practice, and 66; mass mobilization 66–7; mass movement building, and 64; significance of 64–5; UN, and 64; WSF, and 65
World Social Forum 2, 24–5; emergence 32–3; International Council 5–6; methodology 69; success of 29; transnational femist networks 58
worldwide anti-globalization movements 129

Yugoslavia 117; destruction of 118; socialism, and 121

Zapatista 32–3, 40; uprising 2